"In this extraordinary book, Donna Orange helps us hear with our hearts. She challenges us to attend to those silenced by oppression, prejudice, violence, poverty, and other cruelties. This book is essential reading for the neophyte as well as the seasoned clinician, striving to hear the suffering other, as well as the muted voices within ourselves."

Sandra Buechler is a training and supervising analyst at
the William Alanson White Institute, New York, USA

"'I listen therefore I am.' With hearing impaired, one-sided, how does an 'I' take its place in a world of others? Using her own life as such an experiment in nature, Donna Orange openly, poignantly, and brilliantly explores the development of individuality and intersubjectivity, the essence of what it means to be a person. A leader recognized around the world for using psychoanalysis to explore the central questions of philosophy, Orange now brings fresh emotional immediacy and depth of serious thinking to the subject. This is a work of substantial significance, at once a beautiful literary memoir and a contribution of substantial significance."

Warren S. Poland, **MD**, has practiced clinical psychoanalysis
for over 50 years and is the former editor
of the *JAPA Review of Books*

"In *Learning To Hear*, Orange continues her ethical quest. Entwining history, philosophy, and psychoanalysis, she exhorts us towards a mission of ethical hearing. For Orange, ethical hearing is distinct from agentic 'listening' – it is a receptivity to the speech and silence that has been kept in the shadows. This book humanizes its subject, and is an important contribution to the social-ethical turn in psychoanalysis."

Sue Grand, **PhD**, has been practicing couples, family,
and individual therapy for over 40 years

Psychoanalysis, History, and Radical Ethics

Psychoanalysis, History, and Radical Ethics: Learning to Hear explores the importance of listening, being able to speak, and those who are silenced, from a psychoanalytic perspective. In particular, it focuses on those voices silenced either collectively or individually by trauma, culture, discrimination and persecution, and even by the history of psychoanalysis. Drawing on lessons from philosophy and history as well as clinical vignettes, this book provides a comprehensive guide to understanding the role of trauma in creating silence, and the importance for psychoanalysts of learning to hear those silenced voices.

Donna M. Orange, PhD, PsyD, is a psychoanalyst and philosopher living in California. She teaches at the NYU Postdoctoral Program and the Institute for the Psychoanalytic Study of Subjectivity, New York. Recent books include *Thinking for Clinicians* (2010), *The Suffering Stranger* (2011), *Nourishing the Inner Life of Clinicians and Humanitarians* (2016), and *Climate Crisis, Psychoanalysis, and Radical Ethics* (2017).

The Psychology and the Other Book Series

Series Editor: David M. Goodman

Associate Editors: Brian W. Becker, Donna M. Orange, Eric R. Severson

The *Psychology and the Other* Book Series highlights creative work at the intersections between psychology and the vast array of disciplines relevant to the human psyche. The interdisciplinary focus of this series brings psychology into conversation with continental philosophy, psychoanalysis, religious studies, anthropology, sociology, and social/critical theory. The cross-fertilization of theory and practice, encompassing such a range of perspectives, encourages the exploration of alternative paradigms and newly articulated vocabularies that speak to human identity, freedom, and suffering. Thus, we are encouraged to reimagine our encounters with difference, our notions of the "other," and what constitutes therapeutic modalities.

The study and practices of mental health practitioners, psychoanalysts, and scholars in the humanities will be sharpened, enhanced, and illuminated by these vibrant conversations, representing pluralistic methods of inquiry, including those typically identified as psychoanalytic, humanistic, qualitative, phenomenological, or existential.

Series titles:

Unconscious Incarnations
Psychoanalytic and Philosophical Perspectives on the Body, 1st Edition
Edited by Brian W. Becker, John Panteleimon Manoussakis, David M. Goodman

Schelling, Freud, and the Philosophical Foundations of Psychoanalysis
Uncanny Belonging, 1st Edition
Teresa Fenichel

Race, Rage, and Resistance
Philosophy, Psychology, and the Perils of Individualism, 1st Edition
Edited by David M. Goodman, Eric R. Severson, Heather Macdonald

Eros Crucified
Death, Desire, and the Divine in Psychoanalysis and Philosophy of Religion, 1st Edition
Matthew Clemente

For a full list of titles in the series, please visit the Routledge website at: https://www.routledge.com/Psychology-and-the-Other/book-series/PSYOTH

Psychoanalysis, History, and Radical Ethics

Learning to Hear

Donna M. Orange

Routledge
Taylor & Francis Group

LONDON AND NEW YORK

First published 2020
by Routledge
2 Park Square, Milton Park, Abingdon, Oxon OX14 4RN

and by Routledge
52 Vanderbilt Avenue, New York, NY 10017

Routledge is an imprint of the Taylor & Francis Group, an informa business

© 2020 Donna M. Orange

The right of Donna M. Orange to be identified as the author
has been asserted in accordance with sections 77 and 78 of the
Copyright, Designs and Patents Act 1988.

British Library Cataloguing-in-Publication Data
A catalogue record for this book is available from the British Library

Library of Congress Cataloging-in-Publication Data
A catalog record for this book has been requested

ISBN: 978-0-367-33929-6 (hbk)
ISBN: 978-0-367-33930-2 (pbk)
ISBN: 978-0-429-32290-7 (ebk)

Typeset in Times New Roman
by Apex CoVantage, LLC

For all those silenced by abuses of power and destruction of trust, especially those destroyed and abandoned by patriarchal religious groups.

Contents

Permissions

Each of the following is this author's own work:

In Chapter 1, significant portions of "You Have the Right to Remain Silent, or Do You Have the Obligation to Speak" have been reused, with revisions, with permission from *Psychoanalysis, Self and Context* (Taylor and Francis), where it appeared in v. 13, 2 October 2018.

In Chapter 5, significant portions of "Experiential History: Understanding Backwards," have been reused, with revisions, first published as Chapter 3 in *History Flows Through Us: Germany, the Holocaust, and the Importance of Empathy*, ed. Roger Frie, Routledge, 2018. Permission requested from Taylor and Francis.

Chapter 6 uses, in expanded form, a chapter in a forthcoming book from Routledge, *Race, Rage and Resistance: Philosophy, Psychology and the Perils of Individualism*, ed. Eric Severson, David Goodman, Heather MacDonald, where it will be called "Another Ethical Voice." I am told I cannot get permission because the book is not yet out.

In Chapter 7, significant portions of "Multiplicity and Integrity: Does an Anti-developmental Tilt Still Exist in Relational Psychoanalysis?" have been reused, with revisions, first published as Chapter 8 in *Decentering Relational Theory: A Comparative Critique*, ed. Lewis Aron, Sue Grand, and Joyce Slochower, Routledge, 2018. Permission requested from Taylor and Francis.

In Chapter 7, significant portions of "Inversions: A Tale of Two Emmanuels" has been reused, with revisions, with permission received from *Psychoanalysis: Self and Context* (Taylor and Francis), where it appeared in v. 14, 2 January 2019.

Introduction
Learning to hear

Several years ago, my left ear, without medical explanation, suddenly went completely deaf. I could no longer locate sounds, could no longer hear music or voices except monophonically, and missed much of what was said to me and around me. Much of what most people take for granted was gone. I tried hearing aids, but nothing was left to aid. Because I live in a country where single-sided deafness is defined as a non-problem, a cochlear implant became possible only five years later through a clinical trial. Meanwhile, life took on a dull, gray, depressive, and isolating cast. Conversations went on around me, but it often became useless to pretend that I could follow. This invisible disability leaves one alone because only other deaf people realize what is not happening. One cannot hear and is unheard, like victims of normalized violence, suffering in a fog but without the justified outrage.

After the surgery, consisting of implanting hardware between skin and skull, threading wires through drilled holes into the cochlea, it was time to learn to hear again. With persistent and systematic training, I learned to find language within noise, just as one does in learning a second or third language. The electronic input from the implant gradually integrated itself with what I still heard in my acoustic ear. I was not nearly as good as new, but not as impaired as before.

Learning to hear again has become a metaphor for me. Like all metaphors, it both signifies and stumbles. It signifies hearing others' voices and my own, others' cries of injustice and suffering, learning the lessons of history. It tries to signify psychoanalytic listening, intersubjectively implanted with prejudice and presuppositions. It points to the loneliness involved in hearing loss, both literal and metaphorical. It wants to signify hearing ethical demand and responsivity.

But the comparison stumbles because implant-training seems much more self-involved than ethical listening can be. First comes the awareness that only privileged first-world people have advantages like cochlear implants, crucial as they have become for children born deaf, as well as for people of all ages who later become profoundly deaf. In addition, the hours of practice alone on the computer and with audiobooks – even books on the history of slavery and colonialism – scarcely seem intensely relational. On the other hand, perhaps not. Hearing loss, like all vulnerabilities, befalls one. One can be or become characteristically indifferent to the other – we might call this ethical hearing loss, or hardness of heart, to switch metaphors – but to lose the capacity to hear or to mourn with the other, what is this? Can ethical capacity, once gained, be lost? Or regained? We have much to consider.

Also, for example, why consider hearing instead of listening? To listen, surely both a needed skill and perhaps a fine art, also requires lifelong study, whether by musicians or by psychotherapists. Teaching and learning this skill to a high level belongs to clinical and musical curricula, and has been extensively studied in psychoanalysis (Bacal, 1997; Baranger, 1993; Bromberg, 1994; Faimberg, 1996; Lichtenberg, 1999; Makari & Shapiro, 1993; Meissner, 2000; Pine, 2001; Reik, 1949; Schwaber, 1983).[1] It has become ever clearer, in theoretical worlds ranging from the classical through the Kleinian to the various intersubjectivities, that *how* the analyst listens determines, to a very great extent, *what* can be heard and responded to. It has also become clear, as Chris Jaenicke (Jaenicke, 2015) explains, that the analyst's basic assumption about how much one is involved in what the patient experiences, and in everything that happens in analysis, determines what can be heard. The analyst, full of one's own suffering, is always there, more or less self-absorbed or turned toward the other.

My choice to focus on hearing, in the face of an extensive literature on listening – to be noted here but not much discussed – intends to focus on the other. Whom do we need to hear, and what remains unheard? Listening is my activity; hearing is my receptivity, my vulnerability, my willingness to be affected by the other.[2] Arguably, the distinction is not so clear and could be drawn differently, but my intention is to place this book within the ethical turn in psychoanalysis. My questions about hearing unheard and silenced voices intend to challenge us to read history, to read the history of our psychoanalytic and psychotherapeutic disciplines from unfamiliar angles, to read the history of our countries from the vantage point of the oppressed. Reading can help us to hear, as well as to work, as Warren Poland (Poland, 2000, 2006, 2018) often repeats, in the service of the Other.

Thus we will consider in this book what it means to learn to hear silenced voices. Pursuing our metaphor, we will think of hearing those silenced as a kind of ethical capacity, a capacity that demands something from us. Resources will come from philosophy, from psychoanalysis, and from history. Thirty-some years in psychoanalytic practice and supervision have taught me to tune in to what Freud called the unconscious, to voices silenced within ourselves and others by non-responsiveness, by fear of knowing ourselves, by violence of many kinds. It has taught me to notice the ways I am silencing patients or supervisees even while trying to help them, complicating their anguished attempts to escape from confusion and unknowing. My *Besserwisser* (knowing better) attitudes, largely unconscious for me, silence others more often than I want to admit, just as white superiority silences and leaves invisible those whom we exclude and dominate.

History, my favorite childhood study, joins philosophy (especially including phenomenology and ethics) and psychoanalysis in this book. We will examine the results of ignorance and disinterest in history, as well as its resources for understanding psychoanalysis and its capacity for transforming ethical conscious-ness. My last book (Orange, 2017) noted the effects of historical unconsciousness on our capacity to see climate change as the emergency it has since become. Unsilencing the voices of the earth and of those most devastated by our warming of the oceans, destruction of essential forests, desertification, and all the rest has become a question of human survival. The threat has become immediate. Still, we continue as if unaffected, dissociated, unconscious. This one example shows how refusal to know history – chattel slavery and settler colonialism – for the crimes against humanity they continue to be, imminently imperils us all.

Transforming silence

This book develops the thesis that some silences cooperate in violence and oppres-sion, often unwittingly, while other silences speak an ethical word of response to the other. Learning to hear means tracing the path from the silence of indifference, "as if consenting to horror" (Levinas, 1989), to the vulnerable silence that speaks.

Chapter 1, "Silence in Phenomenology: Dream or Nightmare?," compares three mid-twentieth-century Frenchmen who wrote sharply divergent accounts of silence: Jean-Paul Sartre, Maurice Merleau-Ponty, and Emmanuel Levinas. We find heroic silence, pregnant silence, and silence as threat and violence. We will notice the silence that refuses witness to victims of atrocity and their children, and the silence of complicity in violence and violation of human rights.

Chapter 2, "Violence, Dissociation, and Traumatizing Silence," considers the effects of parental and cultural silence about violence, perpetrated or suffered or both, on the next generations. Psychoanalysts have studied the transgenerational transmission of trauma in great depth in recent years. Here we add the specific effect of silence on the child who becomes the psychoanalytic patient, as well as the effect of such silences in the analyst's life on the intersubjective treatment context.

The next two chapters, the heart of the book, concern reading history as a method of learning to hear. Chapter 3, "This Is Not Psychoanalysis!," studies the effects of silence and silencing on the psychoanalytic profession itself, beginning with Freud, and continuing into contemporary groups. As our first chapter made clear, silence not only has a cluster of meanings; it is also ethically ambiguous. Silence may defend and protect what is precious, including the power of those who wield it; it may protect patients, or it may refuse them witness to their suffer-ing or to the injustices perpetrated against them. In the history of psychoanalysis and of the therapies indebted to it, even if split off from it, silence has ranged from obliterating chapters of our own history, erasing people and ideas, to supporting idealizations. The amazing disappearances of Ferenczi, Erikson, and Fromm, to mention only a few, as well of many women, indicate the continuing power of silence to exclude. Outstanding historians of psychoanalysis can teach us to hear.

Chapter 4, "The Seduction of Mystical Monisms in the Humanistic Psychothera-pies," explains that Freudian psychoanalysis, most adherents and reactors would agree, located its intellectual ground in Enlightenment Europe, and thus was full of both individualisms and dualisms. Attempting to rectify both these unjustifiable binaries and the resulting injustices, recent psychoanalysis and other humanistic psychotherapies like gestalt have found inspiration in philosophies that deny dualism and turn toward monisms. These include, most famously, the Being-philosophy of Martin Heidegger (1889–1976), Jungian analysis and the pastoral and ecopsychologies inspired by Carl Jung (1875–1961), and most recently, the "new phenomenology" of Hermann Schmitz (1928–). Each offers a vision of oneness to supersede, obviate, or underpin the apparent binaries: Being (evermore mystical in the later Heidegger), universal archetypes in Jung, and atmospheres in Schmitz. Each one silences the plurality of voices in his own way. We will take each in turn, looking briefly at some of the best uses to which each has been put, and then consider why these monisms may be a seduction and a temptation for humanistic (or better, human dignity-oriented) psychotherapies, including psychoanalysis and gestalt.

Chapter 5, "Reading History as an Ethical and Therapeutic Project," claims that studying history from the vantage point of those most disadvantaged by its victors provides an alternative story of progress, one that takes the stories of conquest as stories of untold suffering. For psychoanalysts, beginning to absorb these histories of slavery and Jim Crow, of settler colonialism and of destruction of indigenous peoples, not to mention the devastation climate crisis is wreaking on the world's isolated and impoverished peoples, creates the possibility of an ethical awakening. Just as, in recent years, psychoanalysts have become trauma sensitive, linking child abuse and torture, just to name two, with many forms of adult suffering, reading history may help us to hear otherwise. We may learn to feel others' struggles as implicating us – our ancestors, our complicity, our continuing profit from the suffering of those we treat and those around us. We may come to wonder what the history we are reading demands of us – no longer so innocent in our gated communities and our doorman buildings – and how it has affected our patients. As this history questions us, can we respond, "What is this to me? Am I my other's keeper?"

In Chapter 6, "Radical Ethics: Beyond Moderation," we examine alternatives to monism and indifference, options which take the vulnerable individual as irreplaceable, as the beginning and end of ethics. Instead of social contracts or utilitarian systems designed to maximize benefit – the greatest good for the greatest number – radical ethics is a phenomenology of ethical experience, whether of a demand upon me created by the other's need and trust (Knud Ejler Løgstrup) or of the summons of preprimoridial (and pre-conscious) responsibility to the other (Emmanuel Levinas). We will consider whether any traditional ethical system has the possibility to meet today's ethical emergencies, such as climate justice creating extreme migration and starvation emergencies, and why we may all face the radical ethical demand.

In Chapter 7, "Ethical Hearing: Demand and Enigma," we will consider in more detail what a radical ethic means, and what it may demand of us, while we are rereading history. For most of us, substitution is not the one-time heroic act of an Arnaud Beltrame, but we may ask what his example means for contemporary psychoanalysis and psychotherapy as we read our own history, the history of our countries, and try to grasp what is demanded of us now.

Many writers and interlocutors, sensitive to the silent voices, have encouraged and helped me in this project. Some live at Pilgrim Place in Claremont, CA, where my beloved community of elders, continuing their lives of service into advanced age, inspire me daily even as they joke that I have "flunked retirement." My neighbors remind me daily of those silenced ones: Refugees detained by the U.S. government, women in religion and academia, the less affluent on the other side of the tracks. Several teachers, most now departed, taught me philosophy as ethics in a Socratic spirit. Some who still teach me to hear are students and members of my study groups and courses, including colleagues from universities and psychoanalytic institutes in Europe, Japan, Taiwan, Australia, Canada, Chile, and the U.S. whose questions and challenges have forced me to clarify and develop the ideas in this book. Recently, for example, Koichi Togashi, Nancy Amendt-Lyon, Matthew Ratcliffe, and Robert Stern have wittingly and unwittingly provided great help. My phenomenology study group, including Dan Bloom, Michal Drabanski, Ruella Frank, Cathleen Hoskins, Rich Hycner, Michael Vincent Miller, Andre Sassenfeld, and Carol Swanson, keep me thinking and stretching, and will perceive their influences here. The Climate Psychology Alliance, based in the UK but with members worldwide, keeps me learning and appropriately worried. Our longtime and precious "philosophy camp," including Don Braue, Doris Brothers, Elizabeth Corpt, Roger Frie, Lynne Jacobs, and Michael Reison, provides both the solid friendships and the endless questioning that makes an effort like this one sustainable. Workshopping this work in progress at NIP in New York and at Dallas Psychoanalytic, both in early 2019, forced me to hear more important silencings, and I am very grateful to the many responsive participants. My editors at Routledge, Kate Hawes and Charles Bath, as well as the highly competent production team, not only produce handsome books out of my fragmentary efforts, but sustain my faith in the worth of this work.

A special thanks goes to the cochlear implant clinicians and researchers whose work has provided literal new hearing to so many. To my surgeon and researcher Eric Wilkinson, my audiologist Dawna Mills, and researcher John Galvin, all from the House Clinic in Los Angeles; to Michael Dorman and his team at Arizona State University; and to the Cochlear Research team at the University of Maryland, especially Josh Bernstein, Kenneth Jensen, and Matt Goupell: It has been a great privilege to work with scientists so devoted to the humanistic and ethical project of improving lost or never-established hearing. You remind me, as biblical scholar James Muilenburg reputedly repeated, that "the God of Israel was a speaking God," (Muilenburg, 1961), and that learning to hear could be a way to describe ethical development.

Another special thanks goes to the Psychology and the Other community, whose conferences and books (Aron & Henik, 2009; Goodman & Severson,

2016; Goodman, 2012; Severson, Becker, & Goodman, 2016; Severson & Goodman, 2017) have become my interdisciplinary home in the past decade. My dear friend David Goodman, with his collaborators Eric Severson, Brian Becker, and others, have created a challenging space and impetus for what many of us are calling an "ethical turn" in the "psy disciplines," allowing us all to find our voices in the face of racial, gender, and climate/economic injustices. You have made me and others, outsiders in each and all the disciplines represented, welcome. I am full of gratitude.

Much of this writing comes from spring ("summer") semester in 2018, when the privilege of working for four months in Freud's home at Berggasse 19 in Vienna came to me as a Freud Fulbright scholar. The administration there made me welcome and comfortable in the library extension called the veranda, where Freud used to watch his children and grandchildren play outdoors. Dr. Daniela Finzi, who directs the Fulbright program and much of the museum activity; Monika Pessler, the museum chair; and Peter Nömaier, the finance director, supported me warmly and consistently. Librarian Sandra Sperber provided both resources and useful conversation. Johanna Frei organizes events so gracefully. Robert Stepniak took a special interest in my technical needs. The extremely capable museum staff shared their coffee, treats, and my broken non-Austrian German. Georg Thaler helped me understand historical matters and pointed me toward extremely useful books. I truly miss these devoted people, and feel very grateful for the chance to live among them for four months.

To all these people, I am profoundly grateful, but most of all to my husband, Don Braue, whose history of religions background challenges my tendency to take Western superiority for granted, and who provides endless practical and emotional support. He gracefully tolerates my working behind a closed door. All my writing of the past ten years has benefited from his editorial eagle-eye and awareness of missing pieces from my explanations and arguments, as well as from his technical capacities and patience. These last qualities he now devotes daily to our grateful Pilgrim Place community so that I must share his attentions.

Finally, in a Winnicottian spirit of acknowledging plagiarism, I want to thank all the people whose work I have used without reference because it has, as phenomenologists say, become sedimented into my thinking. Please take this as both apology and gratitude.

I further regret that I will have surely misread and heard wrongly. I hope you will know that we all are learning to hear each other, but that the ears are more than imperfect.

Notes

1 These references are only a sample of a more extensive literature, and undoubtedly and regrettably omit important contributions.
2 Lisbeth Lipari (2012) understands this contrast exactly opposite to the way I do; hearing, for her, resembles the dead and totalizing "said" in the work of Levinas (1981).

References

Aron, L., & Henik, L. (2009). *Answering a question with a question: Contemporary psychoanalysis and Jewish thought*. Boston: Academic Studies Press.

Bacal, H. A. (1997). Chapter 5 Optimal Responsiveness and Analytic Listening: Discussion of James L. Fosshage's "Listening/Experiencing Perspectives and the Quest for a Facilitating Responsiveness". *Progress in Self Psychology, 13*, 57–68.

Baranger, M. (1993). The Mind of the Analyst: From Listening to Interpretation. *International Journal of Psycho-Analysis, 74*, 15–24.

Bromberg, P. M. (1994). "Speak! That I May See You": Some Reflections on Dissociation, Reality, and Psychoanalytic Listening. *Psychoanalytic Dialogues, 4*(4), 517–547.

Faimberg, H. (1996). "Listening to Listening". *International Journal of Psychoanalysis, 77*, 667–677.

Goodman, D. M. (2012). *The demanded self: Levinasian ethics and identity in psychology*. Pittsburgh, PA: Duquesne University Press.

Goodman, D. M., & Severson, E. R. (2016). *The ethical turn: Otherness and subjectivity in contemporary psychoanalysis* (1st ed.). London and New York: Routledge and Taylor & Francis Group.

Jaenicke, C. (2015). *The search for a relational home: An intersubjective view of therapeutic action*. London and New York: Routledge and Taylor & Francis Group.

Levinas, E. (1989). As If Consenting to Horror. *Critical Inquiry, 15*, 485–488.

Lichtenberg, J. D. (1999). Listening, Understanding and Interpreting. *International Journal of Psycho-Analysis, 80*(4), 719–737.

Lipari, L. (2012). Rhetoric's Otherr: Levinas, Listening, and the Ethical Response. *Philosophy and Rhetoric, 45*, 227–242.

Makari, G., & Shapiro, T. (1993). On Psychoanalytic Listening: Language and Unconscious Communication. *Journal of the American Psychoanalytic Association, 41*, 991–1020.

Meissner, W. W. (2000). On Analytic Listening. *Psychoanalytic Quarterly, 69*(2), 317–367.

Muilenburg, J. (1961). *The way of Israel*. New York, Harper.

Orange, D. M. (2017). *Climate crisis, psychoanalysis, and radical ethics*. London and New York: Routledge, Taylor & Francis Group.

Pine, F. (2001). Listening and Speaking Psychoanalytically: With What in Mind? *International Journal of Psychoanalysis, 82*(5), 901–916.

Poland, W. S. (2000). The Analyst's Witnessing and Otherness. *Journal of the American Psychoanalytic Association, 48*(1), 17–34.

Poland, W. S. (2006). Struggling to Hear. *American Imago, 63*, 223–226.

Poland, W. S. (2018). *Intimacy and separateness in psychoanalysis*. New York: Routledge.

Reik, T. (1949). *Listening with the third ear: The inner experience of a psychoanalyst*. London: Allen & Unwin.

Schwaber, E. (1983). Psychoanalytic Listening and Psychic Reality. *International Review of Psycho-Analysis, 10*, 379–392.

Severson, E. R., Becker, B. W., & Goodman, D. (2016). *In the wake of trauma: Psychology and philosophy for the suffering other*. Pittsburgh, PA: Duquesne University Press.

Severson, E. R., & Goodman, D. (2017). *Memories and monsters: Psychology, trauma and narrative*. Relational Perspectives Book Series 95 (p. 1 online resource). Routledge.

Chapter 1

Silence in phenomenology

Dream or nightmare?

Silence, at best, is ambiguous. Thomas More, in Robert Bolt's *A Man for all Seasons* (Bolt, 1962), depends on this unclarity to claim that his silence does not have the dangerous meaning that Cromwell claims it does. No mere void, silence may protect, deny, attack, or give consent. One may be reduced to silence, either by humiliation or out of failure to find the right word. One may be struck silent by art, by holiness, by outrageousness. Persons or groups may find themselves silenced through acts of familial, cultural, or political domination, even by violence. Probably every human being has some experiences with silence, with silencing others, or having been silenced. David Kleinberg-Levin provides an evocative list, challenging all explanations:

> What comes to mind are these: the heavy silence of one going deep into her grief; the silence of one whom unspeakable horror has rendered speechless; the awkward silence of shame or embarrassment; the aggressive silence of one who is hiding his guilt; the benumbed silence of a deep depression; the silence of an anger which accuses and causes hurt by using silence as a weapon; withholding the kindness of speech; the heroic silence of the political prisoner, who refuses to surrender the names of his comrades even under extremes of torture; the guarded silence of citizens who must endure constant surveillance under the rule of a police state; the silence of timidity; the silence of shyness; the silence of rapt attention; the silence of prayer; the silence of spellbound anticipation; the silence of a joy that needs to be deeply felt.
>
> (p. 100)

No phenomenological account of silence can fail to address this array, if only indirectly.

But what is silence itself? Phenomenology, of course, ever allergic to universalizing definitions and mindful of Wittgenstein's family resemblances, will look to descriptions and contexts. Let us first trace a meandering path through silence in the company of phenomenologists Jean-Paul Sartre, Maurice Merleau-Ponty, and Emmanuel Levinas. Finally, we return to the everyday silences of clinical work, to see what phenomenologists might teach working psychoanalysts, and vice versa.

Pregnant silence

Sartre, writing after the war about the resistance, saw silence as heroic act of freedom. Kleinberg-Levin's list surely has Sartre's "republic of silence" in mind:

> We were never more free than during the German occupation. We had lost all our rights, beginning with the right to talk. Every day we were insulted to our faces and had to take it in silence. Under one pretext or another, as workers, Jews, or political prisoners, we were deported EN MASSE. Everywhere, on billboards, in the newspapers, on the screen, we encountered the revolting and insipid picture of ourselves that our oppressors wanted us to accept. And, because of all this, we were free. Because the Nazi venom seeped even into our thoughts, every accurate thought was a conquest. Because an all-powerful police tried to force us to hold our tongues, every word took on the value of a declaration of principles.
>
> (Liebling & Guthrie, 1947)

Thus, Sartre teaches us first about the effects of violent silencing. He continues, indicating that keeping silence may also be heroic:

> All those among us – and what Frenchman was not at one time or another in this situation who knew any details concerning the Resistance – asked themselves anxiously, "If they torture me, shall I be able to keep silent?" Thus the basic question of liberty itself was posed, and we were brought to the verge of the deepest knowledge that man can have of himself. . . . It was completely forlorn and unbefriended that they held out against torture, alone and naked in the presence of torturers, clean-shaven, well-fed, and well-clothed, who laughed at their cringing flesh, and to whom an untroubled conscience and a boundless sense of social strength gave every appearance of being in the right. Alone. Without a friendly hand or a word of encouragement. Yet, in the depth of their solitude, it was the others that they were protecting, all the others, all their comrades in the Resistance. Total responsibility in total solitude – is this not the very definition of our liberty?
>
> (Liebling & Guthrie, 1947, pp. 498–500)

Merleau-Ponty, explicitly addressing Sartre but implicitly speaking to all who have considered silence a mere lack of noise or the opposite of speech, provides another surprising account in his 1952 "Indirect Language and the Voices of Silence" (Merleau-Ponty, 1964a). Silence speaks, in particular through the work of Cezanne or Klee.[1] From depths before, after, under, and between words or music, but intricately involved in them and providing to them layers of meaning, silence can be full, generous, and generative. "We should consider speech before it has been pronounced," Merleau-Ponty later wrote, "against the ground of silence which precedes it, and without which it would say nothing" (1973, pp. 45–6).

When the conductor raises her baton to evoke a "Kyrie" or the expected notes of Beethoven's Fifth Symphony, when a pause follows an unexpected question, silence creates the breath or ground for music, for painting, or for language. At the end of a talk, a story, or a concert, a moment of silence, unpremeditated, may testify to the depth of feeling produced in the audience. When someone has revealed something shockingly painful, perhaps the loss of a child or a terminal prognosis, a reverent, receptive, compassionate silence must often precede any few words that may be possible. Oh, oh, oh, may be all we can say. Silence may accompany and witness.

Merleau-Ponty, however, meant to speak of a silence even more inclusive and originary than what his earlier words have suggested to me. As in Schelling (Schelling & Wirth, 2000) before him, he came in his last years to identify silence with nature itself,[2] not contrasted with language but as its very underpinning. A language, he wrote, "sometimes remains a long time pregnant with transformations which are to come . . . even if only in the form of a gap, a need, or a tendency" (Merleau-Ponty, 1964b, p. 41). In its indirectness, all language is silence. In his recent *Merleau-Ponty and the Face of the World: Silence, Ethics, Imagination, and Poetic Ontology*, Glen Mazis (2016) places silence at the center of Merleau-Ponty's early account of perception as well as of his mature work on chiasm and intertwining. Silence becomes the invisible source of the visible. Not a literal silence, it occurs in painting, in music, in poetry. Expressive and lyrical, it gives sense to the sensible.

But this silence can be corrupted. We can avoid it, but only at our peril. Long before computers and the internet dominated our daily lives, Merleau-Ponty warned of reducing thinking to data collecting. In the name of science we then test, operate, and transform the data. In this way, he wrote, "we enter into a cultural regimen in which there is neither truth nor falsity concerning man and history, into a sleep, or nightmare, from which there is no awakening" (Merleau-Ponty, 1964b, p. 160). Like Hegel's night in which all cows are black, we have entered the postmodern era Merleau-Ponty did not live to see, but which he surely described. Our headlong rush into the big-data world comes with a loss of connection to what Merleau-Ponty in his 1952 essay would have called the "voices of silence," as Mazis (2016) repeatedly points out.

Of course, such concern about the deadening effects of technical rationality have been common among phenomenologists, beginning with Edmund Husserl (1970) and including especially Heidegger, whose critique in its original form unfortunately included a far-too-casual reference to the production of corpses in concentration camps, as if nothing more had been at stake: "Farming is now a motorized food industry, in essence the same as the fabrication of corpses in gas chambers and extermination camps, the same as the blockade and starving of the peasantry, the same as the fabrication of the hydrogen bomb" (Heidegger, 1994 p. 27).[3] Merleau-Ponty takes a very different path, linking cybernetics to a loss of the world's silent and speaking wholeness, but likewise worried that a reductive data-focus would lead to disastrous consequences. He might not be surprised by our climate catastrophe. When we lose the sense of shuddering and shivering as silence comes to speech, we may also lose reverence for our world, for the nature that we are.[4]

Phenomenologist Bernard Dauenhauer has considered silence as a phenomenon (Bindeman, 2017; Dauenhauer, 1980). He first described two types: First, intervening silence that punctuates speech; second, anticipatory and afterwards silences, expectant and haunting. His third type, deep silence, links him to Merleau-Ponty, though he means perhaps something more recognizable, as he speaks of the silence of intimate contact, of liturgical silence, and of the silence-of-the-to-be-said. This last transcends all saying, but he relates it, with Gadamer, to tact and inexpressibility. Dauenhauer provides such examples as Shakespeare's Richard's refusal to answer his victims before their execution. Zen gardens in Kyoto provide me another example.

Threatening silences

Phenomenologists have spent less time describing silences that menace, but the disadvantaged of the world know them well. No less pregnant than those Merleau-Ponty described in his many writings about painting, or that Wittgenstein might have included in his "showing" as contrasted with "saying," these have quite another feel. In the natural world, we speak of "the calm before the storm." Patients tell their analysts of parents whose silences were worse than beatings or tirades. Border agents refuse to tell children what has happened to the parents from whom they have been violently separated. People historically excluded from being counted as human – whether from skin color, gender, sexual orientation, religion, or whatever – know that silence concerning their stories wipes out their history and threatens their further significance. "Black Lives Matter" protests such menacing silence. Psychoanalysts who fear gratifying may refuse important words of acknowledgment or welcome. Naming can murder, but so can refusal to name.

Frantz Fanon (Fanon 2008; Fanon & Philcox, 2004), psychiatrist and phenomenologist, described in detail the ways that speaking out of silent assumptions shaped the experience of blacks and of those suffering under colonial regimes. He had sat in Merleau-Ponty's courses, but for him, the silence was dangerous. The view or "gaze" that whites directed toward blacks and Arabs, he understood, infected their experience of themselves. Only by recontextualizing their experience, a revolutionary idea, could colonized or enslaved people gain any ground of their own. Diagnosing them as insane, or as inherently defective, silenced their own voices and made them invisible. Fanon's psychiatric work (Fanon, Gibson, Damon, Cherki, & Beneduce, 2014; Gibson, 2017) challenged the colonialist thinking and practice behind the psychiatric hospital and gave the silenced voices. Later chapters will consider silences and dissociation surrounding chattel slavery and violent settler colonialism. Fanon also spoke into these silences, and into the presumptions making them possible. Phenomenological *epoche* remains unavailable to help here, as Fanon clearly saw, because the whites cannot perceive their assumptions that would require bracketing.

Trauma-frozen silences

Another step distant from Merleau-Ponty's silence of "mute radiance," we find the silences involved in traumatic experience. We can distinguish, perhaps, the silence of anticipation, that of abandonment, and the failure of witness, where silence itself becomes trauma *nachträglich* [understood backwards]. Assuming an understanding of psychological trauma as shockingly disorganizing experience[5] that leaves a person disoriented in time and distrustful of self and others, we may be tempted to think of noisy violence, of school shootings, of atomic bombs, of rape. Even though these images are too often accurate, the silence before, during, and after them rarely receives its phenomenological due. If phenomenologist Emmanuel Levinas could write that his entire life had been shaped by the anticipation and memory of the Nazi horror, no wonder he wrote in the postwar years of insomnia, of the noisy and ominous silence of the *il y a* [there is], always portending violence yet demanding response.

> The entire opening of consciousness would already be a turning toward the something over which wakefulness watches. It is necessary, however, to think an opening that is prior to intentionality, a primordial opening that is an impossibility of hiding: one that is an assignation, an impossibility of hiding in oneself; this opening is an *insomnia*.
>
> (Levinas, 2000, pp. 207–8, emphasis in original)

Like single-sided deaf people who suffer from tinnitus, the traumatized hear rumbling noises reminding them that the worst can happen and that all can be lost. Many, of course, scream into the night, at the all-too-present realities in their nightmares. In the daytime, they may be mute. But this rumbling insomnia can also open toward the ethical.

So we should not expect that Levinas would endorse either Sartre's heroic postwar conception of silence, or Merleau-Ponty's mystical, quasi-romantic Schellingian idea. For him, silence gives consent to violence and refuses responsibility. From the immediate work on his return to Paris after liberation, "*Parole et silence*" (Levinas, Calin, Chalier, & Marion, 2009) to his magnum opus *Otherwise than Being* (Levinas, 1981), he insisted on the ethical speaking that does not allow either perpetrators or bystanders to hide from responsibility.

Trauma therapists and students of extreme dissociative conditions have, I believe, provided important questions to phenomenology, about which philosophers have until now been all too willing to keep silent. What kind of silence fails to speak of climate catastrophe, threatening to make further speech on this subject degenerate into a hopeless wail? What kind of silence keeps me from greeting the miserable homeless person on the street asking me for a euro or a dollar? What kind of silence keeps me from asking what part my own ancestors had in supporting slavery, or in the colonizing of the so-called Terra Nullius (empty land whose inhabitants did not count as people), so that indigenous peoples were slaughtered or disastrously reduced? How did these people become nobody for me, so that I cannot even speak their names or their languages?[6] How does a person or a group become "reduced to silence?"

And what about silence as the refusal, out of fear or out of cowardice, to witness to injustice and atrocity? *Shoah* producer Claude Lanzmann speaks of a "conspiracy of silence": "There are some good ways of being silent. There some good ways, and there are very bad ways as well. To talk too much about the Holocaust is a way of being silent, and a bad way of being silent" (Caruth, 2014, p. 208). He does not explain, but clearly he sides with Merleau-Ponty in refusing to oppose speech and silence. Apparently, speech itself can obfuscate historical realities, can minimize, can silence the sufferer of atrocity.

Silence in the phenomenology of Emmanuel Levinas

Like Sartre and Merleau-Ponty, Levinas (1905–1995),[7] whose insomnia we noted earlier, lived before and after the occupation in Paris, but unlike them, spent the five war years in captivity in a labor camp near Hannover, where, as a French officer, he survived, but where the Jewish captives were segregated and much more harshly treated. Not for Jews was the genial "university in the camp" the reality described by fellow phenomenologist Paul Ricoeur (Reagan, 1996). Levinas (1990) wrote:

> There were seventy of us in a forestry commando unit for Jewish prisoners of war in Nazi Germany . . . but the other men, called free, who had dealings with us or gave us work or orders or even a smile – and the children and women who passed by and sometimes raised their eyes – stripped us of our human skin. We were subhuman, a gang of apes. A small inner murmur, the strength and wretchedness of persecuted people, reminded us of our essence as thinking creatures, but we were no longer part of the world. Our comings and goings, our sorrow and laughter, illnesses and distractions, the work of our hands and anguish of our eyes, the letters we received from France and those accepted for our families – all that passed in parenthesis. We were beings entrapped in their species; despite all their vocabulary, beings without language. Racism is not a biological concept; anti-Semitism is the archetype of all internment. . . . It shuts people away in a class, deprives them of expression and condemns them to being "signifiers without a signified." . . . How can we deliver a message about our humanity which, from behind the bars of quotation marks, will come across as anything other than monkey talk?

And then, about halfway through our long captivity, for a few short weeks, before the sentinels chased him away, a wandering dog entered our lives.

One day he came to meet this rabble as we returned under guard from work. He survived in some wild patch in the region of the camp. But we called him Bobby, an exotic name, as one does with a cherished dog. He would appear at morning assembly and was waiting for us as we returned, jumping up and down and barking in delight. For him, there was no doubt that we were men. . . . This dog was the last Kantian in Nazi Germany, without the brain needed to universalize maxims and drives.

(pp. 152–3)

Many have written about this passage, but here I want to ask what it tells the phenomenologist about silence and affirming or negating human dignity. To speak means more than to bark out words ("*Hier is kein Warum!*" [Here there is no why!] from the guard to desperately thirsty Primo Levi (1961) who asks why his small icicle has been swatted away). To speak to the other may mean a joyful or thoughtful greeting from a companion animal, or from someone who cannot speak my language. It may mean recognizing without words that a sufferer is a fellow human who should never be so mistreated. Colleagues who work daily with victims of torture must listen and listen and listen to the unspeakable, bearing witness to the humanity of the other. Ironically, our silent horror at what has been done to these fellow humans begins to undo their tortured silencing, if only a little. This silence trembles, on both sides.

Silence unfrozen

To unfreeze traumatic silences, speaking becomes necessary. Whatever the exact text, "Black lives matter," "Me too," or "Never again," among many, this ethical speaking (sometimes trivialized, of course) insists that the silenced and persecuted and murdered ones are human, and that injustice to them requires active response. Indifference by us who profit from the continued silence – we who live in the houses stolen from the deported and murdered Jews of Europe, for example, or on land stolen from indigenous peoples – deepens the trauma and further isolates those traumatized.

Psychoanalysis, the "talking cure," has long known that speaking the unspeakable (Orange, 2011a) in the right context can restore, if not cure, traumatized people.[8] Voices from the classical tradition, even after the shameful banishment of Sándor Ferenczi, have spoken for the "soul murdered" (Shengold, 1989) and for those nearly destroyed by historical atrocity (Adler, 1995). Relational psychoanalysis has begun to consider relational trauma, and especially the "self states" it may lead us to disavow (Bromberg, 1994, 1998). Intersubjective systems theorists (Arnold, 2013; Stolorow, 2007) have brought trauma – in development and adulthood – into the center of their phenomenological account of pathogenesis and psychoanalytic process. The shattered experiential world of the traumatized becomes a psychotic state to find connection and understanding by a therapist or analyst who is a brother or sister in the worlds of trauma. Often, as Davoine and Gaudillière (2004) write from a European perspective, the patient's madness finds the analyst's history, and connects to undo the wretched silencing.

Attempting to undo silencing psychoanalytically often runs directly into shame. Shame, built into most traumatic experience with its inherent degrading and dehumanizing qualities, does not add to trauma or constitute a defense against awareness of it. Instead, it pre-reflectively disempowers and disentitles the potential speaker. What right have I, so much below any ladder or scale, to speak of mistreatment or injustice done to me? The traumatized person, humiliated in many ways not always evident, has been preemptively silenced by the resulting shame. Why did I not fight off my rapist? Why did I not work harder in the face of the school's rejection of me? Why could I not keep silent after days or weeks of torture? All these questions, and more, disqualify the traumatized from speaking, and from being heard and re-included in human community.

Shamed silence may also result from the community's refusal of witness to massive injustice. Consider, for example, the desperate plight of those psychoanalysts who fled Germany and Austria in the 1930s, only to find that many of their colleagues did not want them, either because they feared competition or because of anti-Semitism (Steiner, 1989, 2011). Already terrified and alone, often without the language skills they needed, and without the medical credentials to practice in the U.S., they and their families faced rejection in Britain and the U.S., as well as terrible losses in Europe. Their traumatic experience has shaped the learning of us who have been their students, but has almost never been spoken or written about until recently (Kuriloff, 2014). We have inherited the fruits of bystandership, reminding me of the words of Emmanuel Levinas speaking of Heidegger's silence, "as if consenting to horror" (Levinas, 1989, p. 458).

Silence as complicity[9]

As usual, Philip Cushman (2018) has written the work on ethics, psychology, and torture that I would have wanted to write, with a thoroughness that never masks his commanding prophetic voice. Reminding me of those originals who made me shudder and cower in shame reading Abraham Heschel's *The Prophets* (Heschel, 1962),[10] calling us psychologists to account for our semi-deliberate moral unconsciousness, Cushman holds us responsible – rightly, in my view – for the evils our neglect of ethical education, as well as our thoughtless "individualism, consumer capitalism, neoliberalism, scientism" (p. 1) have wrought in our name. I (Orange, 2018b) share his trenchant critiques of these ideologies and attitudes precisely, and thus will not repeat them. My own reflections, leaning toward the psychoanalytic, imply a reference to a prophetic character hidden in the psychoanalytic tradition – indeed, in the whole psychoanalytic tradition. Of course I realize that Cushman's work indicts me along with all our colleagues, that the deep and thick ethical failures he explains in the torture context are running, as he says, like a fault line below our professional communities, preventing us from responding adequately to current crises, leaving us befuddled and confused in just the ways he describes, polluting the work we pursue with good intentions. His prophetic warning is more than urgent.

Like Cushmans', my concerns intersect at the crossroads of philosophy (especially phenomenology, philosophical hermeneutics, and ethics), history (including psychoanalytic history, and the histories of settler colonialism and chattel slavery), climate science, and psychoanalysis (Orange, 2017). Not for a moment to minimize the importance of all humanistic psychotherapies, it seems important to notice the ways in which psychoanalytic theories may have obfuscated ethical concerns, just as Cushman illuminates in psychology and the "psy disciplines" generally. Though I particularly want to honor those psychologists/psychoanalysts who have led the fight to expose and to end the involvement of psychologists in the U.S. torture program, we must grant that most of us were silent, and even now inadequately horrified by the acts done in our name. I am reminded of the infamous Göring Institute of psychoanalysis in Berlin during the Third Reich, as well as of the doctors I met in Heidelberg, who no longer even call themselves psychiatrists (now it is the faculty of psychosomatics) because of the atrocities their profession had committed "in those years." (The work of Robert Jay Lifton [Lifton, 1986] should surely be background reading here). Freud's concern with unconscious motivation has not helped enough, in his time or ours, to challenge organized crimes against humanity.

Where is our commensurate shame? Perhaps I am missing Cushman's point, but I am not so sure. Perhaps the same moral fault lines, made up of individualism, scientism, and Irwin Hoffman's masterfully described "doublethinking" (Hoffmann, 2009), leading us to moral fog and evasion, now keep us underreacting to the support that organized psychology gave the George W. Bush torture program, and now threatens to resume. All that is needed for evil to prevail is for good people to do nothing, according to an idea often attributed to Edmund Burke.[11] Cushman explains how the deep structure of the psychological professions, almost never examined and brought into dialogue, make it almost impossible to generate the kind of ethical deliberation that might have put on the brakes, or activated the "good people." But given that our deep assumptive structures continue unquestioned by most, what other horrors may we be supporting or overlooking? Our colleagues of color could tell us the answer if we would give them five minutes (Gump, 2010; Jones, 2015). So could the millions of climate refugees. So Cushman's prophetic demand to consider our sins of individualistic and consumerist mindlessness – Warren Poland (2018) likes to define the unconscious as what we do not want to know about ourselves – also constitutes a call to psychoanalysis, to meaning-and-dialogue-oriented psychotherapy, to a kind of human and ethical work never to be doublethought into a STEM (science, technology, engineering, math) discipline.

Unfortunately, just as Cushman suggests, we contemporary psychoanalysts – like our grandparents who excluded humanistic and ethical voices like Erich Fromm, Erik Erikson, and John Bowlby – we lean, perhaps unintentionally, toward ethical ambiguity. Some advocates of multiple self-states,[12] asked who is responsible for voting in their name in elections, fall silent. No one is responsible when everyone is standing in the spaces.[13] (I do it myself, living intricately implicated in an extreme capitalist system that systemically destroys millions of innocent human lives, and the planet that could support them). The autonomous ego of ego psychology was, of course, too simple to describe complex relationally emergent self-experience, but the developmentally and relationally described ego of Hans Loewald (1979, 2000), for example, appropriated from the parents its moral responsibilities. Without a theory and practice of ethical selfhood,[14] I believe, we cannot expect psychoanalysis to lead the "psy disciplines" in creating moral dialogues, even protests, to resist ethical fogs and ambiguities like those that permitted us to stand by while psychologists participated in torture in our names. If we theorize away the possibility of integrity and responsibility, we are lost.

Pretending to be a hard science will not solve our problem. In a STEM discipline, as in our omnipresent devices, everything functions by rules. If the rules are properly formulated, everything runs just fine. Bending the rules will cause crashes. Even malware runs by the rules, showing us that the rules are indeed value-free.[15] In our human sciences trying to be STEM sciences, though, we tend to ignore those ethical problems that cause crashes in human relationships, that reduce human beings to things, in Cushman's elegant and horrifying language:

> How did we allow this series of betrayals, humiliations, and sadistic acts to be thought of as a subject of legal debate, instead of recognizing it as an ethical scandal? Torture is an utterly reprehensible act, unjustifiable both ethically and practically. It is a betrayal that wounds the very soul of the prisoner (Apuzzo, Fink, & Risen, 2016), degrades the perpetrator, and undermines the moral integrity of the society that is responsible for it. It starkly illuminates what must be considered the most egregious of human mistakes: treating fellow humans as things to be used, not precious lives to be cherished and honored. It . . . is the graphic and perhaps most extreme enactment of an instrumental relationship, one that strikes at the very core of human social existence by its objectification of the other and its denial of the limits of one's own understandings. It is in part what the Hebrew prophets meant by idolatry (see Fromm, 1955, 1966): the process by which humans first uncritically admire and worship inanimate and human-made creations such as wealth, automobiles, social status, national emblems, revanchist fantasies, or demagogic behavior, and by so doing are themselves turned into things.
>
> (p. 10)

No one who remembers Jean Améry's (1980) description of the first time he was tortured could claim that Cushman exaggerates. But Améry preceded his story with a quotation from British novelist Graham Greene who commented on photographs of Vietcong torture emerging in the American and British press at the time:

> The strange new feature about the photographs of torture now appearing in the British and American press is that they have been taken with the approval

of the torturers and are published over captions that contain no hint of condemnation. They might have come out of a book on insect life. . . . Does this mean that the American authorities sanction torture as a means of interrogation? The photographs certainly are a mark of honesty, a sign that the authorities do not shut their eyes to what is going on, but I wonder if this kind of honesty without conscience is really to be preferred over . . . the old hypocrisy.

(p. 23)

Améry commented: "The admission of torture, the boldness – but is it still that? – of coming forward with such photos is explicable only if it is assumed that a revolt of public conscience is no longer to be feared" (p. 23). So these questions, possible and actual long before the George W. Bush administration, make it clear that the climate for shoulder-shrugging in U.S., and in psychology cultures, was fertile soil, with little opposition to be expected, after 9/11. And psychoanalysis, with a stronger intellectual tradition, could do no better?

But ethical scandals tend not to be the topics of our training, conferences, or journals. Not only do we fail to learn the hermeneutic dialogue necessary to consider ethical questions in depth and to confront their meanings, but when breaches of this magnitude do "occur" (note my minimizing, anonymizing language), we do not immediately devote our next national or international conference to them. A few concerned souls may offer one panel, probably not even a plenary. We do not, for the most part, engage in collective soul-searching, asking how we could have been complicit in so much evil, or even what exactly is wrong with torture.

And yet, why should we be surprised? When famous psychoanalysts have committed egregious sexual boundary violations, sometimes even leading to loss of professional licenses, institutions have protected them despite widespread knowledge, as if the offender's privacy were more important than our duty to protect patients and trainees. Sometimes senior colleagues even invite the offender to social gatherings and continue to teach his papers and books, as if to say to trainees that respecting and protecting patients does not matter. Wink, wink, nod, nod. He or she is one of us, and could shoot someone on Fifth Avenue and no one would object. Or senior colleagues may blame the patient, to training committees or licensing boards. Of course, the offender cannot then explain to self or others *why* the transgression was wrong, or *why* the boundary is a boundary. Not to mention the confusion of tongues, and debilitating shame, resulting for the patient or trainee. Our collective failure to engage in ongoing ethical dialogues in our training institutes, journals, and conferences stems from the scientism that Cushman and Hoffman describe, and reinforces it. Discussion about ethics usually comes down to making the rules ever more precise – I have recently seen the draft of a psychoanalytic institute's 20-page ethics code, which does attempt to be a statement of both values and rules. We keep hoping that precision in our rules will rescue us from needing to engage in moral discourse, and moral reasoning. But we must break the silence and resort to genuine education. Cushman (2019) writes: "The absence of philosophically learned moral discourse in the profession leads to a thin, easily manipulated relation with ethics" (p. 13). Without practice in such ethical dialogue, leading to practical wisdom, we are like people who need to learn to swim when already drowning. With only rules to guide us, we become experts at bending them, as Cushman warns.

To summarize my first thought, I believe we should heed Cushman's call to take ourselves seriously as an alternative to the valueless, foggy, procedural, reductive, liquid (Bauman, 1993, 2000) "discourse" of postmodernity. We hermeneuts in psychology and in psychoanalysis (Cushman, 2007, 2011; Orange, 2011b; Stern, 2013) can speak up for racial justice, climate justice, ethical treatment of patients, and opposition to torture, for example. We can invite those who think psychotherapy concerns more than techniques and technologies, and especially those who think it probably concerns something else entirely, to talk ethics with us. Perhaps our conversations, and ethical worries, will bleed out into the larger cultures where they are so urgently needed.

My second thought concerns the reading of history as an ethical project, to be further developed in a later chapter. Scientistic approaches to psychology, psychotherapy, and, worst of all, to psychoanalysis lose track of the old dictum that those who do not study history are doomed to repeat it – a good reason to read the Hoffman report, Cushman's article, and the writings of those closely familiar with this awful story. But worse, by not studying history, including this history, we are already repeating. We continue the fog, the obfuscation "bad things happened," and the evasions. Somebody else did it, far away. Chattel slavery, settler colonialism? Somebody else did it, long ago.

And yet, just last summer, wanting to know more about the history of Maine, where I usually spend summers, and looking to Wikipedia as the handiest resource, I "learned" that Maine's history began with the French and the British. Surrounded by names like Penobscot and Kennebec and Passagassawakeag, and having read Wendy Warren's *New England Bound: Slavery and Colonization in the New World* (Warren, 2016), I remembered that the earliest colonists from Massachusetts had sent others to Maine to take the land and eliminate those few indigenous people who had survived the plagues already brought from Europe. The beauty of Maine hides a brutal, criminal history of over-entitled Europeans appropriating communally held land in the name of religion, but for economic gain. Only a few of its original people remain to protect and honor their Penobscot, Wabanaki cultures. If we look beyond the surface of the history we have been taught, we prepare ourselves for moral questioning.

Thus, I believe that each of us must study some aspect of the history of moral oppression and crimes if we are to develop the needed sensitivities to stop repeating. We already know this in families. Because my nine siblings and I talk about the conditions of our past, it has become possible for one of my younger sisters to write a statement to be read at her funeral: "no one in our generation ever beat their children." Repeating can be stopped, usually through dialogic examination of what went wrong and what it all means, both individually and culturally. Lynching, and its more recent imitators, stops only if we study its history and the attitudes – conscious and unconscious – it expresses. Psychoanalytic devotion to this type of understanding means protecting our precious dialogic legacy from the threat of doublethinking, and from physics envy. In search of scientific legitimacy, we lose and betray the most precious gift we have to offer our patients and the larger world. We also refuse ethical responsibility.

This brings me to my title point, the Miranda warning: You have the right to remain silent. Yes, when I am being approached by law enforcement as if I were a criminal, this precious right may save me. Still, it cannot become my fundamental life organizing principle. When you are starving, falling, being mistreated, being tortured, I may not remain silent. Now we have crossed over from law into ethics. Cushman (2019) asks: "How did we allow this series of betrayals, humiliations, and sadistic acts to be thought of as a subject of legal debate, instead of recognizing it as an ethical scandal?" (p. 10). The difference between parsing out legal distinctions – important as these may be – and responding ethically corresponds to the difference between machine-like rule-following and protecting the vulnerable Other, whose fate, directly or indirectly, may be in my hands. Learning, over and over, the relation and difference between law and morality requires conversation about such matters from childhood through graduate school and professional education to the end of life. Reading books like lawyer Bryan Stevenson's *Just Mercy* (Stevenson, 2014) helps us understand that laws can be seriously unjust, and that, as he often repeats, each person is better than the worst thing he or she has ever done. No moral calculus here, but an ethical conversation about justice beyond law. Reading history, to return to my earlier point, stretches our moral sensibilities to include people whom we might not otherwise notice or include in our concerns. In the face of gross injustices all around us, in which we participate pervasively, we do not have the right to remain silent.[16] We psychologists and psychoanalysts are citizens, and fellow human beings. Philip Cushman has now spoken out, challenging the most fundamental attitudes and assumptions in our professions, breaking our silence on behalf of those who cannot speak for themselves. Who will be next?

In conclusion

Belatedly, we are learning to hear. "Philosophy," Merleau-Ponty wrote in his last work, *The Visible and the Invisible*, "is the reconversion of silence and speech into one another" (Merleau-Ponty and Lefort, 1968, 129/169 [French version]).[17] Finding words for the unspeakably beautiful and the unspeakably horrible, inadequate as these words will always be, even perhaps poetic words, philosophy does only half of its job. In the other half, we lapse back into silence, as Wittgenstein and Ogden (1990) reminded us: whereof we cannot speak, thereof we must remain silent. Silent before that which demands reverence, silence before what exceeds words either by way of sublimity or horror.

The artist faces the same problem as the philosopher: On the wall of Beethoven's house in Heiligenstadt are Kant's (Kant and Beck, 1993) words: The starry heavens above and the moral law within. In this very house where Beethoven wrote both his heartwrenching *Heiligenstadt Testament* expressing his suicidal thoughts over his encroaching deafness,[18] and also wrote some of his greatest music, he faced the problem of silence. To break it he wrote music; to accept silence, he walks in the fields.

So a phenomenology of silence arrives at no definition, but finds an omnipresent feature of human life that punctuates and pervades it, under and beyond all the noise. Silence also threatens, as in deafness and in violence. It protects the guilty, often for generations, and creates false innocence. But it may, at times, express the profoundest reverence.

Notes

1 Bindeman (2017) quotes: "We usually say that the painter reaches us across the silent world of lines and colors, and that he addresses himself to an unformulated power of deciphering within us that we control only after we have blindly used it – after we have enjoyed the work" (p. 66).

2 It remains to study the voice of Spinoza running through *The Phenomenology of Perception* (Merleau-Ponty & Landes, 2012), an influence perhaps deeper than that of Schelling.

3 Heidegger's infamous silence after the war both about the Shoah and his own full-throated support for the regime of its perpetrators underlies the questioning of his philosophy in Chapter 4.

4 There is far more to be said about Merleau-Ponty's phenomenology of silence, but space limitations and also respect force me to refer the reader on to Glen Mazis.

5 Phenomenologist Matthew Ratcliffe (2017) speaks of the anticipation/fulfillment structure of the modalities of intentionality in his work on audio-verbal hallucinations. Psychological trauma violently disrupts this structure, making coherent speech impossible. Similarly, Robert Stolorow (2011) writes in a Heideggerian voice of the disruption of temporality in trauma.

6 Many questions for the phenomenologist/clinician belong here: Does my silence about race, gender, history, violence, further silence my patient? Do I implicitly try to evade responsibility by my silence?

7 Sean Hand has written about the postwar contributions immediately after the war by all three men, and their interactions (Appleby, 1996).

8 See also the thoughtful and challenging work on restorative justice, e.g. (Stauffer, 2015) and moral repair (Walker, 2006, 2010).

9 This section borrows, with some adjustments and with gratefully acknowledged permission, from my response to Cushman (Orange, 2018b).

10 The massive biography (Blight, 2018) of fugitive slave turned writer and orator, Frederick Douglass, alludes repeatedly to Heschel's work, and shows that Douglass understood himself clearly in the tradition of Jeremiah, Ezekiel, and Isaiah, speaking for those silenced and tortured by chattel slavery. See Chapter 5.

11 Here is the long version: "Whilst men are linked together, they easily and speedily communicate the alarm of any evil design. They are enabled to fathom it with common counsel, and to oppose it with united strength. Whereas, when they lie dispersed, without concert, order, or discipline, communication is uncertain, counsel difficult, and resistance impracticable. Where men are not acquainted with each other's principles,

nor experienced in each other's talents, nor at all practised in their mutual habitudes and dispositions by joint efforts in business; no personal confidence, no friendship, no common interest, subsisting among them; it is evidently impossible that they can act a public part with uniformity, perseverance, or efficacy. In a connection, the most inconsiderable man, by adding to the weight of the whole, has his value, and his use; out of it, the greatest talents are wholly unserviceable to the public. No man, who is not inflamed by vain-glory into enthusiasm, can flatter himself that his single, unsupported, desultory, unsystematic endeavours, are of power to defeat the subtle designs and united cabals of ambitious citizens. When bad men combine, the good must associate; else they will fall, one by one, an unpitied sacrifice in a contemptible struggle." Edmund Burke, *Select Works of Edmund Burke*. A New Imprint of the Payne Edition. Foreword and Biographical Note by Francis Canavan (Indianapolis: Liberty Fund, 1999). Vol. 1. Retrieved 7/22/2019 from the World Wide Web: https://oll.libertyfund.org/titles/796

12 Here I distinguish "states" from parts, with Onno van der Hart and others who expertly and compassionately teach us to treat those sufferers from extreme violence who live in parts not even remembered by other parts.

13 I have discussed this problem at length elsewhere (Orange, 2018a), and noted that Bromberg seems recently to be reversing course toward a more integrated sense of self. It is also true that some proponents of this type of postmodern theory involve themselves in ethical critique and political activism.

14 I am not claiming here that we possess a substantialized or reified thing called "a self" (see critiques by Stolorow (1995), but rather that the phenomenological and ethical sense of more- or less-integrated selfhood, responsible for actions, attitudes, and bystanding, needs theorizing in psychoanalysis if we are to escape our ethical fog (Orange, 2013).

15 Cushman (2019) formulates our STEM aspiration problem perfectly when he writes: "When psychology claims a scientistic warrant, it is in the unenviable position of trying to determine good ways for humans to live by using a method that claims it has bracketed off all ideas about good ways to live" (p. 19).

16 Howard Caygill (2002) insistently questions whether Emmanuel Levinas had a right to his partial silence on the subject of Israel. As he notes, these echoes return when we begin to speak of Heidegger's silences in Chapter 4.

17 I am grateful to Sean Williams (2010) for alerting me to this passage as well as to Merleau-Ponty's important connection to Schelling.

18   O how harshly was I repulsed by the doubly sad experience of my bad hearing, and yet it was impossible for me to say to men speak louder, shout, for I am deaf. Ah how could I possibly admit such an infirmity in the one sense which should have been more perfect in me than in others, a sense which I once possessed in highest perfection, a perfection such as few surely in my profession enjoy or have enjoyed – O I cannot do it, therefore forgive me when you see me draw back when I would gladly mingle with you, my misfortune is doubly painful because it must lead to my being misunderstood, for me there can be no recreations in society of my fellows, refined intercourse, mutual exchange of thought . . . what a humiliation when one stood beside me and heard a flute in the distance and *I heard nothing*, or someone heard *the shepherd singing* and again I heard nothing, such incidents brought me to the verge of despair, but little more and I would have put an end to my life – only art it was that withheld me, ah it seemed impossible to leave the world until I had produced all that I felt called upon me to produce, and so I endured this wretched existence – truly wretched, an excitable body which a sudden change can throw from the best into the worst state.

                    (Heiligenstadt Testament, 6 October 1802, emphasis in original)

References

Adler, H. (1995). Recall and Repetition of a Severe Childhood Trauma. *International Journal of Psycho-Analysis*, *76*, 927–943.

Améry, J. (1980). *At the mind's limits: Contemplations by a survivor on Auschwitz and its realities*. Bloomington: Indiana University Press.

Appleby, J. O. (1996). *Knowledge and postmodernism in historical perspective*. New York: Routledge.

Arnold, K. (2013). The Abyss of Madness by George E. Atwood New York, NY: Routledge, 224 pp., $40.95, 2012. *Division 39/Review*, *8*, 21–22.

Bauman, Z. (1993). *Postmodern ethics*. Cambridge, MA: Blackwell Publishers.

Bauman, Z. (2000). *Liquid modernity*. Cambridge and Malden, MA: Polity Press and Blackwell.

Bindeman, S. L. (2017). *Silence in philosophy, literature, and art*. Leiden and Boston: Brill-Rodopi.

Blight, D. W. (2018). *Frederick Douglass: Prophet of freedom* (First Simon & Schuster hardcover ed.). New York: Simon & Schuster.

Bolt, R. (1962). *A man for all seasons: A play in two acts*. New York: Random House.

Bromberg, P. M. (1994). "Speak! That I May See You": Some Reflections on Dissociation, Reality, and Psychoanalytic Listening. *Psychoanalytic Dialogues*, *4*(4), 517–547.

Bromberg, P. M. (1998). *Standing in the spaces: Essays on clinical process, trauma, and dissociation*. Hillsdale, NJ: Analytic Press.

Caruth, C. (2014). *Listening to trauma: Conversations with leaders in the theory and treatment of catastrophic experience*. Baltimore: Johns Hopkins University Press.

Caygill, H. (2002). *Levinas and the political*. London and New York: Routledge.

Cushman, P. (2007). A Burning World, an Absent God: Midrash, Hermeneutics, and Relational Psychoanalysis. *Contemporary Psychoanalysis*, *43*, 47–88.

Cushman, P. (2011). So Who's Asking? Politics, Hermeneutics, and Individuality. In R. Frie & W. Coburn (Eds.), *Persons in context: The challenge of individuality in theory and practice* (pp. 21–40). New York and London: Routledge.

Cushman, P. (2018). The Earthquake That Is the Hoffman Report on Torture: Toward a Re-Moralization of Psychology. *Psychoanalysis, Self, and Context*, *13*, 311–334.

Cushman, P. (2019). *Travels with the self: Interpreting psychology as cultural history*. New York: Routledge.

Dauenhauer, B. P. (1980). *Silence, the phenomenon and its ontological significance*. Bloomington: Indiana University Press.

Davoine, F., & Gaudillière, J.-M. (2004). *History beyond trauma: Whereof one cannot speak, thereof one cannot stay silent*. New York: Other Press.

Fanon, F. (2008). *Black skin, white masks*. New York, Berkeley and California: Grove Press. Distributed by Publishers Group West.

Fanon, F., & Philcox, R. (2004). *The wretched of the earth/Frantz Fanon*; translated from the French by Richard Philcox; introductions by Jean-Paul Sartre and Homi K. Bhabha. New York: Grove Press.

Fanon, F., Gibson, N. C., Damon, L., Cherki, A., & Beneduce, R. (2014). *Decolonizing madness: The psychiatric writings of Frantz Fanon*. New York, NY: Palgrave Macmillan.

Gibson, N. C. (2017). *Frantz Fanon, psychiatry, and politics*. Lanham: Rowman & Littlefield International.

Gump, J. (2010). Reality Matters: The Shadow of Trauma on African American Subjectivity. *Psychoanalytic Psychology, 27*, 42–54.

Heidegger, M. (1994). *Bremer und Freiburger Vorträge*. Frankfurt am Main: Klostermann.

Heiligenstadt Testament, 6 October 1802. http://www.lvbeethoven.com/Bio/Biography HeiligenstadtTestament.html

Heschel, A. J. (1962). *The prophets* (1st ed.). New York: Harper & Row.

Hoffmann, I. (2009). Doublethinking Our Way to "Scientific" Legitimacy: The Desiccation of Human Experience. *Journal of the American Psychoanalytic Association, 57*, 1043–1069.

Husserl, E. (1970). *The crisis of European sciences and transcendental phenomenology: An introduction to phenomenological philosophy*. Evanston, IL: Northwestern University Press.

Jones, A. (2015). A Psychoanalytic Reader's Commentary: On Erasure and Negation as a Barrier to the Future. *Psychoanalytic Dialogues, 25*, 719–724.

Kant, I., & Beck, L. W. (1993). *Critique of practical reason*. New York and Toronto: Macmillan.

Kleinberg-Levin, D. M. (2008). *Before the voice of reason: Echoes of responsibility in Merleau-Ponty's Ecology and Levinas's Ethics*. Albany: State University of New York Press.

Kuriloff, E. A. (2014). *Contemporary psychoanalysis and the legacy of the Third Reich: History, memory, tradition*. New York: Routledge.

Levi, P. (1961). *Survival in Auschwitz: The Nazi assault on humanity*. New York: Collier Books.

Levinas, E. (1981). *Otherwise than being: Or, beyond essence*. Hague, Boston and Hingham, MA: M. Nijhoff, Distributors for the U.S. and Canada and Kluwer Boston.

Levinas, E. (1989). As If Consenting to Horror. *Critical Inquiry, 15*, 485–488.

Levinas, E. (1990). *Difficult freedom: Essays on Judaism*. Baltimore: Johns Hopkins University Press.

Levinas, E. (2000). *God, death, and time*. Stanford, Calif., Stanford University Press.

Levinas, E., Calin, R., Chalier, C., & Marion, J.-L. (2009). *Oeuvres*. Paris: Bernard Grasset and IMEC.

Liebling, A. J., & Guthrie, R. (1947). *The republic of silence*. New York: Harcourt.

Lifton, R. J. (1986). *The Nazi doctors: Medical killing and the psychology of genocide*. New York: Basic Books.

Loewald, H. W. (1979). The Waning of the Oedipus Complex. *Journal of the American Psychoanalytic Association, 27*, 751–775.

Loewald, H. W. (2000). *The essential Loewald: Collected papers and monographs*. Hagerstown, MD: University Pub. Group.

Mazis, G. A. (2016). *Merleau-Ponty and the face of the world: Silence, ethics, imagination, and poetic ontology*. Albany: SUNY Press.

Merleau-Ponty, M. (1964a). *Signs*. Evanston, IL: Northwestern University Press.

Merleau Ponty, M. (1964b). Merleau-Ponty, Maurice: "Eye and Mind": The Primacy of Perception. Trans. Carleton Dallery. In J. Edie (Ed.), *The primacy of perception* (pp. 159–190). Evanston, IL: Northwestern University Press.

Merleau-Ponty, M. (1973). *The prose of the world*. Evanston, IL: Northwestern University Press.

Merleau-Ponty, M., & Landes, D. A. (2012). *Phenomenology of perception*. Abingdon, Oxon and New York: Routledge.

Merleau-Ponty, M., & Lefort, C. (1968). *The visible and the invisible: Followed by working notes.* Evanston, IL: Northwestern University Press.

Orange, D. M. (2010). *Thinking for clinicians: Philosophical resources for contemporary psychoanalysis and the humanistic psychotherapies.* New York: Routledge.

Orange, D. M. (2011a). Speaking the Unspeakable: "The Implicit," Traumatic Living Memory and the Dialogue of Metaphors. *International Journal of Psychoanalytic Self Psychology, 6,* 187–206.

Orange, D. M. (2011b). *The suffering stranger: Hermeneutics for everyday clinical practice.* New York: Routledge, Taylor & Francis Group.

Orange, D. M. (2013). A Pre-Cartesian Self. *International Journal of Psychoanalytic Self Psychology, 8,* 488–494.

Orange, D. M. (2017). *Climate crisis, psychoanalysis, and radical ethics.* London: Routledge.

Orange, D. M. (2018a). Multiplicity and Integrity: Does an Anti-Developmental Tilt Still Exist in Relational Psychoanalysis? In S. Grand & L. Aron (Eds.), *Relational questions for relational psychoanalysis* (pp. 148–172). London: Routledge, in press.

Orange, D. M. (2018b). You Have the Right to Remain Silent, or Do You Have the Obligation to Speak? *Psychoanalysis, Self, and Context, 13,* 335–341.

Poland, W. S. (2018). *Intimacy and separateness in psychoanalysis.* New York: Routledge.

Ratcliffe, M. (2017). *Real hallucinations: Psychiatric illness, intentionality, and the interpersonal world.* Cambridge, MA: The MIT Press.

Reagan, C. E. (1996). *Paul Ricoeur: His life and his work.* Chicago: University of Chicago Press.

Schelling, F. W. J. V., & Wirth, J. M. (2000). *The ages of the world.* Albany: State University of New York Press.

Shengold, L. (1989). *Soul murder: The effects of childhood abuse and deprivation.* New Haven: Yale University Press.

Stauffer, J. (2015). *Ethical loneliness: The injustice of not being heard.* New York: Columbia University Press.

Steiner, R. (1989). It Is a New Kind of Diaspora . . . . *International Review of Psycho-Analysis, 16,* 35–72.

Steiner, R. (2011). In All Questions, My Interest Is Not in the Individual People But in the Analytic Movement as a Whole: It Will Be Hard Enough Here in Europe in the Times to Come to Keep It Going: After All, We Are Just a Handful of People Who Really Have That in Mind . . . . *International Journal of Psychoanalysis, 92*(3), 505–591.

Stern, D. B. (2013). Psychotherapy Is an Emergent Process. *Psychoanalytic Dialogues, 23,* 102–115.

Stevenson, B. (2014). *Just mercy: A story of justice and redemption* (1st ed.). New York: Spiegel & Grau.

Stolorow, R. D. (1995). An Intersubjective View of Self Psychology. *Psychoanalytic Dialogues, 5*(3), 393–399.

Stolorow, R. D. (2007). *Trauma and human existence: Autobiographical, psychoanalytic, and philosophical reflections.* New York: Analytic Press.

Stolorow, R. D. (2011). *World, affectivity, trauma: Heidegger and post-Cartesian psychoanalysis.* New York: Routledge.

Walker, M. U. (2006). *Moral repair: Reconstructing moral relations after wrongdoing.* Cambridge, UK and New York: Cambridge University Press.

Walker, M. U. (2010). *What is reparative justice?* Milwaukee, WI: Marquette University Press.

Warren, W. (2016). *New England bound: Slavery and colonization in early America* (1st ed.). New York: Liveright Publishing Corporation.

Williams, S. (2010). *Silence and phenomenology: The movement between nature and language in Merleau-Ponty, proust, and schelling.* (PhD), University of Oregon, Retrieved from https://scholarsbank.uoregon.edu/xmlui/bitstream/handle/1794/10917/Williams_Sean_phd2010sp.pdf;sequence=1.

Wittgenstein, L., & Ogden, C. K. (1990). *Tractatus logico-philosophicus.* London and New York: Routledge.

Chapter 2

Violence, dissociation, and traumatizing silence

Psychoanalysis, Werner Bohleber (2007) reminds us, began as a theory of trauma. How its emphasis shifted, and to what extent, has remained a matter of dispute, but most observers agree that since the Vietnam War, trauma has returned to the center of psychoanalytic concern. While analysts in many lands still remain focused on unconscious fantasy and innate aggression as the fundamental causes of human suffering, German analysts, like many of their colleagues in the U.S., have refocused on the effects and psychic reprocessing of psychological trauma. The psychoanalysts of a country that created more traumatized people in a more systematic way than any other in history and has therefore also created generations of perpetrators' children and grandchildren, German psychoanalyst Bohleber tells us, must address trauma and its multigenerational effects on victims and perpetrators. Implicitly, he raises the question of how silence – of all concerned, including bystander/participants – permits, affirms, and refuses witness to the crimes, problems also discussed at length by the contributors to *The Collective Silence: German Identity and the Legacy of Shame* (Heimannsberg & Schmidt, 1992, 1993). The victims stand ever more alone, as Jill Stauffer (2015) writes in speaking of "ethical loneliness": "the experience of being abandoned by humanity compounded by the experience of not being heard" (p. 9). Later she notes:

> If any of us are lucky enough to have remained intact and unviolated, we don't want to hear that no matter what we do we might end up destroyed, that the fabric holding together the world that we experience as relatively safe is very fragile. We don't want to know that and so we may find it difficult to hear a story where that is the message. That is one complication in how we hear . . . .[further] a great many of us probably inherit our sense of our own responsibilities from ideas about the autonomous self who is responsible only for actions freely undertaken – in other words, the idea that we bear responsibility only for things we've done and intended.
>
> (p. 78)

Ethical loneliness can only be understood intersubjectively; it intrinsically involves others.

The Viennese philosopher Ludwig Wittgenstein wrote: "whereof we cannot speak, thereof we must be silent" (Wittgenstein, 1994, para 7). Thus he ended his early *Tractatus Logico-philosophicus*, surely one of the most studied – and probably one of the least understood – texts in the history of Western philosophy. When the science-minded *Wiener Kreis* wanted to discuss it with him, he reportedly (Janik & Toulmin, 1996; Monk, 1990) sat in a corner reading Rabindrinath Tagore. But what did he mean about silence?

Most commentators think Wittgenstein, probably one of two most important Western philosophers of the twentieth century, wanted to claim that we could speak only of trivial matters; of ethics and religion we cannot speak, and should not try to. Some read him as disparaging these areas much as Freud did religion in *The Future of an Illusion* (Freud, Robson-Scott, & Strachey, 1962), scornful of infantile longings. (These same wordless longings Takeo Doi (1989) of Japan taught us to cherish as *amae*, not to be thrown away to achieve adulthood). But Wittgenstein, trying to get his first book into print, wrote to a prospective publisher that it was really two works, one written and one unwritten. The unwritten was the more important. You will not be surprised to learn that the publisher rejected his work. Silence does not make exciting reading, and does not pay publishers well.

But we clearly learn that Wittgenstein, though always seeking philosophical conversation, did not share Freud's preference for the "talking cure." He seemed to believe that speaking of the unspeakable was irreverent, and he had no tolerance for idle chatter. And yet, this tortured philosopher, who had lost three brothers to suicide and had seriously considered it himself, was torn between a repeated need to make personal confessions, and a claim that "we must be silent."

About what must we be silent? About what are we unable to speak? Like many of us, who reach not only the limits of our capacity to speak of the good, of *amae*, and of the holy, but also of suffering too terrible to name, he learned to be silent. The Wittgenstein family, housed in a Viennese palace with almost a dozen grand pianos, played by the greatest composers, resembled an emotional prison, where the sons were expected to follow their demanding father into the steel industry. Inclined toward the arts and other pursuits, they could not oppose or satisfy Karl Wittgenstein, and died one after the other. The family required that the dead ones be no longer mentioned. Their spirits of those who departed had to be silenced, in a process Bernard Brandchaft called pathological accommodation (Brandchaft, Doctors, & Sorter, 2010) and Leonard Shengold "soul murder" (Shengold, 1989). Escape from this system of traumatizing malignant narcissism (Shaw, 2014; Turco, 2014) was impossible. Ludwig, the philosopher, fled to England, returning primarily to disinherit himself (Monk, 1990), by giving away his vast fortune after his parents died. But he said little about his suffering, keeping silent.

Similarly, Jacques Austerlitz, the long-mute protagonist in Sebald's novel (Sebald, 2001; Sebald, Bell, & Wood, 2011) explains:

> I realized then . . . how little practice I had in using my memory, and conversely how hard I must always have tried to recollect as little as possible,

avoiding everything which related in any way to my unknown past. Inconceivable as it seems to me today, I knew nothing about the conquest of Europe by the Germans and the slave state they set up, and nothing about the persecution I had escaped. . . . I was always refining my defensive reactions, creating a kind of quarantine or immune system which, as I maintained my existence on a smaller and smaller space, protected me from anything that could be connected, however distant, with my own early history.

(p. 139)

Only his extended conversation with the narrator, like a good psychoanalysis, begins to restore the links (Loewald, 1975).

Silence and dissociation

We psychoanalysts are familiar with many types of dissociation, from the mildest types of "forgetting" what we clearly once knew or intended – perhaps to schedule a dental appointment – to full amnesia after traumatic shocks like murder, rape, and torture. We know the kinds of phenomena formerly called multiple personalities. A patient, horribly tortured in childhood, sits down, and in a voice we have never heard before, not clearly addressed to the analyst, says: "Don't do that. You really should not do that. You could get in trouble" and so on. The astonished analyst realizes only later that she or he has never met this part of the patient before, but the supervisor explains that this is really a great gift to the analyst and to the treatment. The analyst is hearing and seeing directly, for the first time, the internal conversation. Just now enough relational safety has emerged between patient and analyst to make this moment possible, and to make it usable. Another one says someone has been attending her university classes and taking notes in her handwriting, but that she had not been there. She wants help because she wants to be responsible for everything that is done in her name (I worked with her for many years, and heard unrepeatable stories). Such patients need the kind of ethical witness we will later discuss.

Speaking with trauma theorist Cathy Caruth (2014), who links trauma to silencing, extraordinary student and physician of dissociative conditions Onno van der Hart explains that the essence of trauma is "the lack of support, of help, of comfort; being utterly left alone with the experience and having no one listening" (p. 202). He later continues:

the therapist or other person bearing witness needs to be responsive, exhibiting emotional resonance. And that's why sometimes classical psychoanalysis is so contra-indicated. Because with the patient on the couch, he or she doesn't see the therapist and misses the resonance in the eyes. This may be very disruptive to many traumatized people because it reactivates their attachment trauma, the unavailability of their parents, who might have responded with blank faces to them as children or turned away.

(pp. 204–5)

Van der Hart makes it clear that listening need not be literal, and must be expressed. "Resonance in the eyes," as well as with the voice, communicates ethical and therapeutic hearing. The therapy, he says, "is about the patient's grief . . . coming to terms with the fact that what was will never be again" (p. 207). Continued silence abandons the patient, gives consent to horror, and abandons the transformative work of mourning.

In the middle, we meet many everyday clinical experiences, harder to recognize, except by a lurking sense that something is missing in the story or in the treatment. Freud taught us long ago to listen for the gaps in patients' conscious stories, as evidence for the unconscious; in fact, he used such gaps as his most fundamental argument for the existence of unconscious mental life:

> Our right to assume the existence of something mental that is unconscious and to employ that assumption for the purposes of scientific work is disputed in many quarters. To this we can reply that our assumption of the unconscious is *necessary* and *legitimate*, and that we possess numerous proofs of its existence. It is *necessary* because the data of consciousness have a very large number of gaps in them; both in healthy and in sick people psychical acts often occur which can be explained only by presupposing other acts, of which, nevertheless, consciousness affords no evidence.
>
> (Freud et al., 1915, p. 166, emphases in original)

In the beginning, Freud believed, of course, in a mind topographically organized with a dynamic unconscious containing content censored from awareness because it was too painful or anxiety-producing to know. Oedipal desires or castration anxiety were prime examples, generating symptoms, dreams, and slips. Later, in the structural theory, conflict with the demands of the superego or the external world could produce unconsciousness. He could not, however, tolerate the idea that traumatic experience caused unconsciousness, so Ferenczi was banished, and dissociation went unrecognized. Many of Freud's own best ideas, like the complexity of temporality in *Nachträglichkeit* (making sense backwards) or the compulsion to repeat, had to wait for the wars of the mid-century to be worked through, and for the founder to die. I believe we honor Freud, in whose Vienna house I am writing these words, by bringing back his central ideas, understanding better those he introduced but did not develop, and reintegrating some that he exiled.

In the past 40 years, for example, psychoanalysis has retrieved Freud's beloved travel companion and rejected rebel Sándor Ferenczi,[1] and has learned to notice many kinds of dissociation. In one type, familiar in the U.S., patients enter therapy because of some problem at work or home, from just feeling "terrible," or because the medical doctor recommends therapy. The patient cannot explain the suffering and claims to have grown up in a perfectly normal family. "I guess I am just crazy." Sometimes the dissociation yields easily to gentle and respectful questioning, and the patient comes to realize that what we call a "backstory" produced the difficulties, and the work can go forward. Often it turns out that siblings in the family are also struggling. Already, if there is any type of trauma, any history of violence or neglect, we are in the area of dissociation, a kind of split mind like that described by Fairbairn, rather than that of classical repression, where something once known has been censored due to conflict. This common clinical experience, as Winnicott might have said – with some cultural differences – psychotherapists readily recognize.

But often the trouble is less obvious, and the dissociative process may be more complex. Let us think of a patient who feels unwanted and lost. As a child, he or she was required to be nearly invisible, and never learned even to ask for needed things at school, like perhaps for permission to go to the toilet, or for a pencil when one was missing, never mind affirmation, recognition or support. There is a profound disconnection between what the patient believes is right and just for all human beings, and what he is allowed to want for himself. This gap needs understanding, but perhaps neither patient nor analyst can see the link. Affirmation and support from the analyst helps nothing; the gap is too profound. Both people begin to feel hopeless.

One day, however, the analyst wakes up in a state that Italians call *dormiveglia*, between waking and sleeping, realizing somehow that this patient reminds her of her younger self. How had the analyst been deprived of something essential? Her father had come home from war and had never spoken about what he had seen or done there. Even as she grew older, she was never permitted to ask. Even now, as a teaching psychoanalyst, she knew very little of her family's history or why she had been required to be so unobtrusive as a child. She had had to be good, not to earn praise, but to prevent something; she did not know what.

At the next session, remembering the work of Davoine and Gaudillière (2004), she asked her patient if he knew whether either of his parents or any of his grandparents had been in a war. Given the ages of those probably involved, there could have been fascists, war criminals, resistance fighters, exiles, children born in bomb shelters, or all of the above. He began to find out, and to have a personal history, gruesome as it was, that made sense to him. An Austrian psychotherapist recently told me that early in every treatment, she asks what the parents and grandparents were doing during the war, because every person living in her country still carries this history and lives it out today. Often, 75 years later, the patient does not consciously know the stories of atrocities, of resistance, of support or bystanding for the criminal regime, or exactly how the family had been involved. But all this history lives in the house, and in the family relationships, and no real therapy is possible without bringing this history alive and into conversation. Challenging the silencing taboo "not in my family" (Frie, 2017) means bringing everything into question in a country, and in families, where everything seems so normal, but so little can be spoken.

My point is that avoiding our own traumatic history can prevent working with patients' dissociation. Most of us, patients and analysts both, carry unconscious and dissociated scars that we bring into every psychoanalytic process. Only recently is the literature on the transgenerational transmission of trauma

(Grand & Salberg, 2017; Salberg & Grand, 2017) teaching us how dangerous it is to work as analysts without knowing our own history – familial and cultural. One need not be a theoretical relationalist or intersubjectivist to get this point, but it helps! Knowing myself as the daughter of three generations of maternal suicides affects me and my patients and my supervisees; not knowing this could create disasters, or at least leave people terribly alone and misunderstood.

A word about self-disclosure in psychoanalysis, a big topic in relational psychoanalysis: For me, what is called "countertransference self-disclosure" – telling the patient how I feel about her or him – is rarely necessary or to be recommended. The analyst, including personal history and countertransference reactions, is involved at every moment in the patient's experience and in the psychoanalytic process, and can never be neutral. Clinical wisdom, not neutrality, usually teaches us to say less rather than more. And yet, we cannot really hide from our patients, and when we try to, we often repeat the problematic situations that brought them to us anyway. Thus, a kind of open sincerity seems important. If a patient asks me a direct question, I try first not to analyze the motives behind the question, as these will usually come out anyway, but rather to find out what the patient really wanted to know so that I do not say too much, or answer the wrong question. But I make it clear that I will answer as much as I can, out of respect for a fellow human being. Phenomenologist Bernhard Waldenfels (2011, p. 121) often quotes Paul Watzlawick: "One cannot not answer." To refuse to answer communicates something about our regard for the questioner's human dignity and worth, and we try to be sure our answer expresses this respect.

Another kind of self-disclosure may be very subtle. Just saying "we" in some situations indicates to the other that we recognize the experience the patient is describing, without going into any details. The therapist who asks about war history implies that she, too, comes from a family involved in the Nazi times. I imagine that every therapist and patient alive in Japan today is in some way still related to the Great War (in Japan, this expression means World War II). Sometimes this simple question reassures the other that we both belong to the same human community, not a small thing if the patient is consumed by shame. "When someone humiliates us like that, we really want to disappear," a therapist or analyst might comment. Yes, both of us humans have this experience, and it no longer needs to be dissociated or denied.

This linking between experiences and between people has special importance when physical and mental violence have been involved. Violence – beating, torture, rape, mental brainwashing, and so on – constitutes an attack on one's very humanness, on one's trust in others, in one's trust in oneself, and one's trust in the world. Shame, writes South African philosopher Bruce Janz (2011) desubjectifies. Like Georgio Agamben (1999) and Primo Levi (1988), he recognizes that some human destruction is irreversible, and that only others can speak for those destroyed. But like Jill Stauffer (2015), who writes of "ethical loneliness,"[2] he believes that witnessing, even silent witnessing to injustice and horror, "is a moment on the way to a renewed ability to speak" (p. 469), that is, to renewed subject status and subject experience.[3] "The testimony that becomes possible," he writes, "when true shame is felt, where bare life is experienced, is the testimony that both speaks the truth of what happened, and bears witness to the lengths we and others would go to follow a prescribed view of the world" (p. 469). Meanwhile, the "collective silence" (Heimannsberg & Schmidt, 1993) perpetuates shame and dissociation.

Violence

Some kinds of violence can only go on in the dark. Even in the twilight created and perpetuated by normative inequality, silence protects the perpetrator and shames the victims. Already wounded in their basic humanity, sufferers – and sometimes also criminals – find no witness and no relief. Gradually, they disconnect from the memories, losing the capacity to tell their stories or make sense of their lives. This disconnection lives on into the next generations as parents and grandparents either fear or refuse to tell their children of their war experiences, or of extreme humiliations. Even when there has been no guilt, but only terror, silence may rule.

A grandmother had hidden her husband, escaped from a prison camp in Eastern Europe. She refused to speak about this time many years after the end of World War II, fearing that Nazis would still come after her. As a result, the adult grandchildren's sense of this time resembles a dream or a blank, not the nightmare that the grandmother lived.

I heard similar stories in Japan, about grandfathers who had fought in China in the 1930s. Their psychoanalyst grandchildren grew up feeling that something was wrong, but no one would tell them what, and they were not allowed to ask.

In my own country, the unspeakable crimes are settler colonialism (eliminating indigenous peoples so that whites can "possess" the land) and chattel slavery (in which human beings are bought, sold, inherited, kept illiterate, and beaten into submission). In school, we are taught that these things happened, but never who actually did them.[4] Having visited the camps, we may know of the internment of our Japanese citizens during the war, but do not know the names of those who carried out this policy in our names. So, violence haunts our lands like crimes without perpetrators or victims, but only free-floating shame, nightmares, repetition, and confusion.

Silencing women – rarely regarded as crime or outrage – continues to this day as a form of violence so common that it becomes imperceptible (Solnit, 2014). Even when someone objects, she may be called hysterical, shrill, or worse. She is "picking a fight." From the refusal to educate girls worldwide to the disappearing of women's voices in nearly every discipline, our memory fails to explain how we came to this situation. We were born into a normative situation that took our silence for granted as something not needing any justification.

Judith Lewis Herman (2009) asks what happens to the memory of a crime, "in the mind of the victim, in the mind of the perpetrator, and in the mind of the bystander?" (p. 127). She summarizes the answer of Daniel Bar-On

(Bar-On, 1989), who had interviewed adult children of Nazi war criminals: "The fathers did not want to tell; the children did not want to know" (p. 129). The truth became unspeakable, so that all were left in Stauffer's "ethical loneliness," unheard. "Remembering and telling the truth about terrible events are essential tasks," Herman writes, "for both the healing of individual victims, perpetrators, and families and for the restoration of the social order." (p. 129).

Of course, it is important to take care speaking of violence, silence, and dissociation, victims, and perpetrators. Best, perhaps, is to begin with the violence my country has done to others. In November 2018, after changing some yen to dollars for me at Hiroshima Bank, the teller asked me what brought me to her city. "My people did a terrible thing to your people here, and I needed to see." "Oh yes," she responded, "my grandmother," making a big gesture with both hands, "A-bomb." I could only make a deep bow in sorrow. We perpetrators need to speak so that those we have destroyed and injured can speak.

In another experience on that trip – in Kobe, Japan – we had been talking about traumatic memory, again in Europe, and the need for the children of victims, perpetrators, and bystanders to know so that we do not repeat terrible crimes. At lunch, over our beautiful bento boxes, one colleague after another spoke without any questions from me, saying that someone in the family had been in fighting in China in the 1930s, but that no one would ever speak about it. It continues only as a deep dark cloud, present but disconnected from daily life. We call this traumatic dissociation, inflicted by silence. By the time the grandchildren, perhaps psychoanalysts now, begin to ask the questions, the parents and grandparents have died. All the recent studies of transgenerational transmission of trauma, however, teach us that the dreadful truths continue to haunt us like unconscious ghosts.

So what are we to do now, if those who know what happened are dead or unwilling to tell their children what they know? One possibility is to encourage ourselves and our children to read history in detail, possibly in groups, as an almost therapeutic project. We can no longer directly remember the history of the enslavement of African people in our country for 250 years, for example. Learning about it in detail, and allowing the descendants of slaves to teach us about this history and its effects, however, may humble us. The more we learn, the more questions we will ask, and the less innocent we will feel. This seems to me a way of making the unconscious conscious, and undoing dissociation.

Silence and the fogging of memory

In the beginning, much is clear. Torturers, murderers, totalitarian dictators, parents who employ unspeakable violence of uncountable kinds to control their children: These are the victimizers, the perpetrators, the criminals. The tortured, the murdered, the brutalized, incested, and humiliated children: These are victims, often completely innocent. But take even a few steps back, not to mention generations, and we enter Primo Levi's "grey zone" (Levi, 1988, p. 36ff). In his last years, decades after return, he described the moral world of Auschwitz where many prisoners, clearly victims of the Nazi regime, became victimizers to greater and lesser degrees, from assisting in the gas chambers to stealing food. He found understanding in varying degrees for these victim victimizers, cruel as many of them were, far more than for the well-fed Germans and Austrians who pretended not to know of the camps, often located in their own neighborhoods. These people pretended to be victims too, victims of a terrible government (which they had enthusiastically supported, by the way) who committed crimes in their names. They claimed innocence.

But we are not directly concerned with moral equivocation and semi-conscious evasion of responsibility, though this question will return through the back door. Rather, as psychoanalysts, we must ask what unconscious processes lead to the fogging of memory and the confusion of victimhood and perpetration, or as relationalist Jessica Benjamin (2004) would say, doer and done-to. Psychoanalysis, as Warren Poland (2006) teaches, defines itself by just such questions. He writes:

> What makes an attitude uniquely psychoanalytic is concern for the power of unconscious forces, the analyst's working in the service of helping the patient come to know his or her own mind with ruthless candor, unfettered by shame or guilt.
>
> (pp. 223–4)

Assuming we agree, then, that psychoanalysts struggle to help ourselves and our patients to know what unconsciously prevents our candor about historical victim or victimizer status, what have we learned so far? Why, in short, might we not want to know? What maintains the fog, carefully protected by generational clouds of silence? In some cultures, of course, we have the honor of the family, never to my knowledge, listed as among the properly psychoanalytic defenses. But now we have the work of Canadian/German psychoanalyst and historian Roger Frie, author of *Not in My Family: German Memory and the Holocaust* (Frie, 2016). With extraordinary courage, Frie recounts his own journey toward seeing what had always been right there in his life: His beloved grandfather's Nazi status and active participation. His book includes the photograph of his grandfather in the uniform of a Nazi motorcycle club, the image that shocked his grandson into realization. It further describes Frie's later discoveries about the exact work his grandfather did during the war, on the terrifying *Vergeltungswaffen*, rockets aimed mostly at London, only ended because the Allies bombed their launching sites. Not only has Frie needed to protect his own attachment to this grandfather – a powerful unconscious motivator against the candor of which Poland writes – but then he must struggle, as do all thoughtful later-born Germans and Austrians, with other difficult questions that blur the lines between guilt and innocence, victimizers and victims. But I am getting ahead of my story.

First, let us propose some informal working definitions, imperfect but perhaps clarifying. Let us agree to call a *victim* someone who suffers injustice; that is, not only suffers, as one might from an accidental injury, but one who suffers from unjust discrimination or violence. In this sense, one is not a flood victim (even though it is easy to feel victimized by impersonal forces), but one may actually be a victim of an unjust racial or economic system. Clearly, the term may be used in various ways, but for our purposes here, the reality and sense of injustice seems indispensable.

Second, a *perpetrator* creates or inflicts injustice on other human beings. Whatever form this injustice may take, the perpetrator never intends to be on the receiving end of the treatment being inflicted on the victim or victims. If the doer is willing to be done-to in exactly the same way, we are speaking of a game, played within rules. Refusal of reciprocity is indispensable to injustice, and to being a perpetrator. An enormous philosophical literature exists around this question, but for now, we seek only working definitions, so that we can go on to find a phenomenology of memory fog for psychoanalysis.

How can we define "historical trauma"? Let us say that collectively, we are speaking of wars, whether won or lost, of genocides, of all the violence associated with wars, genocides, and totalitarian regimes. But the collective historical traumas do not seek psychoanalysis, nor, for the most part, do the immediate perpetrators: the dictators, the torturers, the murderers. So, the "historical trauma" concerning us here, silenced by the unconscious processes to which we have already referred in passing, mostly hides under a mask of normalization – until it can no longer. The grandson of the Nazi, the granddaughter of the Hiroshima victim or of the death camp survivors from Europe, speak through their symptoms and dreams to a psychoanalyst who is ready to hear more than today's report. These children and grandchildren grew up with anxieties and hints they could not interpret: Parents who will never buy property in the U.S. because they might suddenly need to move again; grandparents who teach their children and grandchildren to trust no one, without saying why; parents who suddenly stop talking when children come into the room, or who fight to mask their sorrow. There are stoical, hard-working parents who simply seem to have some years missing from their lives, or some people unaccountably missing, leaving their children to wonder why. Often, the child begins to wonder why she or he cannot make any impact on such a parent, where the sudden silences or rages come from, whether the child is doing something wrong. The psychic holes transmit themselves, almost automatically, across generations, until an analyst attuned to unconscious forces of history asks why.

Thus we can say that historical trauma, though it belongs originally to those tortured, murdered, dispossessed, or driven away, comes to us more often in the next generations, and need us to be on the alert for it, in whatever forms it may take in our own cultures. In North America, we may see post-traumatic stress, substance abuse, depression in familiar and unfamiliar forms, and returns to the political forms that created the historical trauma of slavery and colonialism in the first place. In France, we have learned from Françoise Davoine to listen for historical trauma in many forms of madness. In each geographical and cultural location, other manifestations appear, but every clinician, as long as we live in a world of war and violence, must learn to pick up and hear these indicators – first in ourselves, and then in our patients. More than once in my years of practice in New York, searching with a patient for liberation from a life incarcerated in parental violence or depression, I dreamed of European concentration camps, only to discover that the patient was having similar dreams. In both instances, the patient later found Holocaust history in the family. Yes, we work in the service of the other, even at night!

Clearly, attention to language claims a high priority. But now we come to the least definable, but perhaps most important word, in the section title – fog. Visually, fog creates a blur that keeps us from seeing what may be so close as to endanger us. Auditorily, fog resembles static or noise that covers the sound or voice that could provide the "ruthless candor," protecting us from knowing what is too painful or guilt inducing to know. In the context of historical trauma, this fog or static may mask historical crimes, as in the case of Roger Frie's family and so many others. An Austrian colleague, as mentioned earlier, tells me that sooner or later in every treatment, she asks where family members were during World War II. Possibilities include the *Wehrmacht* (the regular German armed forces; this means they were probably fighting and dying in Russia), the SS (this elite group included very high numbers of Austrians, and managed all the concentrations camps under Heinrich Himmler), resistance (very small numbers, living in hiding), and very few others. No one was uninvolved, though approximately 90 Austrians are known to have hidden Jews, or helped them to escape. The fog of memory, in Austria, has taken the form of a quick conversion of Austrians into "Hitler's first victims," showing how malleable the victim/victimizer discourse can be. They conveniently forgot – the Allies supported this forgetting after the war to keep Austria in the Western bloc in the Cold War – how enthusiastically they had welcomed the Nazis and persecuted the Jews to extermination. In this fog, my questions, in the birthplace of Sigmund Freud's psychoanalysis, about "where are the Jewish psychoanalysts?" meet puzzled faces. I guess there are two or three here now, they say. Then a visit to the Central Cemetery (*Zentralfriedhof*) shows elaborate, well-tended monuments to Beethoven, Schubert, and Mozart, not far from the Jewish section, untended and with gravestones knocked down and in ruins. Similarly, in the U.S., our political discourse about racial problems often seems to forget that we whites enslaved fellow human beings here for hundreds of years, and cruelly punished any who tried to escape for their own human dignity, or who tried to learn to read.

Fog, of course, can arise in less wretched ways, to protect natural and needed bonds. We see this most commonly when a small child arrives in school with an unusual set of bumps and bruises. Sent to the school psychologist, who asks what happened, we hear that he fell off his bicycle. The pattern of the injuries does not support this story, so we understand that the child is probably afraid of speaking the truth. The truth might mean he will be beaten again, that childcare workers will come and take him away from the family, or some evil we adults cannot imagine. So, he fell off his bike. Or, yes, they hit me because I was bad. I won't do it anymore. The victim has transformed himself into the one who makes the problem, a very simple example of what becomes an automatic form of what Fairbairn will call the moral defense. We are not allowed to ask questions of the parents (*Was hast Du in der Nacht getan?* What were you doing in the war?) because we need their protection. In turn, we protect the perpetrators from having to speak of their own crimes, and in the light of our love and admiration for them, they may come to feel more and more like innocent victims. After all, we did it for our children. It becomes more and more difficult for either generation, or for the grandchildren, to emerge from this foggy unconsciousness into "ruthless candor, unfettered by shame or guilt." But the fog exacts a high price, in personal symptoms and in familial and societal confusion. As we see in both Europe and in the U.S., such fog also leaves us vulnerable to dictators and demagogues similar to those who wreaked havoc in the past. We have no way to say: Look what happens when you listen to the discourse of hatred.

In another version, family violence may be fogged out, hiding its reality from the children, creating more versions of what Ferenczi named "confusion of the tongues" (Ferenczi, 1949) by blaming the child for incest, for beatings, for all forms of humiliation, exploitation, and neglect. Not until the children have children of their own and find themselves confused by the way they treat their own children may they ask for help from an analyst or from their adult siblings. Unable ourselves even to recall much of the worst abuse, our analysis finds us ever deeper in self-blame. If we are lucky, we have siblings also trying to find their way who begin to question us and tell us what they remember. Eyewitnesses can help with revising the meanings we had always accepted. Maybe I am not good for nothing; maybe I was being exploited ruthlessly, denigrated with verbal and nonverbal attacks, even to the throwing of knives, when I did not meet expectations. Maybe you, my brother, were constantly terrified of the next beating, and remember – I do not – that I sometimes tried to protect you. All of us may have needed the fog of memory just to survive; we could not allow ourselves to believe how dangerous our life actually was. As adults, we helped each other with the fog.

Another source of unconscious fogging can be what psychoanalysts now call the intergenerational transmission of trauma. When the parents come from families where the parents are missing – and no one asks for the historical circumstance behind this absence – and those with whom they reside are violent or otherwise hateful, these same parents may have no sense of good-enough parenting. Their now-adult children, who may be more or less grateful to be living, realize that these parents should never have had children, but knew no better. It is hard, even for those beaten down, to know whether one's own parents were more victims or more perpetrators. Though we can easily provide clear instances that belong to each category, we are left with many in question, just as Primo Levi wrote. So, is this more defensive fogging, or something wrong with our categories?

Let me say here clearly that I am not a radical postmodernist. While there is often more than one perspective on the truth, more than one true story to be told about a given event (Rashomon effect), there is truth and there is falsehood. There is justice and there is injustice, even if we do not always know exactly what it is. So how do we emerge from real or neurotic guilt, from useful and destructive shame, into "ruthless candor," at least with ourselves? Psychoanalysis, that invention also called "the talking cure," takes the attitude that careful, attentive listening that stays close to the other's suffering but ready to engage the unconscious demons, often of historical trauma and our own complicity in it – or knowledge that those we love have done terrible things to us and to others – can be liberating. Psychoanalysis expects that we need each other. Turned toward the other, we may sing sorrowfully: I can see clearly now, the fog is gone.

Notes

1 Freud wrote to his daughter Anna Freud: "He has made a full regression to etiological views that I believed and gave up 35 years ago, that the regular cause of neuroses was gross childhood sexual traumas . . . with remarks on the hostility of patients and the necessity to take in their criticism and to acknowledge our mistakes with them. . . . The whole thing is really stupid (Freud, Schröter, & Eitingon, 2004, II, p. 829). I am grateful to Peter Rudnytsky for alerting me to this note.
2 She describes ethical loneliness a double abandonment, the experience of being abandoned by humanity compounded by the experience of not being heard when you testify to what happened. Victims of sexual assault know this loneliness well.
3 Responding to South African philosopher Samantha Vice (2010), Janz paraphrases what he calls her "religious subtext": "The inheritance of an inequitable and unjust advantage bears some resemblance to original sin. Shame is a kind of response to the recognition that this sin is part of one's being, and not just the result of some isolated act. Adam and Eve, after all, became aware of their nakedness and were ashamed. And, silence and humility are classic steps on the via negative, the negative path back towards wholeness and integration with the divine. The negative path is one of renunciation and denial of possessions including, importantly, knowledge and power, which are kinds of possessions" (p. 468).
4 This reminds me of the dissociation described by Roger Frie in *Not in My Family: German Memory and the Holocaust* (Frie, 2017).

References

Agamben, G. (1999). *Remnants of Auschwitz: The witness and the archive.* New York: Zone Books.

Bar-On, D. (1989). Holocaust Perpetrators and Their Children: A Paradoxical Morality. *Journal for Humanistic Psychology, 29,* 424–443.

Benjamin, J. (2004). Beyond Doer and Done to: An Intersubjective View of Thirdness. *Psychoanalytic Quarterly, 73,* 5–46.

Bohleber, W. (2007). Remembrance, Trauma and Collective Memory: The Battle for Memory in Psychoanalysis. *International Journal of Psychoanalysis, 88*(2), 329–352.

Brandchaft, B., Doctors, S., & Sorter, D. (2010). *Toward an emancipatory psychoanalysis: Brandchaft's intersubjective vision.* New York: Routledge.

Caruth, C. (2014). *Listening to trauma: Conversations with leaders in the theory and treatment of catastrophic experience.* Baltimore: Johns Hopkins University Press.

Davoine, F., & Gaudillière, J.-M. (2004). *History beyond trauma: Whereof one cannot speak, thereof one cannot stay silent.* New York: Other Press.

Doi, T. (1989). The Concept of Amae and Its Psychoanalytic Implications. *International Review of Psycho-Analysis, 16,* 349–354.

Ferenczi, S. (1949). Confusion of the Tongues between the Adults and the Child: (The Language of Tenderness and of Passion). *International Journal of Psycho-Analysis, 30,* 225–230.

Freud, S., Robson-Scott, W. D., & Strachey, J. (1962). *The future of an illusion* (Rev. ed.). London: Hogarth Pressand Institute of Psycho-Analysis.

Freud, S., Schröter, M., & Eitingon, M. (2004). *Briefwechsel 1906–1939.* Tübingen: Edition Diskord.

Freud, S., Strachey, A., Tyson, A., Strachey, J., & Freud, A. (1915). The Unconscious. In *The standard edition of the complete psychological works of Sigmund Freud, Volume XIV (1914–1916): On the history of the psycho-analytic movement, papers on metapsychology and other works* (Vol. 14, pp. 159–215). London: Hogarth

Frie, R. (201 6). *Not in my family: German memory and the holocaust.* Oxford: Oxford University Press.

Frie, R. (2017). *Not in my family: German memory and responsibility after the Holocaust.* New York, NY: Oxford University Press.

Friedman, L. (2014). The Discrete and the Continuous in Freud's "Remembering, Repeating and Working Through". *Journal of the American Psychoanalytic Association, 62*(1), 11–34.

Grand, S., & Salberg, J. (2017). *Trans-generational trauma and the other: Dialogues across history and difference.* London and New York: Routledge, Taylor & Francis Group.

Heimannsberg, B., & Schmidt, C. J. (1992). *Das Kollektive Schweigen: Nationalsozialistische Vergangenheit und gebrochene Identität in der Psychotherapie* (Erw. Neuausg. ed.). Köln: EHP, Edition Humanistische Psychologie.

Heimannsberg, B., & Schmidt, C. J. (1993). *The collective silence: German identity and the legacy of shame* (1st ed.). San Francisco: Jossey-Bass.

Herman, J. (2009). Crime and Memory. In K. Golden & B. Bergo (Eds.), *The Trauma controversy: Philosophical and interdisciplinary dialogues* (pp. 127–141). Albany: SUNY Press.

Janik, A., & Toulmin, S. (1996). *Wittgenstein's Vienna* (1st Elephant pbk. ed.). Chicago: I.R. Dee.

Janz, B. B. (2011). Shame and Silence. *South African Journal of Philosophy, 30,* 462–471.

Levi, P. (1988). *The drowned and the saved.* New York: Summit Books.

Loewald, H. W. (1975). Psychoanalysis as an Art and the Fantasy Character of the Psychoanalytic Situation. *Journal of the American Psychoanalytic Association, 23,* 277–299.

Monk, R. (1990). *Ludwig Wittgenstein: The duty of genius* (1st American ed.). New York: Free Press: Maxwell Macmillan International.

Poland, W. (2006). Struggling to Hear. *American Imago, 63,* 223–226.

Salberg, J., & Grand, S. (2017). *Wounds of history: Repair and resilience in the transgenerational transmission of trauma.* London and New York: Routledge, Taylor & Francis Group.

Sebald, W. G. (2001). *Austerlitz.* München: C. Hanser.

Sebald, W. G., Bell, A., & Wood, J. (2011). *Austerlitz* (Modern Library trade pbk. ed.). New York: Modern Library.

Shaw, D. (2014). *Traumatic narcissism: Relational systems of subjugation.* New York: Routledge, Taylor & Francis Group.

Shengold, L. (1989). *Soul murder: The effects of childhood abuse and deprivation*. New Haven: Yale University Press.

Solnit, R. (2014). *Men explain things to me*. Chicago, IL: Haymarket Books.

Stauffer, J. (2015). *Ethical loneliness: The injustice of not being heard*. New York: Columbia University Press.

Turco, R. N. (2014). Traumatic Narcissism: Relational Systems of Subjugation, by Daniel Shaw, Routledge, New York and London, 2013, 167 pp. $36.97. *Psychodyn. Psi.*, *42*(4), 721–725.

Vice, S. (2010). How Do I Live in This Strange Place? *Journal of Social Philosophy*, *41*, 323–342.

Waldenfels, B. (2011). *Phenomenology of the alien: Basic concepts*. Evanston, IL: Northwestern University Press.

Wittgenstein, L. (1994). *Tractatus logico-philosophicus*. London and New York: Routledge.

Chapter 3

This is not psychoanalysis!

Perhaps the most famous, though by no means the last, silencing in the history of psychoanalysis occurred in the Vienna Psychoanalytic Society on 1 February 1911. Alfred Adler had in the previous meeting delivered a paper on "the masculine protest as the central problem of neurosis." Now Freud responded, according to meticulous note-taker Otto Rank (Wiener Psychoanalytische Vereinigung, Nunberg, & Federn, 1962), saying that "this is not psychoanalysis" (p. 146), explaining at length why his views and Adler's were incompatible. His own understandings, of course, defined psychoanalysis, as he was to repeat later in various contexts. Adler left the Society soon after this meeting.

According to Nunberg and Federn (Wiener Psychoanalytische Vereinigung et al., 1962), as reported by Martin Bergmann (2011), Alfred Adler presented to the Vienna Psychoanalytic Society his view that "masculine protest" was present in all women. Freud responded by saying, "Adler's writings are not a continuation upward, nor are they a foundation underneath; they are something else entirely. This is not psychoanalysis" (p. 146 in Nunberg and Federn, vol. 3). According to Bergmann, the assembled "disciples" in their comments "showed that they did not understand that at this moment the boundaries of psychoanalysis were being defined for the first time" (Bergmann, 2011, p. 667).[1]

These "disciples" increasingly did understand that discussion within the Wednesday group, which became the Vienna Psychoanalytic Society, could occur only within these boundaries. As Adler, Jung, Tausk, and Stekel departed, each taking others along, the minutes, written by Otto Rank, proceed as if nothing had happened (Bos, 1996). But their voices had gone silent in the service of orthodoxy. By 1914, Freud saw that only official authority could protect from the pitfalls inherent in the practice of psychoanalysis. In *On the History of the Psycho-Analytical Movement*, he wrote:

> I considered it necessary to form an official association because I feared the abuses to which psycho-analysis would be subjected as soon as it became popular. There should be some headquarters whose business it would be to declare: "All this nonsense has nothing to do with analysis; this is not psycho-analysis."
> (S. Freud, A. Strachey, Tyson, J. Strachey, & A. Freud, 1914. p. 43)

For many years, Freud himself remained that headquarters, so that the requirements of orthodoxy shifted as his views developed. In his last years he himself commented: "when a man is endowed with power it is hard for him not to misuse it" (Freud, 1937, p. 249).

Another institutional control emerged early, in the form of journals, all under the strict control of Wednesday group members. When Stekel, editor of the *Zentralblatt*, departed from the Wednesday group, Freud directed all the others to leave the journal, thus removing the possibility of independent conversation. Bos (1996) notes that even today, psychoanalytic journals effectively control access to conversation, deciding what is and is not within the bounds of psychoanalysis as the journal editors understand it.

Over time, all members came to understand that they could not question Freud, even when he changed his own views (Bergmann, 2011), replacing the early topographical theory with the structural theory, including the dual instinct claim. After the initial whiplash, non-Kleinian analysts simply have left the death instinct out of discussion. Americans opted for a more optimistic, though unembodied, ego psychology. Loyalty kept most analysts silent, in a compliance and conformity that reminded Erich Fromm of attitudes and practices within dictatorships (Fromm, 1958). When Fromm criticized Ernest Jones's orthodoxy-supporting attack on Ferenczi's sanity in the Freud biography (Jones, 1957), Jacob Arlow responded that "in psychoanalysis there is no monolithic structure with a 'party line,'" (Arlow, 1958, p. 14). (Rudnytsky, 2015). Fromm, as we shall see, had already learned otherwise.

Silencing in psychoanalysis, as well as among those excluded who formed other psychotherapeutic groups, has been and continues to be far more complicated than mere gagging, or even thought control, by authoritarians. At least three historical/relational phenomena have interlocked:

1   The institutional structures of psychoanalysis, including the training analysis and the tendency to protect the leaders from criticism.
2   The historical trauma of persecution, migration, and extermination, generating the silences of the ashamed.
3   Self-silencing, protecting individual psychoanalysts from exclusion and psychoanalysis from creative contributions.

Let us consider each in turn, understanding that they refuse to stay separated.

Institutional structures

Soon after the incident described previously, Freud invited his six most trusted followers/disciples – Otto Rank, Hans Sachs, Max Eitingon, Ernest Jones, Sándor Ferenczi, and Karl Abraham – to form a secret committee, the signet-ring group. Jung seems to have known he was excluded (Cremerius, 1990). This group served as both "kitchen cabinet" and international defense team until 1924, when Rank left over the birth trauma, and Abraham died in 1925. Even later, Eitingon and

Jones remained close, supporting Freud in interpreting Ferenczi's innovations as reflecting pathology (Freud, Schröter, & Eitingon, 2004). At any cost, even in the face of the Nazi takeover in Berlin, they felt they had to protect psychoanalysis (Steiner, 2011).

Psychoanalytic institutions may have inherited a tendency toward secrecy and ambiguity from this period. Historian of psychoanalysis Riccardo Steiner (2011) seems to attribute this style of non-communication especially to Ernest Jones, who early on suggested the secret-ring group to Freud and served as President of the International Psychoanalytical Association (IPA) during the dangerous years of the 1930s, but more careful research into the Freud-Jones correspondence would clarify much. Did Freud know that Jones did not really want the Jewish analysts in Britain? Though we now have the Freud-Jones correspondence, much is still hidden, and we do not know whom or what this silence intends to protect.

The training analyst system, developed in Berlin and reluctantly accepted by Freud after his cancer convinced him that he would not forever be able to control the future of his movement,[2] became, and remains to this day, another important source of silencing in psychoanalysis. Not only does it include requirements that candidates be analyzed by already anointed "training analysts" who report to training progression committees and hold complete control over the fate of these candidates; the training analysts themselves have survived rigorous tests of orthodoxy and compliance over many years. Many, though not all, institutes outside the IPA have rejected the training analyst system. Unfortunately, many of these have developed informal, even cultish, means of enforcing compliance and accommodation (Brandchaft, Doctors, & Sorter, 2010). Independent thinkers either go silent or become courageous outsiders.

Freud himself believed that analysis was learned one-to-one, surely an unsystematic but often deeply effective and convincing approach rather like apprenticeship.[3] Freud himself was the ultimate *Meistersinger*, to whom seekers from everywhere traveled. Like Wagner's hero, he knew his *Wissenschaft* (science) was even more an art. But art (including literature and music) under authoritarians, as artists were soon to learn under the National Socialists, becomes either perverted into propaganda, stolen, or destroyed. It had also, as Freud himself expected, been difficult to maintain a sense of creativity in psychoanalysis once it became subservient to the medical profession. Not surprisingly, relational and intersubjective innovations came to prominence in psychoanalysis in the U.S. only in the years after psychologists lodged a legal challenge to the hegemony of medical psychoanalysis. Some psychiatrists participated in the newer thinking, of course, but I think of names like Stephen Mitchell, Robert Stolorow, Jessica Benjamin, George Atwood, Lewis Aron, Adrienne Harris, and many more, all psychologists excluded from the institutes of the American Psychoanalytic Association until the late 1980s, and thus also from the IPA. I think it safe to say that Freud would have firmly disapproved of the rigid rules for admission to the IPA that he and the early analysts founded to protect psychoanalysis. None of these psychologists, not to mention brilliant clinical social workers, could be members today.

And yet, the training analysis system itself, gradually generating the elaborate and closed hierarchy of training analysts, became a requirement only when the founders saw that they were truly mortal, Freud in the mid-1920s with his cancer, Jung later with his cardiac problems. Both had recommended training analysis earlier (Roazen, 2002), but both had wanted, for as long as possible to keep real control over who became an analyst. The training analysts inherited this control from the founders, and long maintained it. The cost of this system increased over the years, in the stifling of creativity, when saying something unorthodox could result in never becoming a training analyst, never being truly included, locally or internationally. Psychoanalysis became risk-averse, and the costs – largely invisible and silent – lay on young and idealistic analysts, as well as on patients, who had to be "analyzable."

Because historian of psychoanalysis Paul Roazen's voice has now gone mute, let me quote his concluding words on silences around the training analysis system and elsewhere:

> The issue of training analyses seems to me the tip of a large over-all historical subject, which as I say has kept me fascinated as a matter of scholarship for four decades now. Once it was a question of keeping quiet the fact that Freud had analyzed his own daughter Anna. In the future, I hope that Freud's neglected interests in phylogenetics, as well as telepathy, will receive the full attention that they deserve; it is no tribute to his memory to narrow him down to what might be plausibly acceptable today. The whole question of money in the history of psychoanalysis also needs to be adequately explored. I anticipate that the uncensored publication of Freud's various correspondences, which will go on after anyone alive today is still around, will continue to be challenging and instructive. . . . The field is, I think, inherently strong enough to withstand the kind of examination which all important subjects deserve. *Silence itself belongs at graveyards, not to the life of the mind.*
>
> (Roazen, 2002, p. 77, emphasis added)

But organized psychoanalysis found other ways of silencing people, and we have, no doubt, intergenerationally inherited the effects of these tendencies to consider people heretics – or at least untrustworthy as keepers of the orthodoxy of the time. One, the habit of describing one's opponents as "insufficiently analyzed," (cf. Bergmann, 1997) became a particularly pernicious form of dismissiveness and humiliation, against which those so silenced or excluded could rarely find any defense. Another, particularly malignant and more than a tendency, excluded gay and lesbian people for putative "pathology." Although Freud himself did not share this view, psychoanalysis in the U.S. silenced, shamed, and attempted "conversion" of gay analysts and patients. Believable stories circulate of senior American psychoanalysts who threatened gay colleagues if they came out or tried to practice psychoanalysis openly.

Protecting orthodoxy and orthodoxy as protection

From the beginning, the circle around Freud took on a religious tone, even while it continued to examine from various angles the psychological motivations for religious belief (Cooper-White, 2018), culminating in *The Future of an Illusion* (Freud, 1928). Max Graf, father of "Little Hans" and member of the early Wednesday group, describes the atmosphere there:

> I have compared the gatherings in Freud's home with the founding of a religion. However, after the first dreamy period and the unquestioning faith of the first group of apostles, the time came when the church was founded. Freud began to organize his church with great energy. He was serious and strict in the demands he made of his pupils; he permitted no deviations from his orthodox teaching. Subjectively, Freud was of course right, for that which he worked out with so much energy and sequence, and which was as yet to be defended against the opposition of the world, could not be rendered inept by hesitations, weakening, and tasteless ornamentations. Good-hearted and considerate though he was in private life, Freud was hard and relentless in the presentation of his ideas. When the question of his science came up, he would break with his most intimate and reliable friends. If we do consider him as a founder of a religion, we may think of him as a Moses full of wrath and unmoved by prayers, a Moses like the one Michael Angelo brought to life out of stone – to be seen in the Church of San Pietro in Vincoli in Rome. After a trip to Italy, Freud never tired of talking to us about this statue; the memory of it he kept for his last book.
>
> In the meantime, Freud's theories spread ever further all over the world . . . inspired adherents appeared everywhere, new pupils, new apostles. One day Freud brought into our circle a tall, good-looking physician from Switzerland. Freud spoke of him with great warmth; it was Professor Jung from Zürich. Another time he introduced a gentleman from Budapest – Doctor Ferenczi. Branches of the Freudian church were founded in all parts of the world.
>
> (Graf, 1942, p. 472)

Even Freud's family knew he was a dominant personality: His grandson Anton Freud (1996) wrote:

> Ordinary emperors and kings have only one court. Grandfather had two. . . . The first court was the psychoanalytic one. . . . The second court belonged to grandfather's private life. You do not have to be Galileo to notice that this one revolved around grandfather too.[4]

My earlier, and surely incomplete, reading of Freud's authoritarian style attributed his tendency to exclude, shun, and silence dissenters to his intense desire to be regarded among the greatest of Western groundbreakers, with Copernicus and Darwin. Complexifying the clear theories of infantile sexuality, the Oedipus, and the drives, not to mention diluting the pure gold of analytic practice with the copper of suggestion, could not be tolerated. The great Moses might become a forgotten nobody.

But living and working in Freud's Vienna,[5] including several months in the unrenovated veranda of his house from which he watched his children play in the garden, has taught me something else. We later-born (*nachgeborene*) psychoanalysts know and do not know that more or less 200,000 Jews lived within walking distance of Freud's house – I do not exaggerate much – in 1900. We do and do not know that all of them were gone by the end of 1938. Freud and his immediate family escaped to London, but despite his efforts to get visas for them, his four sisters met a fate described in detail by Cooper-White (2018). She quotes a Treblinka survivor who testified that one (either Marie, age 81, or Pauli, age 78) approached the camp commander,

> showing him an identifying document, saying she was the sister of Sigmund Freud and asking to be given light office work. The commander said there must have been a mistake and told her that in two hours there should be a train to Vienna. She could leave all her valuables and documents here, have a bath, and after the bath she would receive her documents and a travel permit to Vienna . . . [she] went to the bath house, from which she never returned.
>
> (pp. 261–2)

Cooper-White also lists the names and fates of the 11 Jewish members of the Vienna Psychoanalytic Society (itself disappeared from the IPA before the end of 1938) who were unable to emigrate after the *Anschluß* [Germany's 1938 annexation of Austria]. The end came swiftly in Vienna. The streets near Freud's house are lined with *Stolpersteine*, remembering the names and death camps of those who used to live in the houses, often with a note that "there were 57 others," or that "in this house, 110 were gathered to wait for transport." One lives in a spectacularly beautiful crime scene, with a determined veneer of normality. I am informed by local psychoanalysts that only two, or possibly three, Jewish psychoanalysts live and practice in Vienna today. When I told them my own experience of psychoanalysis had been primarily and extensively among Jewish colleagues and patients, they seemed mildly surprised. Where did these people come from, they wondered?

But the clouds had long been threatening. Not only did Vienna, long a haven for Eastern European Jews, including Freud's parents, elect a rabidly anti-Semitic mayor in 1997 from whom Emperor Franz Josef could no longer protect his city, the very success of Jewish leaders in business, in the arts, in the intellectual life of the *Wiener Moderne* or *Jung Wien*, encouraged a deadly envy, harking back to the worst medieval stereotypes. And this was only the secular form of hatred. The Catholic Church, deeply engrained in Austrian life even to this day – no shopping on Sunday even now! – also nurtured the deep roots of anti-Jewish hatred dating before anyone's memory. Here is an example, probably known to both Freud and Hitler. Years ago, when I was studying Heidegger in order to teach his early work, I learned of his Catholic background and influence by the popular Austrian preacher Abraham a Sancta Clara (1644–1709), who like Heidegger was born near Messkirch but died in Vienna. He was a rabid anti-Semite, proclaiming:

> After Satan Christians have no greater enemies than the Jews. . . . They pray many times each day that God may destroy us through pestilence, famine and war, aye, that all beings and creatures may rise up with them against the Christians.

> (quoted by Wistrich, 2001, p. 1)

According to biographer Robert Safranski (1998), Heidegger's earliest writing celebrated the setting of a monument to Sancta Clara. Robert Michael, author of *A History of Catholic Antisemitism: The Dark Side of the Church* (2008) believes that Mayor Karl Lueger found in Sancta Clara the most important impetus for his anti-Semitism. So, it was shocking, walking around in the first district, to find a street named after Sancta Clara, then a statue of him in the *Volksgarten* public park near the Albertina museum and *Staatsoper* opera house, and later a plaque honoring him in a church whose name I cannot remember.

So, when we read in Cooper-White that anti-Semitism shaped the early history of psychoanalysis, we recognize something. It is still in the air there – *unheimlich*, as Freud would have said – and unconsciously, like the air we breathe, not know-ing it is poisonous. If we do not seem Jewish, it comes out. On a warm spring eve-ning my husband and I visited one of the charming *Heuriger* (new-wine gardens) not far up the *Straßenbahn*. When we paid our bill, the friendly waiter, eager to show off his English, told us he had learned it working in the U.S., but returned to Austria because he couldn't bear working for poor wages for a Jew. He expected us to understand and agree. It all happened so fast that we scarcely believed we had heard him, and he was gone.

So Freud's authoritarian style now takes on an additional meaning for me, that of a *pater familias* absolutely determined to protect his own, and never to give in to those who would dilute his "discoveries" or leave us weak and vulnerable, whether to the anti-Semites, to the medical profession wanting to exclude lay analysts, or to other thinkers with strong alternative theories, like Adler. We may regret the losses Freud's doctrinaire style produced, but the context, perhaps, makes his style more forgivable.

We, however, are left with this legacy of silencing. Douglas Kirsner (2000) has described this remainder in four large U.S. "classical" institutes in horrifying detail. The powerful have been able to protect their own crimes and manip-ulations, while excluding and ignoring those who would speak out or think otherwise, all in the name of psychoanalysis. Though this is harder to document, rumor has it that the dissident institutes (non-IPA) have not been immune to such problems. In Kirsner's view, they exist in medical and non-medical institutes worldwide. He writes:

> Institutional structures and problems surrounding training are not fundamentally different around the world. Cremerius has argued plausibly that, historically, training, especially the training analysis, became transformed into an instrument of power that promoted conformity, isolation and stagnation in psychoanalytic institutes (Cremerius, 1990). Psychoanalytic institutions are normally organized as guilds which, in my view, are really internally focused cliques. They aim at the perpetuation of their ways of thinking (what they assume to be their body of knowledge that they pass on to their students) and tend to foreclose approaches that challenge their assumptions. They are not part of a wider university culture which, despite its many faults, at least rests on some wider protocols and accountability structures.
>
> (Kirsner, 1999, p. 428)

Kirsner primarily attributes the problems in institutional psychoanalysis to its power structures unchallenged by university checks and balances, academic freedom, and the evidence checking available in most academic fields.[6] Secretive progression committees, lengthy training analyses (Kirsner, 2010), the training analyst system, and so on, have closed down the open inquiry he found in studying the first decades of psychoanalysis, when none of these structures existed. Though Kirsner does not make this comparison, Daniel Shaw's studies of the operation of cults and their malignantly narcissistic leaders (Shaw, 2014) come to mind. Given the economic system in which analysts depend on referrals from others within the institutional structure, leaving the cult may seem foolhardy or impossible. Even though it seems to me that the traumatic history of emigration also played a role in the authoritarian attitudes of psychoanalysts in the U.S. and elsewhere, I find Kirsner's studies and analyses indispensable.

Even after Freud, we have the stories of excommunication and shunning. One method, shamelessly practiced by Ernest Jones, exercised against Ferenczi and others, was refusal to publish and condemnation to the ranks of insanity. Freud himself described Ferenczi to Max Eitingon (Freud et al., 2004, p. 764, 1.XI. 1931) as neurotic, but no psychoanalyst thought oneself exempt from neuroses. Jones placed Ferenczi, arguably Freud's most important interlocutor for 25 years (Dupont, 1995; Falzeder, 2002; Falzeder & Brabant, 2000; Falzeder, Brabant, & Giampieri-Deutsch, 1996), outside the range of those who should be taken seriously, effectively disappearing him from psychoanalytic history and discourse until his clinical diary (Ferenczi & Dupont, 1988) appeared in the late 1980s. But the damage had been done. Although interpersonalists never forgot Ferenczi's mutuality (Wolstein, 1989), and many relationalists took up his ethic of care (Berman, 2003, 2009; Orange, 2011), the Freudian tradition, as well as the Kleinian and Lacanian schools, still prefers to forget or dismiss this maligned ancestor.[7] Silencing impoverishes, seriously and often irreparably.

Silencing after Freud

Let us also consider Erich Fromm (1900–1980) as an example of institutional shunning both by the Freudian establishment, and even among dissidents. Born in Frankfurt in a rabbinical family (Fromm, 2000a), he studied law, sociology, philosophy, psychology, and psychoanalysis in the Heidelberg school with Frieda Fromm-Reichmann, to whom he was briefly married and whom, after their separation, he helped to escape from Nazi Germany while emigrating himself to Geneva and in 1934 to New York. Crucial early influences, by his own account, included Talmudist Salman Baruch Rabinkow, sociologist Alfred Weber (brother of Max Weber, but in Fromm's words, "a humanist, not a nationalist and a man of outstanding courage and integrity" (Fromm, 2000a, p. 251), Johann Jakob Bachofen[8] (for the mother emphasis), Freud, Ferenczi, and Georg Groddeck (the only German analyst he knew as full of "truth, originality, courage, and extraordinary kindness", p. 252). Fromm had already in 1930 joined the Frankfurt School for Social Research and had completed his analytic training. After the war he cofounded the William Alan White Institute, and taught at the New School for Social Research until 1959. By this time, he had written *Escape from Freedom* (Fromm, 1941) and *The Art of Loving* (Fromm, 1956) and begun to live most of the time in Cuernavaca, Mexico, where he taught and wrote (Fromm, 1959, 1961, 1964, 1967, 1976, 1987; Fromm & Marx, 1966) until 1974. Then he lived in Muralto, Switzerland until his death.

Though Fromm was and remains enormously prominent as a social philosopher, his relationship to organized psychoanalysis concerns us here. In 1924, with Frieda Fromm-Reichmann, Fromm helped to found the *Therapeutikum* in Heidelberg. After a brief training analysis in Berlin with Hanns Sachs, one of Freud's five inner circle of the famous rings, Fromm and Fromm-Reichmann, with Karl Landauer and Heinrich Meng, founded the South German Institute for Psychoanalysis in Frankfurt in 1929; Fromm joined the Frankfurt School the following year, though after the public book-burning on 10 May 1933, he and most Jewish-German analysts prepared to leave. After his emigration to the U.S. in 1934, he began – while still working with Horkheimer – to collaborate with Harry Stack Sullivan and Clara Thompson, and began his work with dissident Karen Horney. In 1943, Horney prevented him, as a lay analyst, from joining her newly founded institute. He then allied himself more firmly with Sullivan and Thompson to found the William Alanson White Institute in New York where he taught, ever since the home of interpersonal psychoanalysis. This institution, along with Theodor Reik's NPAP (National Psychological Association for Psychoanalysis) became a refuge for non-medical analysts like Fromm.

Importantly, however, Fromm regarded himself as a Freudian, especially when the name of C.G. Jung came up. Despite his extensive later critiques of Freud as authoritarian, and his claim by 1937 that the unconscious was structured more by relatedness and culture than by sexual instincts, he found Freud's central insight that most human motivation remains unconscious to be incontrovertible. (We might even regard him as the first relational psychoanalyst, but he would have surely responded that this honor belonged to Ferenczi (Fromm, 2000b)). So

Fromm's exclusion from the IPA, as recounted in detail by Paul Roazen (2001) and more compactly by Rainer Funk (2000) and George Hogenson (Hogenson, Naifeh, & Smith, 2003), counts as a horror story, easily to be confused with forms of silencing within totalitarian regimes. Of course, the story begins in the *Nazizeit*, but it does not end there.

By early 1933, when Hitler came to power, two-thirds of the analysts loyal to Freud had already left Germany, most notably Max Eitingon, founder of the DPV (German Psychoanalytical Society, *Deutsche Psychoanalytische Verein*), for Palestine, and Hanns Sachs for Boston. Only Aryans (but orthodox Freudians) Felix Boehm and Carl Müller-Braunschweig were left to try to keep the DPV within the IPA, communicating constantly with Ernest Jones in Britain and Anna Freud in Vienna. At first, they all tried – while all the remaining Jewish analysts except Edith Jacobson (imprisoned by the Nazis for her refusal to break patient confidentiality) left (Brecht, 1988). "Non-Aryans" had lost even civil rights. Even after Matthias Göring (cousin of Reichsmarschall Hermann Göring) took over the DPV, Freud himself encouraged Boehm and Müller-Braunschweig to keep psychoanalysis going in the Third Reich, just as long as they kept out revisionists like Herald Schulz-Hencke (a Gentile married to a Jewish woman, so only temporarily protected, anyway) and Wilhelm Reich. Better to have the National Socialists control psychoanalysis than to permit dissidents or leftists.[9] Jones wrote to Anna Freud on 20 July 1936 about Göring ("a cousin of the famous addict"): "It was easy to get on excellent terms with Göring, who is a very sympathetic personality. We can easily bend him our way, but unfortunately so can other people" (quoted in Roazen, 2001, p. 19).[10] Summarizing this context for Fromm's expulsion from the IPA, I quote at length from historian of psychoanalysis Peter Loewenberg:

> Freud was clearly more interested in preserving the organization and presence of psychoanalysis in the Third Reich than he was in the dignity and self-esteem of his Jewish colleagues or in the conditions that are necessary for psychoanalysis to function as a clinical therapy. . . . It is painful and mortifying to read the record of how the leaders of an honored institution, in order to save the organization and promote the careers of the new successors to leadership, humiliated and cast out a large majority of its members to accommodate to a totalitarian state. That a "scientific," or for that matter a "humanistic," society would exclude qualified members for ethnic, racial, religious, or other extrinsic grounds for the sake of the existence of the institution, defies the autonomy of science from political ideology and the morality of valuing individuals which is the humane liberal essence of psychoanalysis itself.
>
> (Roazen, 2001, p. 23)

Fromm, who had joined the DPV before emigrating in 1934, soon received a letter from Müller-Braunschweig asking for his dues. Short of funds, Fromm said he would pay in installments, but then in 1935, wrote to ask Müller-Braunschweig, who forwarded Fromm's letter to Jones in London, about the rumor that Jewish analysts had been excluded (*ausgeschlossen*) from the DPV. (The DPV, as a result of a July 1936 agreement between Jones, Brill, Müller-Braunschweig, and Boehm, continued to be a member of the IPA and became part of the Göring Institute). "The DPV celebrated Freud's eightieth birthday, but no Jews were allowed" (Goggin & Goggin, 2001, p. 105; Roazen, 2001, p. 26). Jones (in Roazen, 2001), in his usual evasive style, wrote to Fromm:

> Dr. Müller-Braunschweig forwarded to me your letter of complaint considering the resignation of the Jewish members. It is not literally true that they have been excluded . . ., but after a considerable discussion in Berlin between them and their colleagues, a discussion at which I also was present, they subsequently decided it would be in everyone's interest for them to send in their resignation. It was plain to me that there was no alternative, and indeed I may tell you that I am daily expecting to hear the whole German-Society itself being dissolved [Roazen comments that there was no evidence for this].
>
> As regards the question of communicating with you, you will doubtless understand that it is far from easy to write from Berlin. There also appears to be a misunderstanding in the matter for which I am more to blame than Dr. Müller-Braunschweig. They assumed that I would notify the German members living abroad, whereas this was not-quite clear in my mind. I notified those in England and evidently thought this would suffice. You are the only other member in this category, and I had thought that you were now a member of the New York Society.
>
> (pp. 24–5)

Jones, knowing that as a lay analyst Fromm would have had difficulty joining any American component society of the IPA, then offered him "Nansen" or direct membership; that is, something analogous to a "Nansen" passport for refugees, with membership not dependent on belonging to a component society. Fromm accepted, and Jones immediately confirmed his membership in the IPA in 1936.

The next episode, reported by Roazen (2001, pp. 31–2), occurs after the war. Fromm, living and teaching in Mexico, discovered in the early 1950s that he was no longer listed as a direct member of the IPA.[11] So he wrote to Ruth Eissler, IPA Secretary in 1953:

> I would greatly appreciate it if you would be kind enough to inform me on the following question: I have been a member-at-large of the International Psychoanalytic Association since about 1934, when I had to resign from the German Psychoanalytic Association [*sic*]. I find that my name does not appear any more on the [IPA] Association's list of members-at-large, although I never resigned, nor was I ever notified of a termination of my membership. Could you be kind enough to let me know what my status as a member is?
>
> (p. 31)

Eissler's replies, "a study in cant and dissimulation," (Hogenson et al., 2003, p. 129), begin as follows:

> Membership in the I.P.A. depends on membership in a Component Society of the I.P.A. You are listed as a member of the Washington Psychoanalytic Society, which is not in itself a Component Society of the I.P.A. but is an Affiliate Society of the American . . . [she follows by saying the old DPV no longer exists, not true, and irrelevant to Fromm's question] . . .
>
> Membership-at-large in the I.P.A. may be acquired in exceptional cases, by those who were previously members of a component society of the I.P.A. A number of lay analysts in this country, who are not members of the American Psychoanalytic Association but who reapplied for membership in the I.P.A. were willing to be screened by the Joint Screening Committee of the International and the American Associations. This Committee was established at the Congress at Amsterdam [1951] in order to help in the appraisal of foreign lay analysts for reinstatement of their membership in the I.P.A. It consists of three ex officio members: The President of the American Psychoanalytic Association; the Chairman of the Board on Professional Standards of the American Psychoanalytic Association; and a member of the Central Executive of the International Psychoanalytic Association who is a member of the American Psychoanalytic Association.
>
> At present applications for reinstatement should be sent to me, as Chairman of the Joint Screening Committee, and should include a detailed curriculum vitae, including present activities.
>
> I hope that this gives you the information which you requested.
>
> (Roazen, 2001, p. 32)

We may note several aspects of this response: It does not explain how Fromm came to be dropped from his at-large membership; it does not acknowledge his already substantial contributions to psychoanalysis and related fields; it more than hints that there would be prejudice against him both for being foreign and for being a lay analyst; and it suggests that someone with extensive training and achievements will have to start all over to document them.[12]

Fromm called her out, asking her to state clearly what the IPA (and/or she) was doing:

> I take it that if I want to continue my status as a member-at-large of the International Psychoanalytic Association, I would have to present the application for re-instatement. Before I make a decision, I would very much like to understand the situation a little better, and I would greatly appreciate it if you could enlighten me on the question of what is meant by a "screening" of previous members-at-large. Does it mean that it is considered that they lost their status as members-at-large, and that the screening amounts practically to a new application for membership? Or if not, according to what principles

is such a screening carried out? Would, for instance, the fact that my psycho-analytic views do not correspond to the views of the majority be one of the factors to be taken into consideration at the screening, and a reason for denial of membership?

I have to confess even to an ignorance concerning the principles governing the American Psychoanalytic Association with regard to the acceptance of members. Is there any rule that as a matter of principle the American Associa-tion excludes all non-medical analysts?

(Roazen, 2001, p. 33)

It is unclear whether Fromm knew at this point that a number of lay analysts in the U.S. had gained IPA membership after the 1951 Congress. He clearly had come to suspect that this "screening" meant to protect "the movement" from heterodox views, that it was a bureaucratic form of silencing dissent and creativity. Eissler's next response, still attempting to hide her tracks, was decisive for him:

At the 17th International Psychoanalytic Congress in Amsterdam, 1951 [where Müller-Braunschweig's new group – the DPV – won admittance], the Joint Screening Committee of the I.P.A. and the A.P.A. was established for the purpose of giving those lay analysts in North America who are not members of the A.P.A., and who had lost membership in the I.P.A. through the change of statutes of the International, the opportunity to be reinstated to membership. The American Psychoanalytic Association does not recognize lay analysts as members except those who had been members before 1939. All those lay analysts who used to be members at large in the I.P.A. and reside in North America have to reapply for membership through the Joint Screen-ing Committee. Most of the former lay-members at large have done so. The reinstatement depends on the recommendation of the committee, which con-sists of three ex-officio members; the President of the American Psychoana-lytic Association; the Chairman of the Board of Standards of the American Psychoanalytic Association, and a member of the Central Executive of the I.P.A., who is also a member of the A.P.A. . . .

I am, of course, not in the position of anticipating the recommendations of the Joint Screening Committee. Personally, though, I would assume that anyone who does not stand on the basic principles of psychoanalysis would anyway not be greatly interested in becoming a member of the International Psychoanalytic Association.

(Roazen, 2001, p. 34)

Fromm wrote back saying that of course he agreed with the "basic principles" of psychoanalysis, but saw that these might be narrowly or broadly understood. Ruth Eissler had made it clear to him that he would never be told why he had been dropped, and that he would never likely be "reinstated."

Even Otto Fenichel, Viennese psychoanalyst and emigre to Los Angeles, who shared Fromm's political positions, thought Fromm deserved to be excluded for being psychoanalytically unorthodox (Prince, 2009). The Goggins' (Goggin & Goggin, 2001) comment on the 1951 readmission of the DPV to the IPA:

> By supporting the admission of the DPV into the IPA, the leadership of the world psychoanalytic community had chosen to place theoretical orthodoxy as a more significant factor in readmission than the Nazification of the members being admitted.
>
> (p. 173)

Little wonder, then, that two years later, Fromm could so easily be excluded for heretical views.

The upshot of this story: Psychoanalysis silenced a pioneering, interdisciplinary, and creative voice. With Erich Fromm speaking at the IPA and writing in the psychoanalytic journals, we might have arrived at the ethical turn decades earlier, challenging the isolation of clinical work from the cultural, social, and ethical/ political contexts in which it tries to understand human suffering. Erich Fromm himself went on to become widely known for his peace and justice work, and for writings like *To Have or To Be?* (Fromm, 1976). Let us hear this prophetic voice, lost to most of psychoanalysis, once more:

> To experience my unconscious means that I know myself as a human being, that I know that I carry within myself all that is human, that nothing human is alien to me, that I know and love the stranger, because I have ceased to be a stranger to myself. The experience of my unconscious is the experience of my humanity, which makes it possible for me to say to every human being "I am thou." I can understand you in all your basic qualities, in your goodness and in your evilness, and even in your craziness, precisely because all this is in me, too. Not only clarity and tolerance in general to my fellow man follows from this experience, but specifically the capacity of the analyst to understand his patient. He may know a great deal *about* a patient, but he will know *him*, understand him, only when he has found in himself, even though in a lesser degree, all the tendencies and desires he tries to discover in his patient's unconscious.
>
> (Fromm, 1964, pp. 77–8, emphasis in original)

Unsilencing

Besides reading the silenced voices in psychoanalytic history, besides bringing Adler, Ferenczi, Fromm, and so many others back into our conversations, besides attempting to deconstruct authoritarian structures that do the silencing even now, what else can we psychoanalysts do about the problem of silencing? I do have a few suggestions, mostly addressed to my fellow senior colleagues, concerning training and our ongoing communal life, and do hope others will supplement them.

1   In training, let us teach our students to read every text critically, asking for its intellectual coherence, underlying philosophical assumptions, and practical clinical implications. What does the author, from whatever school of thought, take for granted, about human nature, about race and gender and sexuality, about what matters and what is real? How would it be to be this author's patient? Would the ideas have applicability to some patients more than others? Does this author model intellectual humility? Just as children need, early on, to become critical readers of all media, books, television, and social media if they are to become participating citizens, our candidates deserve the same respect from us. Everything we say to them will then be grist for this critical mill. An institute where such open inquiry prevails will less likely become a pathological accommodation factory like those described by Kirsner and Brandchaft, or a cult like those addressed by Shaw.

2   Psychoanalysts can engage in more interdisciplinary study. Though medically trained himself – few professional routes were open to Jews in late-nineteenth-century Vienna – Freud always adamantly opposed reducing psychoanalysis to a medical specialty, and I believe, would have supported those of us (Cushman, 2013, 2019; Hoffmann, 2009; Orange, 2010) opposed to the conflation of the STEM (science, technology, engineering, and mathematics) fields with psychoanalysis. Freud linked psychoanalysis with history, the arts, literature, and the like, and welcomed into the study and practice of psychoanalysis scholars from these areas. Both Freud and Jung left medical psychiatry, which both found reductionistic, for psychoanalysis and analytical psychology. (We will consider Jung further in a later chapter).

3   Senior psychoanalysts can take a special interest in examining the ideas of the psychoanalytic dissidents. We need not agree, but our candidates need exposure to these ideas, as well as to the history of repression. What we do not remember, we are doomed to repeat.

4   We can support our younger colleagues, coaching them on strategy, but more importantly, encouraging them to speak up. Given the experiences of many of us, it would be foolish tell them to take these risks without warning them and without standing by them. My younger colleagues need to hear from me my story of being booed – loud and long – in Hamburg in August, 2001 at a suicidality conference. My crime had been to suggest that instead of attempting or committing suicide as an act of hatefulness against their analysts, suicidal patients might actually be suffering. They might deserve our compassion, accompaniment, and mourning. This experience shocked me into silence for a year or two, but fortunately, enough support gradually came my way to help me to find my voice again. Our younger colleagues will need solid and ongoing support from us if they are to find the courage to dissent from orthodoxies.

5   We need to prepare our younger colleagues for the publication grind. Jour-
     nals, of course, hoping to be considered responsible and rigorous, set up peer-
     reviewing systems. These can be helpful or brutal, often in the service of
     orthodoxy. Often the reviewer insists that the writer should have considered
     or cited "canonical" literature, or claims that the author is outside the main-
     stream of the journal's concerns – not relational enough, for example. The
     baffled or downhearted author often gives up, and another innovative voice
     may have been silenced. Of course, not every young author has the capacity
     to write well, or to think both innovatively and coherently, but when we find
     a younger colleague who is almost there, we ought to help, and tell our war
     stories, too. I, for example, saved all my worst reviews, just so I would be able
     to show them to younger authors when they became discouraged.

6   Following Martin Bergmann's suggestion (Bergmann, 1997), let every psy-
     choanalytic training program include a course on the history of psycho-
     analysis. Our next chapter will recommend reading history generally as a
     psychoanalytic and ethical project; here we might think of reading psycho-
     analytic history psychoanalytically. What is it we do not want to know about
     our own origins and history, and what are we doing to protect ourselves,
     individually and as a profession, from knowing our history? Do we really
     believe that psychoanalysis was born full-grown and complete? How often
     do we simply silence or shun the messengers?

7   When colleagues make comments or raise questions at conferences or meet-
     ings, we can welcome them, showing that we value their participation and
     are interested and curious whether we agree or not. We want to be sure that
     this colleague will find the courage to speak up in the future, and that others
     who are not yet speaking will find their voices. Speakers and presenters, I
     believe, can set a tone in psychoanalytic and other professional settings that
     fights against silencing, supports hearing divergent voices, and encourages
     participation.

8   Senior psychoanalysts can speak out, as Emanuel Berman (2010) and
     Lewis Aron (2010) have recently done, against renewed efforts (Blass, 2010)
     to restrict the title of psychoanalyst to those who subscribe to a narrowly
     prescribed theory and practice and to exclude the many worldwide who have
     devoted themselves to psychoanalytic work but who understand it differently;
     readers, for example, of Ferenczi, Balint, Winnicott, Kohut, and the relational
     psychoanalysts.

Conclusion

Writing this chapter, I found myself in Austria, with another history, from which
both Sigmund Freud and Heinz Kohut, among so many others, were barely able
to flee from the racist ideology and extreme violence that destroyed most of their
neighbors. When I began to speak of these topics there, my colleagues at the Freud
Museum gave me an article (Pappenheim, 1989) on psychoanalysis in Vienna

before 1938, especially from the founding of the First Republic to the *Anschluß*. As Else Pappenheim remembered, and as Freud's correspondence also shows as she reported, he was far less interested in Austria's ever more fascist politics than were his social-democratically inclined followers, but even considered the fascists a lesser danger than those he called the Bolsheviks. No wonder he stayed here after many warnings. So, reading psychoanalytic history may also teach us, though much is probably still to be written.

Silencing is not inevitable; nor is hearing. Each, like the "hate and fear" in the *South Pacific* song, has to be carefully taught, and can be learned. We have looked at a few instances, among many, that have generated a legacy and culture of silencing in psychoanalysis. And yet, we can learn to hear each other, and to encourage each other's voices. We will need a culture change toward an inclusive and pluralistic psychoanalysis like that practiced and encouraged by Lewis Aron, as well as by seekers of common ground like Steven Stern (2017) and Peter Shabad (2017, 2001).

Notes

1 Bergmann and others thoughtfully considered psychoanalytic dissidents during and after Freud's lifetime, and the ways dissidence tended to be understood as resistance (Bergmann, 2004).

2 Notably, both Freud and Jung accepted the institutionalization of training analysis in psychoanalysis and analytic psychology, respectively, only when each faced a fatal illness (Roazen, 2002).

3 It has been my privilege to work rather extensively with Gestalt therapists, whose successful group training methods often need supplementing with personal, one-to-one, more psychoanalytically oriented therapies, at least for the best therapists, in my experience. Though such therapy is not required for their training, I often recommend it to supplement their group training, which I greatly admire and which reminds me that there is more than one way to learn.

4 I am grateful to Dr. Daniela Finzi, director of scholarship at the Freud Museum in Vienna, for locating this quotation for me. I had found it on the wall in the exhibition, *Der Wohnung geht es gut* (It goes well with the apartment), just above the table with assigned places for all Freud family members. (*Gewöhnliche Kaiser und Könige haben nur einen Hof. Großvater hatte zwei . . . Der erste Hof war der psychoanalytische . . . . Der zweite Hof gehörte Großvaters Privatleben. Man braucht kein Galileo zu sein, um zu bemerken, daß auch dieser um Großvater kreiste*). www.freud-biographik.de/frdpro.pdf

5 This section draws on my response to former Fulbright Senior Scholar Pamela Cooper-White's presentation of her new book, *Old and Dirty Gods: Religion, Anti-Semitism and the Origins of Psychoanalysis*, at The Freud Museum, Berggasse 19, Vienna, Austria. Event co-sponsored by Fulbright Austria. See also Beller (1989).

6 Later, Kirsner (2007) published a study of one of Ernest Jones's efforts to help refugee analysts from Vienna, but he does not link this history to the institutional problems.

7 For more information about the Freud-Ferenczi relationship, see not only the three volumes of correspondence now available to us (Dupont, 1995; Falzeder & Brabant, 2000; Falzeder et al., 1996), but also Andre Haynal's account (Haynal, 2002). Haynal, like my previous reading, complexifies the story of Freud's authoritarian tendencies, including his fear of abandonment by Ferenczi (cf. p. 103).

8 This widely influential author (1815–1887) of *Das Mutterrecht* (Bachofen, Catt, & National American Woman Suffrage Association Collection [Library of Congress], 1861) returns in Chapter 5 in the discussion of Jung influences. As Fromm remained consistently critical of Jung's Aryanist mystical monism and his support for the Nazi regime, we can see that Jung and Fromm drew different conclusions from Bachofen's work.

9 On 17 January 1932, Freud had written to Jeanne Lampl-de Groot: "I have begun the battle against the Bolshevistic aggressors Reich, Fenichel" (quoted in Roazen, 2001, p. 13).

10 Göring had issued an edict two years earlier that all German-speaking psychotherapists must read *Mein Kampf* and practice according to its ideas.

11 The only direct member was Werner Kemper, who had cooperated with Bohem in supporting "the extermination of homosexuals and soldiers experiencing 'battle fatigue'" (Goggin & Goggin, 2001, p. 122).

12 The IPA still has daunting requirements for analysts who want to join without membership in component training institutes – undocumented aliens, one might say. Many of us, like Fromm, have given up.

References

Arlow, J. (1958). Freud, Friends and Feuds. *The Saturday Review* (14 June), pp. 14 and 54.

Aron, L. (2010). On: Responding to Rachel Blass' Article "Affirming 'That's Not Psycho-Analysis!' On the Value of the Politically Incorrect Act of Attempting to Define the Limits of Our Field". *International Journal of Psychoanalysis, 91*(5), 1279–1280.

Beller, S. (1989). *Vienna and the Jews, 1867–1938: A cultural history.* Cambridge, England and New York: Cambridge University Press.

Bergmann, M. S. (1997). The Historical Roots of Psychoanalytic Orthodoxy. *International Journal of Psycho-Analysis, 78,* 69–86.

Bergmann, M. S. (2004). *Understanding dissidence and controversy in the history of psychoanalysis.* New York: Other Press.

Bergmann, M. S. (2011). The Dual Impact of Freud's Death and Freud's Death Instinct Theory on the History of Psychoanalysis. *Psychoanalytic Review, 98*(5), 665–686.

Berman, E. (2003). Ferenczi, Rescue, and Utopia. *American Imago, 60*(4), 429–444.

Berman, E. (2009). Ferenczi and Winnicott: Why We Need Their Radical Edge: Commentary on Paper by Michael Parsons. *Psychoanalytic Dialogues, 19*(3), 246–252.

Berman, E. (2010). On "Affirming 'That's Not Psycho-Analysis!'". *International Journal of Psychoanalysis, 91*(5), 1281–1282.

Blass, R. B. (2010). Affirming "That's Not Psycho-Analysis!" On the Value of the Politically Incorrect Act of Attempting to Define the Limits of Our Field. *International Journal of Psychoanalysis, 91*(1), 81–99.

Bos, J. (1996). Rereading the Minutes. *Annual of Psychoanalysis, 24,* 229–255.

Brandchaft, B., Doctors, S., & Sorter, D. (2010). *Toward an emancipatory psychoanalysis: Brandchaft's intersubjective vision.* New York: Routledge.

Brecht, K. (1988). Adaptation and Resistance: Reparation and the Return of the Repressed. *Psychoanalysis and Contemporary Thought, 11*(2), 233–247.

Cooper-White, P. (2018). *Old and dirty gods: Religion, antisemitism, and the origins of psychoanalysis.* Milton Park, Abingdon, Oxon and New York: Routledge.

Cremerius, J. (1990). Training Analyis and Power: The Transformation of a Method of Training and Learning Into an Instrument of Power in Institutionalized Psychoanalysis. *Free Associations, 1*(20), 114–138.

Cushman, P. (2013). Because the Rock Will Not Read the Article: A Discussion of Jeremy D. Safran's Critique of Irwin Z. Hoffman's "Doublethinking Our Way to Scientific Legitimacy". *Psychoanalytic Dialogues*, *23*(2), 211–224.

Cushman, P. (2019). *Travels with the self: Interpreting psychology as cultural history*. New York: Routledge.

Dupont, J. (1995). The Correspondence of Sigmund Freud and Sándor Ferenczi: Volume 1, 1908–1914. Edited by Eva Brabant, Ernst Falzeder, Patrizia Giampieri-Deutsch, under supervision of André Haynal. Transcribed by Ingeborg Meyer-Palmedo. Translated by Peter T. Hoffer. Introduction by André Haynal. Cambridge, MA and London: The Belknap Press of Harvard University Press. 1993, p. 584. *International Journal of Psychoanalysis*, *76*, 623–625.

Falzeder, E. (2002). *The complete correspondence of Sigmund Freud and Karl Abraham 1907–1925*. London and New York: Karnac.

Falzeder, E., & Brabant, E. (2000). *The correspondence of Sigmund Freud and Sándor Ferenczi, volume 3, 1920–1933*. Cambridge, MA and London: Harvard University Press.

Falzeder, E., Brabant, E., & Giampieri-Deutsch, P. (1996). *The correspondence of Sigmund Freud and Sandor Ferenczi volume 2, 1914–1919*. Cambridge, MA and London: Harvard University Press.

Ferenczi, S., & Dupont, J. (1988). *The clinical diary of Sándor Ferenczi*. Cambridge, MA: Harvard University Press.

Freud, S. (1928). *The future of an illusion*. New York: H. Liveright.

Freud, S. (1937). Analysis Terminable and Interminable. *International Journal of Psycho-Analysis*, *18*, 373–405.

Freud, A. (1996). Mein Großvater Sigmund Freud. »Die Biographen aber sollen sich plagen ...« Beiträge zum 140. Geburtstag Sigmund Freuds C. Tögel. Sofia, Österreichisches Ost- und Südosteuropa-Institut pp. 7–20. This Quote comes from pp. 13–14.

Freud, S., Schröter, M., & Eitingon, M. (2004). *Briefwechsel 1906–1939*. Tübingen: Edition Diskord.

Freud, S., Strachey, A., Tyson, A., Strachey, J., & Freud, A. (1914). On the History of the Psycho-Analytic Movement. In *The standard edition of the complete psychological works of Sigmund Freud, volume XIV (1914–1916): On the history of the psychoanalytic movement, papers on metapsychology and other works* (Vol. 14, pp. 1–66). London: Hogarth.

Fromm, E. (1941). *Escape from freedom*. New York: Rinehart.

Fromm, E. (1956). *The art of loving* (1st ed.). New York: Harper.

Fromm, E. (1958). Freud, Friends, and Feuds. *The Saturday Review* (14 June), 11–13, 55.

Fromm, E. (1959). *Sigmund Freud's mission: An analysis of his personality and influence*. New York: Harper.

Fromm, E. (1961). *Man for himself: An inquiry into the psychology of ethics*. New York: Holt, Rinehart & Winston.

Fromm, E. (1964). Humanism and Psychoanalysis. *Contemporary Psychoanalysis*, *1*(1), 69–79.

Fromm, E. (1967). *You shall be as gods: A radical interpretation of the old testament and its tradition*. New York: Holt, Rinehart and Winston.

Fromm, E. (1976). *To have or to be?* (1st ed.). New York: Harper & Row.

Fromm, E. (1987). *The sane society*. New York, NY: Fawcett.

Fromm, E. (2000a). Autobiographical Sidelights by Erich Fromm. *International Forum of Psychoanalysis*, *9*(3–4), 251–253.

Fromm, E. (2000b). The Social Determinants of Psychoanalytic Therapy. *International Forum of Psychoanalysis*, *9*(3–4), 149–165.

Fromm, E., & Marx, K. (1966). *Marx's concept of man.* New York: F. Ungar.

Funk, R. (2000). Erich Fromm's Role in the Foundation of the IFPS. *International Forum of Psychoanalysis, 9*(3–4), 187–197.

Goggin, J. E., & Goggin, E. B. (2001). *Death of a "Jewish science": Psychoanalysis in the Third Reich.* West Lafayette, IN: Purdue University Press.

Graf, M. (1942). Reminiscences of Professor Sigmund Freud. *Psychoanalytic Quarterly, 11*, 465–476.

Haynal, A. (2002). *Disappearing and reviving: Sándor Ferenczi in the history of psychoanalysis.* London and New York: Karnac.

Hoffmann, I. (2009). Doublethinking Our Way to "Scientific" Legitimacy: The Desiccation of Human Experience. *Journal of the American Psychoanalytic Association, 57*, 1043–1069.

Hogenson, G. B., Naifeh, S., & Smith, N. (2003). Roazen, Paul: The Exclusion of Erich Fromm from the IPA. *Contemporary Psychoanalysis,* 2001, *37*(1), 5–42. *Journal of Analytic Psychology, 48*(1), 127–130.

Jones, E. (1957). *Sigmund Freud life and work, volume three: The last phase 1919–1939.* London: Hogarth Press.

Kirsner, D. (1999). Life Among the Analysts. *Free Associations, 7*(3), 416–436.

Kirsner, D. (2000). *Unfree associations: Inside psychoanalytic institutes.* London: Process Press.

Kirsner, D. (2007). Saving Psychoanalysts: Ernest Jones and the Isakowers. *Psychoanalytic History, 9*(1), 83–91.

Kirsner, D. (2010). Training Analysis: The Shibboleth of Psychoanalytic Education. *Psychoanalytic Review, 97*(6), 971–995.

Michael, R. (2008). *A history of Catholic antisemitism: The dark side of the church.* New York: Palgrave Macmillan.

Orange, D. M. (2010). *Thinking for clinicians: Philosophical resources for contemporary psychoanalysis and the humanistic psychotherapies.* New York: Routledge.

Orange, D. M. (2011). *The suffering stranger: Hermeneutics for everyday clinical practice.* New York: Routledge and Taylor & Francis Group.

Pappenheim, E. (1989). Politik und Psychoanalyse in Wien vor 1938. *Psyche – Zeitschrift für Psychoanalyse, 43*, 120–141.

Prince, R. (2009). Psychoanalysis Traumatized: The Legacy of the Holocaust. *American Journal of Psychoanalyis, 69*, 179–194.

Roazen, P. (2001). The Exclusion of Erich Fromm from the IPA. *Contemporary Psychoanalysis, 37*(1), 5–42; quoted from Loewenberg's preface to Cocks, G. (1998). *Treating mind & body: Essays in the history of science, professions, and society under extreme conditions* (p. ix). New Brunswick, NJ: Transaction Publishers.

Roazen, P. (2002). The Problem of Silence: Training Analyses. *International Forum of Psychoanalysis, 11*(1), 73–77.

Rudnytsky, P. (2015). Freud, Ferenczi, Fromm: The Authoritarian Character as Magic Helper. *Fromm Forum, 19*, 5–10.

Safranski, R. (1998). *Martin Heidegger: Between good and evil.* Cambridge, MA: Harvard University Press.

Shabad, P. C. (2001). *Despair and the return of Hope: Echoes of mourning in psychotherapy.* Northvale, NJ: J. Aronson.

Shabad, P. C. (2017). The Vulnerability of Giving: Ethics and the Generosity of Receiving. *Psychoanalytic Inquiry, 37*(6), 359–374.

Shaw, D. (2014). *Traumatic narcissism: Relational systems of subjugation.* New York: Routledge and Taylor & Francis Group.

Steiner, R. (2011). In All Questions, My Interest Is Not in the Individual People But in the Analytic Movement as a Whole: It Will Be Hard Enough Here in Europe in the Times to Come to Keep It Going: After All, We Are Just a Handful of People Who Really Have That in Mind. . . . *International Journal of Psychoanalysis, 92*(3), 505–591.

Stern, S. (2017). *Needed relationships and psychoanalytic healing: A holistic relational perspective on the therapeutic process.* Abingdon, Oxon and New York, NY: Routledge and Taylor & Francis Group.

Wiener Psychoanalytische Vereinigung, Nunberg, H., & Federn, E. (1962). *Minutes of the Vienna psychoanalytic society.* New York: International Universities Press.

Wistrich, R. S. (2001). *Hitler and the Holocaust/Robert S. Wistrich* (Modern Library ed.). New York: Modern Library.

Wolstein, B. (1989). Ferenczi, Freud, and the Origins of American Interpersonal Relations. *Contemporary Psychoanalysis, 25,* 672–685.

Chapter 4

The seduction of mystical monisms in the humanistic psychotherapies

Attachments to authorities, sages, and gurus can impede ethical hearing.[1] These bonds deprive the listener of the critical distance needed to evaluate the message, let alone the messenger, often regarded as a seer, a messiah, an *Übermensch*. This connection further removes from the listening adherents any responsibility or concern for singular others outside the inner group formed around the leader, who dominates through preaching a kind of mystification to those who understand. Everyone and everything become included into the one and the all, without differentiation. While ownness (Heideggerian *Eigentlichkeit*, usually translated as authenticity) and individuation (Jung) may gain prominence, otherness and plurality drop out of consideration. Historian of religion John Hutchison (1977) differentiates among uses of the word "mystical," which generally refers to knowledge gained through immediate experience, not as the result of a process of reasoning. He notes, on the on one hand, that the immediate union sought and gained may consist in *communion* of two or more beings, and cites Martin's Buber's work as example for this kind of thinking. On the other hand, he explains that "the mystical union of ontological union or absorption" concerns "unitive consciousness or cosmic consciousness transcending all plurality or duality" (pp. 29–30). Examples come from Asian religions, as well as from Plotinus, and from Western mystics. In this chapter, we consider three examples of such mystical monisms, their more or less evident connections to National Socialist ideas, and their attractiveness to various schools of psychotherapy.

Freudian psychoanalysis, most advocates and detractors would agree, located its intellectual ground in rationalistic Enlightenment Europe, and thus was full of both individualisms and dualisms, but has generally abhorred what I am calling mystical monism.[2] (Chapter 3 considered its authoritarian and self-protective aspects). Its dualisms included mind and body, of course, but also masculine and feminine, active and passive, fantasy and reality, good and evil, and came to involve psychoanalysis versus psychotherapy, analyzable and unanalyzable, conscious and unconscious, ego versus external world, phallic versus castrated, heterosexuality versus homosexuality, object seeking versus pleasure seeking, and treatment versus care (Aron & Starr, 2012). In each case, the second member of the pair was for the most part disparaged. Generally, however, Freudian psychoanalysis – and also its heretical/creative offshoots – have firmly held that patient and analyst are two people, while transference and countertransference confusions constitute just that – confusion.

Attempting to rectify both untenable binaries and the resulting injustices, recent psychoanalysis and other humanistic psychotherapies like gestalt have found inspiration in philosophies that deny both dualisms and actual separateness and turn toward monisms.[3] Monisms, in brief, fuse the many into the one. These include, most famously, the Being-philosophy of Martin Heidegger (1889–1976); analytic psychology, as well as the pastoral and ecopsychologies inspired by Carl Jung (1875–1961)[4]; and most recently, though less famously, the "new phenomenology" of Hermann Schmitz (1928–). Each offers a vision of oneness to supersede, obviate, or underpin the apparent binaries: Being (evermore mystical in the later Heidegger), universal archetypes and the collective unconscious in Jung, situations and atmospheres in Schmitz. We will take each in turn, noting some uses to which each has been put, and then consider why these mystical monisms may be a seduction and a temptation for humanistic (or better, human dignity-oriented) psychotherapies, including psychoanalysis and gestalt.

Martin Heidegger

Martin Heidegger's 1927 *Zein und Zeit* (*Being and Time*) (Heidegger, 1962), arguably the most important and influential philosophy text of the twentieth century,[5] attempted and claimed nothing less than to overthrow and replace the entire history of Western philosophy from Plato on. Not only did he reject the universalizing he also called metaphysics, but also the entire Enlightenment development on which theories of equal justice and inalienable human rights had been based. Henceforth human life (*Dasein*) would be understood as thrown or situated, temporal, and oriented toward its own death.

Of the three thinkers considered in this chapter, Heidegger has appealed most to my collaborators and to me (Stolorow, Atwood, & Orange, 2009; Stolorow, 2007, 2011b). His refusal of the subject-object distinction, his contextualizing experience as being-in-the-world, his analysis of experience as *Befindlichkeit* [How-one-finds-oneself-ness], his view of life as temporality – all this combined with his genial capacity to address the history of philosophy as a story that could be turned on its head – gave us new resources to think forward in intersubjective psychoanalysis. But the price has been high. His student Hans Loewald felt so betrayed by Heidegger's Nazi activity in the mid-1930s[6] that he turned from philosophy to psychiatry and psychoanalysis (Loewald, 2000). Still, on the basis of *Zein und Zeit* (*Being and Time*) (Heidegger, 1962), ever on his desk, he gave psychoanalysis both a non-dualistic way to read Freud, and a relational and independent neo-Freudian voice. Thus, Heidegger, through my collaborators and Loewald, has been an inextricable influence on my own work, no matter how much I have come to regret this influence. His malignant silence after the war about the Shoah and about his own support for the Nazi regime places him in a philosophical horror zone.

Our first attempt to grapple with the underlying evil was a psychobiographical piece, attempting to explain, especially using the letters to Hannah Arendt, how someone of his background could have fallen where he did (Stolorow et al., 2009). Clearly, however, with the publication of more of Heidegger's papers from the 1930s (Heidegger, 2000; Heidegger & Ruckteschell, 2004), and now with the so-called *Black Notebooks* (Heidegger, 2016), more is needed. This more recently available material will take both Heidegger scholars and less schooled readers some time to digest. Meanwhile, though, a few things are clear: First, Heidegger's unoriginal anti-Semitism (Bernasconi, 2017) – including his rants against world *Judentum* and its putative *Machenschaft* (calculation) and *Weltlosigkeit* (worldlessness) – ran much deeper and longer than his Nazi rectorship years of 1933–1934. As Krell notes, (2015, p. 135), some sentences defy comment:

> The world Jewish order, prodded by the emigrants who were allowed to leave [!] Germany, it is everywhere unstoppable, and for all the power it is developing it nowhere has to participate in deeds of war, whereas it is our sole lot to sacrifice the best blood of the best of our own people. (GA 96:262)

His treatment of Jewish colleagues in the 1930s, including Husserl, who had chosen Heidegger to succeed him in his professorship in Freiburg, cannot be reduced to political expediency, or even to cowardice. Second, it also has become clear that the more we learn of Heidegger's later writings, the more we need a new hermeneutic, i.e. new frames and questions, to approach not only his postwar writings but also and especially his evasive interview in *Der Spiegel*, "Nur ein Gott kann uns retten" ("Only a God Can Save Us") (Heidegger, 1966).

Although it will be impossible to do any justice here either to Heidegger's contributions or to the controversies surrounding him, the recent publication of his *Black Notebooks* requires us to note first, his Nazi and anti-Semitic connections, and second, the extent to which these pervade and call into his question all his work. The first task is a work in progress, thanks to historians, biographers and philosophical critics (Bernasconi, 2010; Fried, 2018; Trawny & Mitchell, 2015). This second question remains a matter of serious dispute among thoughtful Heidegger scholars, and among other thinkers indebted to his work. Those who believe his anti-Semitism is separable from his philosophy find stumbling blocks not only in the *Schwarze Hefte* (Krell, 2015) – Di Cesare (2018); Farin & Malpas (2016); Heidegger & Trawny (2014, 2015); Mitchell (2017); Trawny & Mitchell (2015); Zhok (2016) – but much earlier: On 2 October 1929, Heidegger wrote in a letter to Viktor Schwoerer that either "we restore genuine forces and educators emanating from the native soil to our German spiritual life, or we abandon it definitely to the growing Jewification (*Verjudung*)" (cited in: Faye, 2009, p. 34). Robert Bernasconi cites Heidegger's letter to Ernst Jünger in the 1930s, wherein he claimed "that the human being is more essentially a subject when the human being conceives him- or herself as nation, people, or race" (2010, p. 55).[7] But we must look back further still.

Heidegger's most thorough biographer, Rudiger Safranski, entitled his book *Ein Meister aus Deutschland: Heidegger und seine Zeit*, published in English translation as *Martin Heidegger: Between Good and Evil* (Safranski, 1998).[8] Safranski, writing long before the existence of the *Black Notebooks* was known, not to mention published, already provided clues to reading them. Very early, Safranski notes that the Heidegger family numbered among its distant relatives the rabid anti-Semitic preacher Abraham a Sancta Clara (1644–1709), like Heidegger born in Messkirch. The young Heigegger's first public speech enthusiastically honored this man. Though Heidegger later claimed to have treated his Jewish students well, and does not seem to have shared the racial biology views predominant in Nazi Germany (Bernasconi, 2010), there is no evidence of a period not pervaded by ordinary anti-Semitism. In 1929, well before the Nazis came to power and one could have felt compelled by fear to make such statements, Heidegger wrote to a colleague lamenting "*Die Verjudung des deutschen Geistes*" (Rockmore, 2017).[9] Heidegger's later reference to his rectorship as a "mistake" completely evades the question of how long he held racist views before and after the Nazi period, as well as the question about how much his völkisch views shape even his masterpiece *Sein und Zeit* (*Being and Time*), a question already clear to Karl Löwith in 1939 (Löwith, 1939 [1991]). Does *Dasein* refer, for example, to the existence of all human beings, or only some? His tendency to refer to "German *Dasein*" surely raises such questions, as does his eloquent identification with Black Forest peasant life in "Why Do I stay in the Provinces?"[10] Then we find in Heidegger's infamous rectoral address:

> Spirit is the determined resolve to the essence of Being, a resolve that is attuned to origins and knowing. And the *spiritual world* of a Volk . . . is the power that comes from preserving at the most profound level the forces that are rooted in the soil and blood of a Volk, the power to arouse most inwardly and to shake most extensively the Volk's existence. A spiritual world alone will guarantee our Volk greatness.
>
> (Heidegger, "Rectoral Address," in [Wolin & Heidegger, 1993, pp. 33–4])

Such talk makes it difficult to disentangle Heidegger's philosophy from his *völkisch* politics, even long before we learned of the *Black Notebooks*. This was completely clear to Jürgen Habermas (Habermas, 1989), just after the *Historikerstreit* to be described ahead. In Karl Löwith's (1939 [1991]) words, "Given the significant attachment of the philosopher to the climate and intellectual habitus of National Socialism, it would be inappropriate to criticize or exonerate his political decision in isolation from *the very principles* of Heideggerian philosophy itself" (p. 182, emphasis in original).

For our purposes, however, his early and his later work, after the 1933–1934 rectorate,[11] raise problems about what I am calling mystical monism. He dismissed all competing philosophies for not considering the "*Seinsfrage*," the question of being or *Sein* (later *Seyn)*, for not placing in the center that *Dasein* for whom its own existence is a question for it, matters to it. Humanism misses the *Seinsfrage* (Heidegger & Beaufret, 1949; Heidegger & Krell, 1993). Increasingly, rejecting Jews as rootless, he railed against presumed international Jewish conspiracies and calculations. "One of the stealthiest forms of gigantism and perhaps the most ancient is the cleverness of calculation, pushiness, and intermixing whereby Jewry's worldlessness is established" (Heidegger & Trawny, 2014, GA 95: 97).

For psychoanalysts and for existential psychotherapists generally, the question must be: To what extent it is possible to clean up Heidegger, to expunge the problematic elements, and to continue to frame our theory and practice in Heideggerian terms? A recent exchange (Friedman, 2016; Stolorow, 2016) between Lawrence Friedman, who asks whether a usable Heidegger exists for psychoanalysis, and Robert Stolorow, whose recent works (Stolorow, 2007, 2011a) depend heavily on his understanding of Heidegger, may be instructive. Neither directly raises the questions that concern me in this chapter, though both are surely aware of them.

Here I include Heidegger among "mystical monists," intending to suggest the danger of a cult-like followership for his work. When writers or readers measure every idea against, or reference every idea to, *Seyn* (often rendered in English texts as "Beyng"), they may eclipse the many in the one, joining the ranks of monists. Heidegger's devotion to poetic and religious mysticism has been well-studied (Bambach, 2003, 2013; Caputo, 1978). In the history of philosophy, we can think of Parmenides, of Plotinus (the One and the emanations), of Spinoza's one substance (*Deus sive Natura* [God or Nature]), or of Hegel's absolute spirit. Monism favors the one over the many.

Placing Heidegger among the monists will evoke protests among those who find his thinking rich and diversified. Consider however, the Protagorean "man is the measure" style of *Dasein*, not to mention "German *Dasein*." Then think of the normalizing and reductionistic "it all comes down to" found in one of Heidegger's most notorious sentences:

> Agriculture is now a motorized food industry – in essence, the same as the manufacturing of corpses in gas chambers and the extermination camps, the same as the blockading and starving of nations, the same as the manufacturing of atom bombs. [from a lecture related to *Über den Humanismus*, quoted in Wolfgang Schirmacher, *Technik und Gelassenheit: Zeitkritik nach Heidegger*].
>
> (Schirmacher, 1983, p. 25)

Here as elsewhere, he turns to a concept of essence (*Wesen*) to avoid German responsibility, and his own. That terrible technology did it. The possibility that technology can be used for good or ill disappears, as do the people its users had destroyed. The incapacity to see other human beings as individuals, rather than as part of the German *Volk*, or possibly as threats to it (Jews, Americans, Bolsheviks, Jesuits, and the like) leaves him an essentialist and a monist. Threats to the one essence degenerate in technology, or in the *Machenschaft* (calculation) of the *Beiträge* (contributions to philosophy) and the *Black Notebooks*. Individuals, whether perpetrators, victims, or both, disappear.

But why "mystical" monism? In his younger years, Heidegger was entranced with mystics such as Meister Eckhart and Teresa of Avila, though as John D. Caputo writes, Hedeggerian *Gelassenheit* (letting-be) and thinking still exceed Eckhart's "poverty of thought" (Caputo, 2016, pp. 209–216). Later, he adopted the hyper-Germanic poet Hölderlin. Whatever their virtues, such mystics eclipse both ordinary miseries, as well as excruciating human suffering inflicted by war, torture, and genocide. Poets like Paul Celan, who tackle crime and suffering head on, find no one there when they visit Heidegger's hut. Perhaps the mystical monism makes human suffering unreal, or at least tends to normalize it.[12] We must at least ask whether mystical monisms, even under the name of ontology, eclipse the possibility of an ethics beyond rules and norms (Braue, 1984). This question needs more development than this project allows, but surfaces as a question in the three thinkers this chapter considers.

Before turning to Jung, this project requires me to note once again Heidegger's notorious and malignant silence (Knowles, 2019; Lang, 1996) about his unapologetic (Day, 2010) Nazi party membership and advocacy, as well as about the massive atrocities he had implicitly supported.

Silence gives consent, goes the old maxim. Heidegger's silence about his and his own people's participation in a regime responsible for the most deliberate and organized genocide in human history suggest that for him, these crimes were not very problematic. Philosophers (Levinas, 1989) (Rockmore, 1992) and cultural critics (Lang, 1996) have written about this closely held silence. The *Der Spiegel* interviewer made repeated attempts to get him to speak clearly about the war years, and about his participation (Heidegger, 1966, 1976). He would not. Long before the *Black Notebooks* appeared, John D. Caputo wrote: "even after death what Heidegger left behind for us was no *Retractiones* but the 1966 *Der Spiegel* interview, which, far from being a posthumous *retractio*, only perpetuated the cover-up, the protracted backpedaling" (1993, p. 132). A psychoanalysis devoted to clear-eyed searching for what we do not want to know can scarcely find such a thinker usable.

C.G. Jung

Carl Gustav Jung (1875–1961), Swiss psychiatrist, founded analytical psychology as an alternative and competitor to Freud's psychoanalysis. His lifelong concern with religious topics, even as he insistently rejected the Christian religion and the Jewish G-d, has kept him in the first rank of important influences on contemporary pastoral theology and spirituality (Ulanov, 1997a, 1997b), as well as on related ecopsychologies such as deep ecology (Ryland, 2000). Born in Kesswil, Switzerland, Jung was the son of a rural Protestant pastor and of a mother both depressed and given to communing with spirits.[13] Late in life, Jung produced his most famous work, the autobiographical *Memories, Dreams, and Reflections* (Jung & Jaffé, 1989) in which he recounted his childhood dreams and visions, but most memorably, expressed his early and formative conviction that he was two personalities: No. 1, ordinary Swiss schoolboy, and No. 2, some impressive and important man from two centuries earlier. Scholars now agree that Jung probably wrote only the first three chapters of this book, while his longtime secretary, Aniela Jaffé, wrote the rest, likely close to Jung's intentions. According to family legend, referenced throughout life by Jung, his paternal grandfather had been an illegitmate son of Johann Wolfgang Goethe, "the great-grandfather."

Jung grew from the lost and depressed child he describes into a brilliant and scholarly student, and a widely admired young psychiatrist, at the Burghölzli clinic in Zürich, Switzerland's best mental hospital, where he worked with director Eugen Bleuler to develop and refine the word association test. As a very young doctor, he was known as a brilliant clinician who could bring mute patients to speak. By 1901, he had already submitted his medical dissertation, "On the Psychology and Pathology of so-called Occult Phenomena," including accounts of seances led by his cousin Helly Preiswerk, references to Goethe's "intuitive perception" with accounts of visualization and imagination, and comparison of Nietzsche's *Zarathustra* with Kerner's *The Seeress of Prevorst* (Kerner, 1845), an account of clairvoyance. Though Jung's early work, no matter the topic, was strictly scientific, his interest in the "so-called occult" helped him to look for meaning in the words and actions of patients that others dismissed as without significance. For this reason, his work has appealed to phenomenologists (Atwood, 2011), even those of more Freudian lineage.

To bring psychoanalysis to Switzerland, Jung began in 1906 to correspond with Sigmund Freud. Each recognizing the extraordinary talent of the other, the two connected quickly, though the relationship was both fragile and fraught from the beginning. The almost-20-years-older Freud, needing a successor outside his circle of Viennese Jewish followers, saw Jung's brilliance and encouraged his immediate attachment. The letters between the two show an intense, extremely intelligent, but incipiently conflictual relationship from the outset. Jung recalled that their first meeting lasted 13 hours. Freud had already established his most important ideas: Dream interpretation, infantile sexuality, the Oedipus, and unconscious motivation. Jung came to learn, but not to follow. Steeped in a vast cultural literature of Aryanist mysticism, as well as in the evolutionary thinking – ontogeny recapitulates phylogeny – along the lines of Ernst Haeckel (1834–1919), he was also pursuing his own path. To those who later thought Freud's importance to Jung overstated, however, Jung rejoined in 1957: "Without Freud's "psychoanalysis" I wouldn't have had a clue" (Jung, 1973, *Letters*, II, p. 359).

Jung, a voracious reader, absorbed several strands of esoteric, often sun-worshiping, usually Aryanist, mysticism (Noll, 1994) before he met Freud (who, by the way, had also taken some interest in parapsychology and the occult [Bishop, 2000]). Jung read the Theosophists, whose leader Helena Blavatsky preached intuition and spiritual ecstasies as the route to knowing divinity. From his *Gymnasium* (academic high school) days, piqued by the opposition of his teacher Jakob Burckhardt (Bair, 2003), Jung had read Johann Jakob Bachofen, whose *Das Mutterrecht* (Bachofen, Catt, & National American Woman Suffrage Association Collection [Library of Congress], 1861), became a point of reference for the rest of Jung's career. Bachofen's belief that before patriarchy triumphed in Europe, mothers had ruled, became an important facet of Jung's collective unconscious (Noll, 1997b). But these passions were bound to bring him into conflict with Freud, who, as Hans Loewald wrote, profoundly distrusted "the undisciplined mystical-visionary inclinations that led Jung into nebulous regions of alchemy, astrology, and the occult, regions from which it is hard to return with a clear mind" (Loewald, 1977). Freud's own project, on the contrary, belonged to what Max Weber (Weber, Gerth, & Mills, 2009) called the disenchantment of the world (*Die Entzauberung der Welt*).

During his years with Freud (1907–1912), Jung became more and more convinced that Freud's sexually motivated personal unconsciousness could be only a small part of the truth, that it remained too concrete and Jewish. He developed, ever more clearly, the idea that ancient Indo-European/Aryan archetypes live in a collective unconscious, from which the individual individuates with the help of an analyst, also a spiritual guide. Jung published his long and complicated account of these ideas in *Transformations and Symbols of the Libido* (Jung & Hinkle, 1916). But the journal version appeared in 1912 as two articles in the *Jahrbuch für psychoanalytische und psychopathologische Forschungen*. When Freud read what his "crown prince" was writing, the relationship ended. Already deep into the visions that would shape his remaining life and work (Dohe, 2016; Noll, 1994, 1997a), Jung resigned as president of the International Psychoanalytical Association in 1914.

Two lifelong influences emerged from Jung's early years: Goethe, especially his *Faust*, and Nietzsche, especially *Zarathustra*. An extended study could consider their presence in all his work; here we must restrict ourselves to general remarks that may: 1) illuminate the importance of reading Jung within Germanic culture; and 2) assist in clarifying the questions about mystical monisms this chapter has set for itself.

Jung read Goethe at least from adolescence, and seems early to have identified with Faust, who, in order to learn the profoundest wisdom, made his famous pact with the devil. From his own experience and that of his patients, Jung came to believe that one must be willing to visit hell, to identify with religious symbols like Christ or Wotan, to give up living as a "persona," if one wants to become oneself, an individual not merged with the crowd. To emerge from the crowd, one must have the courage to live close to the frightening power of the archetypes of the collective unconscious. Goethe's Faust had long been his model.

Jung's early ideas of the collective unconscious – monistic because it denied real differences – and of the archetypes were already developing in the years with Freud. The most-quoted version from 1943–1945,[14] "The Relations between the Ego and the Unconscious" and "On the Psychology of the Unconscious" appear as V.7 of the *Collected Works in English* (Jung & Hinkle, 1916, 1991). They actually form the last of several later revisions Jung made of two texts, "New Paths in Psychology" (1912) and "The Structure of the Unconscious" (1916). Fortunately, the editors of the *Collected Works* have allowed us to see at least these two versions, so that we can compare. What we cannot see in the *CW* is the translation errors and omissions, which are many and often significant (Dohe, 2016). Not only did his translators protect Jung, deleting many anti-Semitic remarks throughout his work, but he himself was his own best revisionist. In addition, the Jung family, with the help of Sonu Shamdasani, continues to keep some of Jung's papers away from scholars. Thus, we must read with care, knowing that we do not have the whole story.

In the 1943–1945 version, Jung defined his central ideas thus:

> The collective unconscious, being the repository of man's experience and at the same time the prior condition of this experience, is an image of the world which has taken aeons to form. In this image certain features, the archetypes or dominants, have crystallized out in the course of time. They are the ruling powers, the gods, images of the dominant laws and principles, and of typical, regularly occurring events in the soul's cycle of experience.
>
> (pp. 94–5)

He went on to explain that these universal ideas correspond to things in the everyday world, and show up in common speech in our talk of gods, demons, and magic. Despite his relentless critique – in part, perhaps, indebted to Nietzsche – of organized Christianity, Jung's archetypes link him to the history of religions – the famous historian of religion Mircea Eliade[15] spoke at Jung's Eranos conferences. The link to India came through the linguistic studies distinguishing Indo-European from Semitic languages. Jung's fascination with ancient Mithraic cults, as well as his absorption of Norse/Germanic/Icelandic sagas, established him in the popular imagination as religion-friendly, in contrast to the atheist Freud, that "godless Jew," as he called himself. Thus, pastoral psychologists, as well as people who think of themselves as "spiritual not religious," and in particular, seekers of connection to something larger than themselves, and to the earth considered as sacred space, have turned to the work of Jung for inspiration.

But when they hear my professional identification as a psychoanalyst, and ask immediately, "then you are a Jungian, yes?" I say little, but the next question comes: "He wasn't really a Nazi, was he?" if they have heard some rumors.

So, let us begin. No, Jung was not a Nazi in the sense that Heidegger was. He never joined the NDSAP or went around giving Nazi salutes. Living in

Switzerland, he was not forced into the life-and-death choices that many elsewhere in Europe were. But Jung had idealized "the blonde beast," and used this expression. He had from a very early age, and long after World War II, made comparisons between Germanic and Jewish psychology, to the detriment of the latter. He loved the Wagnerian Nordic epics, and published "Wotan" (*CW* 10, pp. 371–99) in 1936, celebrating the advent of a great Germanic archetype, a huge eruption of the collective unconscious that he had long seen coming. He hoped a new and positive side would emerge. Later he doctored this piece, adding a quotation from the Eddas (medieval Icelandic epic poems) to make it seem that he already knew the Nazis were dangerous. Within a year, he seems to have known this clearly. But in the early 1930s, he welcomed Hitler as a savior and messiah for the Germanic peoples. Radio Berlin interviewed Jung on 30 June 1932. He described "Hitler as a strong masculine leader of his people" (see also Cocks, 1997; Dohe, p. 198), going on to praise him "as the spearhead of the phalanx of the whole people in motion" (McGuire, Hull, & Bollingen Foundation Collection (Library of Congress), 1977, p. 78). Somewhere between late 1936 and 1939, he saw the danger. To his *Zarathustra* seminar in its penultimate session in 1939, he said "the old gods are coming to life again in a dark time when they should have been superseded long ago, and nobody can see it" (quoted in Bishop (2000) by Jung, p. 166). Even then he could describe the Nazis only in mythological terms.

In addition, Jung worked within the National Socialist system without joining the party. He joined the International General Medical Society for Psychotherapy in 1928. In 1933, Matthias Göring (he was Reichsmarschall Hermann Göring's cousin)[16] asked Jung to accept the presidency (Cocks, 1997). The Freudians had already been expelled as a group, though Jung tried to allow individual exceptions in the early years of the regime. Later in 1933, Göring included in the *Zentralblatt*, the organization's journal, an announcement that all members were expected to read *Mein Kampf*, and practice according to its ideas. This notice appeared above Jung's signature, to his dismay. Jung did not protest, so his silence was taken by many as consent. He privately explained that the Nazi government could make all psychotherapy disappear with the stroke of a pen, as he put it, so he was trying to help. His critics saw him as a Nazi sympathizer. It is even possible to conjecture that he believed that in absence of Jewish psychoanalysis, his analytic psychology could gain ascendance in German-speaking Europe. In fact, his closest collaborator in these years believed exactly this about his motivation.

Jung always claimed that he differed with Freud on scientific, not religious, grounds. But in the very late 1933 issue of the *Zentralblatt* mentioned earlier, Jung took pains to distinguish Germanic from Jewish psychology, an odd choice of topic unless he had consented to the *Gleichschaltung* (conformity), or unless his personal bias led him there. He was the prophet of universals, but when it came to race, he re-emphasized this particular difference again and again.

Later, in 1946, (Jung, 1970, p. 464), Jung claimed to have criticized Nazi Germany so sharply that he ended up on a Nazi "blacklist." Several scholars have observed that there never existed any publicly accessible blacklist, so Jung could not have known this. He also said the Nazis had banned his books. They did not; they banned Freud's. Anyone can check this on the city of Berlin's website. Unfortunately, we are led by Jung himself to see that he was too eager to protect his reputation. But perhaps worse, he could not see the problem in his repeated comparisons of Germanic and Jewish psychologies, even in 1933 and 1934, when he wrote at length on this topic in the *Zentralblatt*. He claimed a "total inability to understand why it should be a crime to speak of "Jewish" psychology" (*Neue Zürcher Zeitung*, quoted in Bishop, p. 176). His very close collaborator Aniela Jaffé wrote that Jung "dragged [the difference between Jewish and non-Jewish psychology] into the limelight at this particular moment when being a Jew was enough to put one in danger of one's life . . . [this] must be regarded as a grave human error" (Jaffé, 1971, pp. 84–5). We have no evidence that Jung ever recognized these errors, nor did he recognize the racism and colonialism of his views on Africans, black Americans, and on indigenous peoples everywhere whom he regarded as primitives. Fortunately, some members, such as Samuels (2018), of the International Association of Analytic Psychology have recently taken a forceful position with respect to Jung's anti-black and colonialist racism, but they do not mention the anti-Semitism. Nor can the statement be found, as of this writing, on the IAAP's website.

As with Heidegger, we must ask ourselves how much of his work is innocent and usable. The worldwide popularity of Jung, especially among those who have not actually read him, does not answer this question. For those on the receiving end of his biases, the question may be fairly easy, akin to remaining in a religion with a history of exploitation, colonization, and abuse. It requires semi-deliberate indifference to history and to those excluded and affected. Unfortunately, the clouds of mysticism, the attraction of the monistic collective unconscious – endlessly blurring real differences and plurality of cultures – silences the dissenters and occludes the concerns of those who begin to ask questions. Although adherents make much good use – even therapeutic use – of Jungian ideas, I believe the accounts provided by scholars like Carrie Dohe (Dohe, 2016) and others (Goggin & Goggin, 2001) should concern us greatly. Fortunately, we have thoughtful Jungian analysts like Andrew Samuels (Samuels, 1992, 1996; Samuels, Shamdasani, Heuer, & Von Der Tann, 1993), unflinching in his recounting of details and connections, to help us with confronting the worrisome history.

Hermann Schmitz

Hermann Schmitz, founder and prodigious writer of "new phenomenology" (Schmitz, 1980, 1985, 1996, 2005b, 2007, 2010, 2011, 2014a, 2014b, 2014c, 2018; Schmitz & Grossheim, 2008) has attracted enough of a following among European gestalt therapists to invite a close look. Unschooled and untrained in gestalt therapy myself, unlike outstanding commentators within the gestalt community, I can pick up only some philosophical threads. My reading of Schmitz's *Adolf Hitler in der Geschichte* (Schmitz, 1999) resembles that of Amendt-Lyon

(2019), Höll (2018), and Gutjahr (2018), all of whom share my horror of his moral equivalences and minimizing of the Nazi destruction of the Jews. "Holocaust", to Schmitz, means only what happened to Germans in WW1. All three authors show clearly that such talk should make everyone careful of anything such an author says on other subjects.

Additionally, we must consider the probability that Schmitz represents a holdover from the proto-Nazi, völkisch era, profoundly anti-Semitic and Aryan-oriented, that also gave us Nietzsche, Wagner, Heidegger, Jung,[17] and also the National Socialists. Whether Schmitz or some of these people can be called Nazis may be open to question, but they share cultural and intellectual roots. Heidegger, of course, joined the Nazi Party, supported it openly in 1933–1934, and never, to my knowledge, gave up his membership. Both Jung and Schmitz hold a kinship to Ludwig Klages, a völkisch anti-Semite to whom we will return. Though, as we shall see, Schmitz depicts Hitler's anti-Semitism as a bizarre phobia, he never clearly states his own opposition to "atmospheric" or "situational" anti-Semitism. Instead, he normalizes the Nazi period.

In my view, of the many imperative questions to ask about Schmitz's Hitler book, the most important is: Why did he write it? Superficially, this book bears no resemblance to Schmitz's dozens of philosophical texts developing a highly systematic "new phenomenology," organized around notions of *Leiblichkeit* (lived-bodyness),[18] atmospheres, and situations. Instead, this book contains countless excerpts from Hitler's speeches, apparently intended to support the Schmitz interpretation of the whole situation of the *Nazizeit*. Is the Hitler text part of the Schmitz philosophical *oeuvre*, or an outlier? If part of the philosophical *Werke*, which of these ideas does it intend to illustrate, and then how should we regard these ideas themselves? If we are to regard the book as an outlier, as if a musicologist wrote one book on skiing, then we can at least ask of a philosopher, why go on this particular detour and make the outrageous mistakes that prevent even the author from any form of retraction?[19] I will be arguing for the first interpretation: To see the Hitler book as integral to Schmitz's work,[20] to bring its implications out of hiding, and to challenge Schmitz's admirers to discuss it clearly, just as Heidegger's admirers have had to do with the so-called *Schwarze Hefte, or Überlegungen* (Farin & Malpas, 2016; Mitchell, 2017).

Hermann Schmitz presents *Adolf Hitler in der Geschichte* (1999) as an extended essay in the history of ideas. He proposes to present the entire history of Western (*Abendländische*) culture and philosophy as a "situation" into which Adolf Hitler came almost as a matter of course.[21] For the first two-thirds of the book, he traces the history of the Greeks, the early and medieval Christians, the Protestants, the Enlightenment, Marx. On page 264 of a 405-page text, Hitler appears as the next "thinker," with most of the rest of the book given to quotations from Hitler's innumerable speeches, showing how he fit the "situation" explained in the first sections of the book. A final section considers the future as the regeneration of the Roman/German empire, indebted, of course to new phenomenology.

Schmitz explains his concept of "situation" (*die Situation*) in the opening chapter:

I define situation by three characteristics: 1. Wholeness [*Ganzheit*], that is, holding together in itself, and closed-off-ness toward the outside; 2. Meaningfulness [*Bedeutsamkeit*], consisting of states of affairs (or matters of fact), programs and problems through which the whole, so to speak, has something to say . . . ; 3. Inner diffusion [*Binnendiffusion*] (otherwise by me [HS]) called chaotic multiplicity [*chaotische Mannigfaltigkeit*] of the whole meaningfulness in the sense that not all that comes up in the matters of fact, programs and problems, is single.

(Schmitz, 1999, p. 21)

Schmitz goes on to say that what looks like a unique phenomenon in history can be better read as part of a situation, so defined. We find here "the thesis of his book: Hitler was no unpredictable phenomenon, but rather a thinker emergent from the Western tradition, read as a Schmitzian 'situation.'" Nothing that occurs within the situation is extraordinary; thus, Schmitz's refusal to name the destruction of the Jews as "Holocaust" or "Shoah" is completely predictable from his thesis. It should not surprise us that the word "situation" appears literally hundreds of times in this book, and its companion word "atmosphere" (*die Atmosphäre*) at least 20.[22]

The "failure of Western thought" (*Verfehlung des Abendländischen Denkens*) means to Schmitz that Hitler was a matter of course, and that we need to learn from this failure and turn to new phenomenology to recognize such problematic situations and atmospheres.

Let us look more closely. In a typical section entitled *"Das volkspädagogische Motiv"* [the theme of German groundedness], Schmitz quotes Hitler equating German *"Boden"* (soil) with Austrian *"Heimat"* (home place), and continues:

What he contrasts to the presumably spaceless [or placeless?] Jewish type, Hitler explains thus:

"And this Jewish thought is typically spaceless, completely unbound in relation to ground, earth, soil, because it is not originally productive [*urproduktiv*], because it is not basically creative (AH, Speech in Munich, 10 October, 1928)." [Schmitz continues:] Here Hitler circles with words and stamps a hard-to-understand neologism, to awaken something around earth and soil in the psychic sense that he calls "ground" so that it is only possible in such a way. I understand what is meant as according to Hitler an indispensable rooting of original productivity in a shared implanted [or implanting] situation.

(Schmitz, 1999, pp. 308–9)

What is Schmitz doing here? Earlier, he had further distinguished the *"implantierenden Situationen"* (implanted situations) as "in which the personal situation strikes such deep roots, that they are not easily, and if at all, ripped out only with considerable wounds" (p. 24). Here, Schmitz attributes to Hitler a rhetoric of excluding all Jewish work from productivity and creativity because it is not rooted or grounded in soil or homeland, a typical anti-Semitic rhetoric also found in Heidegger's *Black Notebooks*. So, seeing Hitler's strategy or his appeal in this way is not original; what we must notice is Schmitz's appeal to his "situations" as if they create inevitability. According to Schmitz, the long history of Western thought and its failure to account correctly for subjectivity in the lived body, and to notice its situations, created an inevitability to Hitler and his reception. No one is responsible for anything in Schmitz's story, not for ideas, not for plans, not for deeds.

Here we must note that Schmitz's Hitler book follows the infamous *Historikerstreit* generated by the reaction in 1986 and 1987 to West German historian Ernst Nolte's revisionist account of the Nazi period. Nolte (1987), Andreas Hilgruber (1986), and others claimed that Hitler modeled the treatment of the Jews on the Bolsheviks' gulags, and that there was nothing unique, no moral difference about the Holocaust. Nolte infamously wrote that only the "technical process of gassing" separated the National Socialists' deeds from all other eliminations of enemy groups. The equivocating sense of Hillgruber's title – *Zweierlei Untergang: die Zerschlagung des Deutschen Reiches und das Ende des europäischen Judentums* (*Double Defeat: The Shattering of the German Empire and the End of European Jewry*) – evokes special outrage with its implication that the second event just happened by itself.[23] It was time, thought the conservative historians, for Germans to stop feeling guilty, and to develop some national pride. The response by philosopher Jürgen Habermas (1993 [1986 in *Die Zeit*]), "A Kind of Settlement of Damages On Apologetic Tendencies In German History Writing," challenged all this moral equivalency and took Nolte to task for alleging that because Chaim Weizmann had expressed support to Churchill in 1939, that the Jews were thus responsible for the war and for their own destruction. Nolte even believed that Hitler persecuted the Jews primarily because he was afraid of Soviet rat-cage torture. Habermas's response was followed by those of historians Hans Mommsen, Jürgen Kocka, and Eberhard Jäckel. When the furor died down, it was clear that the revisionists had lost this round and that many Germans of that generation were serious about engaging with Germany's actual history.

Ten years later, in a different strategy, Schmitz, more believably, to be sure, describes Hitler at length as Jew-phobic, not a Jew-hater, and quotes Hitler repeatedly calling Jews "germs" like tuberculosis that must be eradicated from the Aryan body to keep it safe and pure. "*Treiben wir das jüdische Volk nicht bald aus, so wird dieses in kurzer Zeit unser Volk verjudet*[24] *haben*" ("if we do not drive the Jews out soon, our people will be jewished") (1923 speech, quoted by Schmitz, 1999, p. 283). In other places, Hitler claims that *Judentum* is a contagious poison. Clearly, Schmitz is onto something here, as his voluminous quotes bear out. This hatred was expressed in terms of germs and contagion, to generate fear and justify extermination.

And yet, nowhere does Schmitz express any horror of the views he is quoting, as if somehow his highlighting this "phobic" character of Hitler's anti-Semitism makes it more acceptable. Amendt-Lyon (2019) notes that Schmitz fails even to use scare-quotes. But failure to be horrified makes this book difficult, even nightmarish, to read. Schmitz compares Hitler's "Jewish-phobia" with that of Ludwig Klages's version,[25] noting that they both wanted to be rid of the Jews for different reasons:

> Both thinkers [Hitler and Klages] were forceful opponents of Jewishness, Klages because he saw the failure of western thought in the will of the god Yahweh, Hitler, because in his view the Jewish "trading folk" made everything into something that could be exchanged at will and thus destroyed ordinary processes in situations.
>
> (Schmitz, 1999, p. 294)

This strange passage, treating Hitler as a "thinker," suggests, perhaps, that Schmitz sees Hitler's phobia as slightly deranged, but still effective, given its programmatic translation by Heinrich Himmler, another figure (another thinker?) much quoted in this book. This obsession also fits into the background created by the völkisch, mystical, Aryan, sun-worshiping, anti-Christian and anti-Semitic influence among German-speaking intellectuals of people like Klages. Klages, after all, like Schmitz, tries to explain "*die Verfehlung des abenländisches Denkens*" [the failure of Western thinking]. It's always the Jews. It remains unclear to me whether Schmitz distances himself from Klages; I do not find this repudiation. Perhaps this silence, a key to the whole book, accounts for Schmitz's refusal to use the words "Holocaust" (except for German suffering), "Shoah," and other appropriate words for the genocide, even as he seems to want to account for it.

Before we speak of ethics, let us turn back to our question: Why did Schmitz write this book? Apart from the awful possibility that he was taking up the work of Nolte and his ilk, but simply pursuing a different strategy, what else is possible? His philosophical works on situations and atmospheres come later (Schmitz, 2005a, 2014a). (I must confess to not having read the works that just preceded the Hitler book, so these concepts may have been in development). Joachim Landkammer, whose helpful review of the Hitler book (Landkammer, 2018) clarifies many aspects, decided to consider it written "as a test case for the new phenomenology." Many have noted that these concepts are anything but phenomenological, even new-phenomenological; did Schmitz need them to justify what he had done in the Hitler book? Or had they been developed ad hoc, as if to give a philosophical reading of German twentieth-century history, by making it seem as if it all just happened, and no one did anything? In this case, Schmitz would seem quietly to be resurrecting the conservative side of the *Historikerstreit*. Or were situations and atmospheres, like the mystical völkisch spheres of Klages and Jung, always hiding in plain sight, and needed only their "test case" to make their implications clear? Whatever the truth of this matter, the later work on atmospheres, those even more mystical versions of situations, now made so popular in some gestalt therapy circles by Matthies (2017) and Griffero

(2014), needs the same kind of philosophical questioning that extremes of post-modern skepticism evoked.

Why this turning toward the vague and the mystical, both in reading history and in clinical thinking? In reading history, we may always suspect that contextualizing may devolve into minimizing, or even into justifying. When we learn that our "founding fathers" in the U.S. owned slaves, fathered children with their slaves, and wrote our constitution to protect slavery as well as white male supremacy, we then hear rejoinders that, well, that was the atmosphere at the time. Everybody was colonialist and racist, not to mention masculinist, so that was that. In an altogether other order of magnitude, it takes – as Amendt-Lyon, Höll, and Gutjahr make blazingly clear – more than rationalization to minimize and normalize the planned, systematic, industrialized murder of millions of human beings on racist grounds. It takes a whole new phenomenology, full of concepts custom-built for minimizing and normalizing. What Schmitz has created is a caricature of phenomenology, with a book on Hitler to show just how grotesque it is. It belongs on the shelf with the Holocaust deniers.

But once again, what is the attraction for psychotherapists? Gestalt therapists generally, down to earth in the here and now, resist the temptation to big theorizing. Until now, most of them have been satisfied with a view of contact and dialogue, indebted to their founders and to Martin Buber. But Jungians too, as well as existentially oriented therapists and psychoanalysts under the influence of Heidegger, have fallen into the same trap. We can surely hypothesize that working with the traumatized and the devastated might lead us to search for more answers, and answers from stranger realms, than we already have handy. We might further notice that when our work succeeds to some extent, so that suffering lightens, so that human misery lessens, so that when devastated and dissociated human lives become defragmented or even somewhat integrated and creative, we often cannot say why. When we can find no answers to our own distress or to the misery of those who seek help from us, we turn to those who seem to know, who can invent new ideas. But handle with care!

Some years ago, in a book written for psychoanalysts and other clinicians who felt incapable of reading philosophy (Orange, 2010), I tried to explain the importance of learning to do it:

> we need to think and question every time we become enamored with a single thinker or school of thought. Every psychoanalytic or psychotherapeutic hero or heroine can become our guru, even our cult leader. Seduced by such authorities – either world class or local – we can abandon our human responsibility to think and question. Instead, we are tempted to interpret the world, our clinical experience, and worst of all, our patients through the voice of the cult leader. We may join groups (including training institutes) that exclude, dominate, and disallow dissenting voices. I believe that reading philosophy is the best antidote for this trouble that has beset our field from the time of Freud. As philosophy students, we become "perpetual beginners" like

Edmund Husserl, father of the phenomenological movement (Moran, 2000, p. 62). As beginners, we remain less likely to think we already know or to place too much faith in the "knowing" of others, even those others whom our own training prepares us to treat with too much reverence. If philosophers themselves become cult leaders or gurus, they are no longer really philosophers for those who follow (Orange, 2010, pp. 4–5).

In other words, careful and critical reading of philosophy and of our psychotherapeutic literatures forms the best antidote to uncritical and cult-like acceptance of pseudo-philosophers like Schmitz and epigones like Griffero.

Finally, a word about contextualizing. Nothing exists by itself: This idea both Hermann Schmitz and the best of psychotherapists, gestalt included, hold in common. When contextualizing means explaining away and minimizing, as Schmitz does in *Adolf Hitler in der Geschichte* (1999) (see also the critiques by my very capable gestalt colleagues), it becomes the silence that phenomenologist Emmanuel Levinas called "as if consenting to horror" (Levinas, 1989, p. 485).[26] Tolerating such talk, we become accomplices.

On the other hand, compassionate contextualizing can mean reframing the experience of a shame-ridden and devastated human being, so that the patient's life begins to have a backstory and a sense of dignity begins to return to the sufferer. Not all contextualizing is the same, or serves the same purposes. We must read with care.

With admiration for those gestalt colleagues and for the philosophers helping them to read Schmitz, as well as gratitude for all those who have helped me to read Heidegger and Jung, I close with a few more words from Emmanuel Levinas in the same essay:

> The diabolical is not limited to the wickedness popular wisdom ascribes to it and whose malice, based on guile, is familiar and predictable in an adult culture. The diabolical is endowed with intelligence and enters where it will. To reject it, it is first necessary to refute it. Intellectual effort is needed to recognize it. Who can boast of having done so? Say what you will, the diabolical gives food for thought.
>
> (Levinas, 1989, p. 448)

Notes

1 In an earlier work (Orange, 2010), I suggested learning to read philosophy as an antidote to cults and authoritarian tendencies in psychoanalysis and in related psychotherapies.

2 In part, as we shall see, this aversion resulted from C.G. Jung's relentless monistic attacks on Freudian psychoanalysis. Freud himself, unofficially but clearly as we gain gradual access to his correspondence, was fascinated by telepathy (Freud, 1910), but was never comfortable absorbing it into the official theory of psychoanalysis (Freud, 1922; S. Freud, A. Strachey, Tyson, J. Strachey, & A. Freud, 1921).

3 To avoid a lengthy and abstruse disquisition on the forms of monism, I quote the following from the *Stanford Encyclopedia of Philosophy*: "monism . . . is the theory that

there is only one fundamental kind, category of thing or principle; and, rather less commonly, [contrasted] with pluralism, which is the view that there are many kinds or categories. In the philosophy of mind, dualism is the theory that the mental and the physical – or mind and body or mind and brain – are, in some sense, radically different kinds of thing. Because common sense tells us that there are physical bodies, and because there is intellectual pressure towards producing a unified view of the world, one could say that materialist monism is the 'default option'." https://plato.stanford.edu/entries/dualism/

4 It has been argued (Capobianco, 1993) that Heidegger and Jung belong together, that Heidegger's unconcealing can be used to illuminate the Jungian unconscious.

5 Books outside philosophy may have affected history more, of course, e.g. Mao's writings, Hitler's *Mein Kampf*, even *Freud's Interpretation of Dreams* or Friedan's *The Feminine Mystique*. In philosophy, many (perhaps even I) would vote for Ludwig Wittgenstein. But Heidegger is alive and well in the German New Right parties like AfD (*Alternativ für Deutschland*). See Göpffarth on Heidegger's "German *Dasein*" today (Göpffarth, 2019). He suggests that *Dasein* and *Volk* imply each other for Heidegger. The problem with technological *Gestell* is that "it neglects traditional, spiritual forms and hollows out the *authentic Dasein* of the *Volk*" (n.p.). Current far-right users of Heidegger hope to cloak their own ideology in an innocent cover of Heideggerian philosophy, putatively anti-racist.

6 To my knowledge, Loewald wrote about this only once: "Philosophy has been my first love. I gladly affirm its influence on my way of thinking while being wary of the peculiar excesses a philosophical bent tends to entail. My teacher in this field was Martin Heidegger, and I am deeply grateful for what I learned from him, despite his most hurtful betrayal in the Nazi era, which alienated me from him permanently" (Loewald, 2000), xlii-xliii. See also (Oppenheim, 2016).

7 In 1935 Heidegger wrote: "The temple work standing there brings the *Volk* into the enjoined relation of its world. At the same time it lets the earth rise up as the native ground on which the Dassein of a *Volk* rests" (OA, 26, quoted in Bernasconi, 2010, p. 62).

8 The German title alludes unapologetically to Paul Celan's famous Holocaust poem *Todesfuge,* wherein a repeating refrain runs: "*Das Tod ist ein Meister aus Deutschland*" (Death is a master from Germany).

9 Rockmore, p. 218 n. 3: "The vulgar term *Verjudung*, which is not contained in standard dictionaries, was common in contemporary forms of anti-Semitism and was used by Hitler in *Mein Kampf*, especially in his discussion of "*Volk und Rasse*," (Hitler, Hitler, & Third Reich Collection (Library of Congress), 1925).

10 Translator Thomas Sheehan notes that this piece, *Warum bleiben wir in der Provinz?* appeared one month after Heidegger left the rectorship in Freiburg. (Heidegger, 1934 [2010]).

11 During his rectorship, he not only spoke in Nazi jargon, but enforced the *Gleichschaltung* (conformity) and the strictures against Jews.

12 By normalizing suffering, I do not mean to accuse Buddhists. Very much to the contrary: They acknowledge it clearly in their first noble truth. Japanese Buddhist Hiroyuki Itsuki writes, for example: "we are born weeping, and we all die alone" (Itsuki, 2001, p. 12). Life is hell, he claims.

13 All my biographical material depends greatly on the monumental work of Deirdre Bair (Bair, 2003).

14 Jung prefaced the 1916 version, the first joint publication of the early essays, with these words: "The psychological concomitants of the present war – above all the incredible brutalization of public opinion, the mutual slanderings, the unprecedented fury of destruction, the monstrous flood of lies, and man's incapacity to call a halt to the bloody demon – are uniquely fitted to force upon the attention of every thinking person

the problem of the chaotic unconscious which slumbers uneasily beneath the ordered world of consciousness. This war has pitilessly revealed to civilized man that he is still a barbarian, and has at the same time shown what an iron scourge lies in store for him if ever again he should be tempted to make his neighbour responsible for his own evil qualities. The psychology of the individual is reflected in the psychology of the nation" (p. 3). The 1943–1945 preface makes no reference to current events.

15 Like Jung, Eliade – who could have been a topic for this chapter had he more psycho-therapeutic followers – received criticism for far-right and Aryanist influences. Robert Ellwood writes of Jung, Campbell, and Eliade: "A tendency to think in generic terms of peoples, races, religions, or parties, which as we shall see is undoubtedly the pro-foundest flaw in mythological thinking, including that of such modern mythologists as our three, can connect with nascent anti-Semitism, or the connection can be the other way" (Ellwood, 1999, p. x). Eliade wrote to Mihail Sebastian in 1939: "The Poles' resistance in Warsaw is a Jewish resistance. Only yids are capable of the blackmail of putting women and children in the front line, to take advantage of the Germans' sense of scruple. The Germans have no interest in the destruction of Romania. Only a pro-German government can save us. . . . What is happening on the frontier with Bukovina is a scandal, because new waves of Jews are flooding into the country. Rather than a Romania again invaded by kikes, it would be better to have a German protectorate" (Sebastian, 2000, p. 238). Again, this is not Jung, but illustrates the climate around him.

16 We met him earlier in Chapter 3. The story of Erich Fromm, also related in Chapter 3, belongs to this story of the fate of psychoanalysis in the Third Reich.

17 See, for example, the extremely well-documented work of Richard Noll (Noll, 1997b), who shows the origins of völkisch mysticism in the romantics, in Wagnerism, in sun worship, in the turn to Eastern religions, blood and soil, Mithraic cults, matriarchical ideas, and how these and many others fused in glorifying all things Aryan. This read-ing, of course, places me close to those German historians who understand the Nazi period, at least in part, as an outgrowth of earlier widespread cultural tendencies among German-speaking elites.

18 As my Gestalt therapy colleagues have noted in their contributions mentioned previ-ously, Schmitz intends this idea to overcome Cartesian body/mind dualism but may be replacing it with a new one: Leib/Körper (lived body/material body).

19 Lothar Gutjahr, who knows Schmitz's full work better than I do, informs me that Schmitz did mention this book in later work, implying its full inclusion in his thinking, and linkage to his other ideas (personal communication).

20 My brief contribution highlights this book in part because it is until now untranslated. Readers who know Schmitz only through the few works that have been translated, and through Italian philosopher Antonio Griffero's much more accessible version of Schmitz, may not realize that the Hitler book comes from the same pen, typewriter, or computer. All quotations from the Hitler book are my translations, and thus open for correction.

21 Without mentioning Schmitz, David Farrell Krell makes the similarity with Heidegger clear: "Heidegger is doing everything he can to resist the realization that a terrifying criminality has overtaken his beloved Germany; by equating victims and victimizers he hopes to lay everything that is happening in Germany at he feet of the machina-tions of modernity. The problem is not Germany but occidental history" (Krell, 2015, p. 149).

22 Schmitz uses, at least in this book, both of these terms most frequently in the plural – situations and atmospheres. They have not been terms in Gestalt psychology or therapy, but are being absorbed now by those who admire Schmitz's "Neue Phänomenologie."

23 Hillgruber did not understate the horror of the Holocaust, but did not want to spread or diffuse the responsibility, as Schmitz's strategy does, to the point of disappearance. Hillgruber was known for the "no Hitler, no Holocaust" view.

24 As we noted earlier, Heidegger too used this non-standard term.
25 Ludwig Klages (1872–1956), founder of the German Graphology Circle and much involved in the Munich Cosmic Circle, contrasted the modern world with a more mystical Greek and matriarchal society, following the work of J.J. Bachofen (1815–1887). A rabid anti-Semite, he was close to C.G. Jung, and influenced his developing concept of the collective unconscious.
26 Levinas was writing of Heidegger's *Spiegel* interview, but could have written the same of Schmitz's whole book: "and death? But doesn't this silence, in time of peace, on the gas chambers and death camps lie beyond the realm of feeble excuses and reveal a soul completely cut off from any sensitivity, in which can be perceived a kind of consent to the horror?" p. 487.

References

Amendt-Lyon, N. (2019). The Boundaries of Gestalt Therapy and the Limits of Our Imagination: Hermann Schmitz's Adolf Hitler in History and "New Phenomenology". *Gestalt Review, 22*.

Aron, L., & Starr, K. (2012). *A psychotherapy for the people: Toward a progressive psychoanalysis*. Abingdon, UK: Routledge.

Atwood, G. E. (2011). *The abyss of madness*. New York: Routledge.

Bachofen, J. J., Catt, C. C., & National American Woman Suffrage Association Collection (Library of Congress). (1861). *Das mutterrecht. Eine untersuchung über die gynaikokratie der alten welt nach ihrer religiösen und rechtlichen natur*. Stuttgart: Krais & Hoffmann.

Bair, D. (2003). *Jung: A biography* (1st ed.). Boston: Little, Brown and Co.

Bambach, C. R. (2003). *Heidegger's roots: Nietzsche, national socialism and the Greeks*. Ithaca, NY: Cornell University Press.

Bambach, C. R. (2013). *Thinking the poetic measure of justice: Hölderlin, Heidegger, Celan*. Albany: State University of New York Press.

Bernasconi, R. (2010). Race and Earth in Heidegger's Thinking During the Late 1930s. *The Southern Journal of Philosophy, 48*, 49–66.

Bernasconi, R. (2017). Another Eisenmenger? On the Alleged Originality of Heidegger's Anti-Semitism. In *Heidegger's Black notebooks: Responses to anti-semitism* (pp. 168–185). New York: Columbia University Press.

Bishop, P. (2000). *Synchronicity and intellectual intuition in Kant, Swedenborg, and Jung*. Lewiston, NY: E. Mellen Press.

Braue, D. A. (1984). *Māyā in Radhakrishnan's thought: Six meanings other than illusion* (1st ed.). Delhi: Motilal Banarsidass.

Capobianco, R. (1993). Heidegger and Jung: Dwelling Near the Source. *Review of Existential Psychology and Psychiatry, 21*, 50–59.

Caputo, J. D. (1993). *Demythologizing Heidegger*. Bloomington: Indiana University Press.

Caputo, J. D. (2016). The poverty of thought in Heidegger and Eckhart. In T. Sheehan (Ed.), *Heidegger: The man and the thinker*. New Brunswick, NJ: Transaction Publishers.

Cocks, G. (1997). *Psychotherapy in the Third Reich: The Göring institute* (2nd ed.). New Brunswick, NJ: Transaction Publishers.

Day, M. (2010). A Spectre Haunts Evolution: Haeckel, Heidegger, and the All-Too-Human History of Biology. *Perspectives in Biology and Medicine, 53*, 289–303.

Di Cesare, D. (2018). *Heidegger and the Jews: The Black notebooks* (English ed.). Medford, MA: Polity.

Dohe, C. B. (2016). *Jung's wandering archetype: Race and religion in analytical psychology.* London and New York: Routledge.

Ellwood, R. (1999). *The politics of myth: A study of C.G. Jung, Mircea Eliade, and Joseph Campbell.* Albany, NY: SUNY Press.

Farin, I., & Malpas, J. (2016). *Reading Heidegger's black notebooks 1931–1941.* Cambridge, MA: The MIT Press.

Faye, E. (2009). *Heidegger, the introduction of Nazism into philosophy in light of the unpublished seminars of 1933-1935.* New Haven: Yale University Press.

Freud, S. (1910). Letter from Sigmund Freud to Sándor Ferenczi, November 15, 1910. In E. Brabant, E. Falzeder, & P. Giampieri-Deutsch (Eds.), *The correspondence of Sigmund Freud and Sándor Ferenczi volume 1, 1908–1914* (pp. 232–233). Cambridge, MA and London: Harvard University Press.

Freud, S. (1922). Dreams and Telepathy. *International Journal of Psycho-Analysis, 3,* 283–305.

Freud, S., Strachey, A., Tyson, A., Strachey, J., & Freud, A. (1921). Psycho-Analysis and Telepathy. In *The standard edition of the complete psychological works of Sigmund Freud, volume XVIII (1920–1922): Beyond the pleasure principle, group psychology and other works* (Vol. 18, pp. 173–194). London: Hogarth.

Fried, G. (2018). *After Heidegger?* London and New York: Rowman & Littlefield International.

Friedman, L. (2016). Is There a Usable Heidegger for Psychoanalysts? *Journal of the American Psychoanalytic Association, 64*(3), 587–624.

Goggin, J. E., & Goggin, E. B. (2001). *Death of a "Jewish science": Psychoanalysis in the Third Reich.* West Lafayette, IN: Purdue University Press.

Göpffarth, J. (2019). Rethinking the German Nation as German Dasein: Intellectuals and Heideggers Philosohy in Contemporary German New Right Nationalism. *The Journal of Political Ideologies.* Retrieved from www.academia.edu/38302855/Rethinking_the_ German_nation_as_German_Dasein_Intellectuals_and_Heidegger_s_philosophy_in_ contemporary_German_New_Right_nationalism?email_work_card=view-paper.

Griffero, T. (2014). *Atmospheres: Aesthetics of emotional spaces.* Farnham Surrey, England and Burlington, VT: Ashgate Pub.

Gutjahr, L. (2018). Nourishing Notions or Poisonous Propositions? Can "New Phenomenology" Inspire Gestalt Therapy? *Gestalt Review,* (22).

Habermas, J. (1989). Work and Weltanschauung: The Heidegger Controversy from a German Perspective. *Critical Inquiry, 15,* 431–456.

Habermas, J. (1993 [1986 in *Die Zeit*]). A Kind of Settlement of Damages on Apologetic Tendencies in German History Writing. In E. Piper (Ed.), *Forever in the shadow of Hitler?* (pp. 34–44). Atlantic Highlands: Humanities Press.

Heidegger, M. (1934 [2010]). Why Do I Stay in the Provinces? In T. Sheehan (Ed.), *Heidegger, the man and the thinker* (pp. 27–30). New Brunswick and London: Transaction Publishers.

Heidegger, M. (1962). *Being and time.* New York: Harper.

Heidegger, M. (1966). "Only a God Can Save Us": The Spiegel Interrview (W. Richardson, Trans.). In T. Sheehan (Ed.), *Heidegger: The man and the thinker* (pp. 45–68). New Brunswick and London: Transaction.

Heidegger, M. (1976). Nur noch ein Gott kann uns retten [Only a God Can Save Us]. *Der Spiegel, 30*(May), 193–219.

Heidegger, M. (2000). *Introduction to metaphysics.* New Haven: Yale University Press.

Heidegger, M. (2016). *Ponderings: Black notebooks.* Bloomington: Indiana University Press.

Heidegger, M., & Beaufret, J. (1949). *Über den Humanismus*. Frankfurt am Main.: V. Klostermann.

Heidegger, M., & Krell, D. F. (1993). *Basic writings: From Being and time (1927) to the task of thinking (1964)* (Rev. and expanded ed.). San Francisco, CA: HarperSanFrancisco.

Heidegger, M., & Ruckteschell, P. v. (2004). *Nietzsche Seminare 1937 und 1944*. Frankfurt am Main: Vittorio Klostermann.

Heidegger, M., & Trawny, P. (2014). *Überlegungen: (Schwarze Hefte)*. Frankfurt am Main: Vittorio Klostermann.

Heidegger, M., & Trawny, P. (2015). *Anmerkungen: (Schwarze Hefte)*. Frankfurt am Main: Vittorio Klostermann.

Hillgruber, A. (1986). *Zweierlei Untergang: die Zerschlagung des Deutschen Reiches und das Ende des europäischen Judentums*. Berlin: W.J. Siedler.

Hitler, A., Hitler, A., & Third Reich Collection (Library of Congress). (1925). *Mein Kampf*. München: Verlag Franz Eher Nachfolger.

Höll, K. (2018). Lothar Gutjahr's "Nourishing Notions or Poisonous Propositions? Can 'New Phenomenology' Inspire Gestalt Therapy?". *Gestalt Review, 22*.

Hutchison, J. A. (1977). *Living options in world philosophy*. Honolulu: University Press of Hawaii.

Itsuki, H. (2001). *Tariki: Embracing despair, discovering peace*. Tokyo and New York: Kodansha.

Jaffé, A. (1971). *From the life and work of C. G. Jung* (1st Harper colophon ed.). New York: Harper & Row.

Jung, C. G. (1957). *Psychology of the unconscious: A study of the transformation and symbolisms of the libido*. New York: Dodd, Mead.

Jung, C. G. (1970). *Civilization in transition* (2nd ed.). Princeton, NJ: Princeton University Press.

Jung, C. G. (1973). *Letters*. Princeton, NJ: Princeton University Press.

Jung, C. G., & Hinkle, B. M. (1916). *Psychology of the unconscious: A study of the transformations and symbolisms of the libido: A contribution to the history of the evolution of thought*. New York: Moffat, Yard and Co.

Jung, C. G., & Hinkle, B. M. (1991). *Psychology of the unconscious: A study of the transformations and symbolisms of the libido: A contribution to the history of the evolution of thought*. Princeton, NJ: Princeton University Press.

Jung, C. G., & Hinkle, M. B. M. (1916). *Psychology of the unconscious: A study of the transformations and symbolisms of the libido: A contribution to the history of the evolution of thought*. New York: Moffat, Yard and company.

Jung, C. G., & Jaffé, A. (1989). *Memories, dreams, reflections* (Rev. ed.). New York: Vintage Books.

Kerner, J. A. C. (1845). *The seeress of Prevorst: Being revelations concerning the inner-life of man, and the inter-diffusion of a world of spirits in the one we inhabit*. New York: Harper & Brothers.

Knowles, A. (2019). *Heidegger's fascist affinities: A politics of silence*. Stanford, CA: Stanford University Press.

Krell, D. (2015). Heidegger's Black Notebooks, 1931–1941. *Research in Phenomenology, 45*, 127–160.

Landkammer, J. (2018). Von Homer bis Hitler Die "Neue Phänomenologie" und die Versuchung der Geschichtsphilosophie. Retrieved from http://archiv.sicetnon.org/artikel/rezensio/schmitz.htm.

Lang, B. (1996). *Heidegger's silence*. Ithaca, NY: Cornell University Press.

Levinas, E. (1989). As If Consenting to Horror. *Critical Inquiry, 15*, 485–488.

Loewald, H. W. (1977). Transference and Countertransference: The Roots of Psychoanalysis Book Review Essay on the Freud/Jung Letters. *Psychoanalytic Quarterly, 46*, 514–527.

Loewald, H. W. (2000). *The essential Loewald: Collected papers and monographs*. Hagerstown, MD: University Pub. Group.

Löwith, K. (1939 [1991]). The Political Implications of Heidegger's Existentialism. In R. Wolin (Ed.), *The Heidegger controversy* (pp. 167–185). Cambridge, MA and London: MIT Press.

Matthies, F. (2017). Bedeutung von Situation und leiblicher Kommunikation. *Neue Phaenomenologie*. 28 Mai 2017 http://friedhelm-matthies.de/wp-content/uploads/2017/08/Friedhelm-Matthies-Bedeutung-von-Situation-und-leiblicher-Kommunikation.pdf

McGuire, W., Hull, R. F. C., & Bollingen Foundation Collection (Library of Congress). (1977). In *C. G. Jung speaking: Interviews and encounters*. Princeton, NJ: Princeton University Press.

Mitchell, A. J. (2017). *Heidegger's Black notebooks: Responses to anti-semitism*. New York: Columbia University Press.

Moran, D. (2000). *Introduction to phenomenology*. London and New York: Routledge.

Noll, R. (1994). *The Jung cult: Origins of a charismatic movement*. Princeton, NJ: Princeton University Press.

Noll, R. (1997a). *The Aryan Christ: The secret life of Carl Jung* (1st ed.). New York: Random House.

Noll, R. (1997b). *The Jung cult: Origins of a charismatic movement* (1st Free Press Paperbacks ed.). New York: Free Press Paperbacks.

Nolte, E. (1987). *Der europäische Bürgerkrieg, 1917–1945: Nationalsozialismus und Bolschewismus*. Berlin: Propyläen Verlag.

Oppenheim, M. (2016). Beyond Betrayal: Responsibility in Heidegger, Loewald, and Levinas. In D. Goodman & E. Severson (Eds.), *The ethical turn: Otherness and subjectivity in contemporary psychoanalysis* (pp. 186–208). London and New York: Routledge.

Orange, D. M. (2010). *Thinking for clinicians: Philosophical resources for contemporary psychoanalysis and the humanistic psychotherapies*. New York: Routledge.

Rockmore, T. (1992). *On Heidegger's Nazism and philosophy*. Berkeley: University of California Press.

Rockmore, T. (2017). Heidegger after Trawny. In A. Mitchell & P. Trawny (Eds.), *Heidegger's Black notebooks: Responses to anti-semitism* (pp. 152–168). New York: Columbia University Press.

Ryland, E. (2000). Gaia Rising: A Jungian Look at Environmental Consciousness and Sustainable Organizations. *Organization and Environment, 13*, 381–402.

Safranski, R. (1998). *Martin Heidegger: Between good and evil*. Cambridge, MA: Harvard University Press.

Samuels, A. (1992). National Psychology, National Socialism, and Analytical Psychology: Reflections on Jung and Anti-Semitism Part II. *Journal of Analytic Psychology, 37*(2), 127–148.

Samuels, A. (1996). Jung's Return from Banishment. *Psychoanalytic Review, 83*(4), 469–489.

Samuels, A. (2018). Open Letter from a Group of Jungians on the Question of Jung's Writings on and Theories About 'Africans'. *British Journal of Psychotherapy, 34*(4), 673–678.

Samuels, A., Shamdasani, S., Heuer, G., & Von Der Tann, M. (1993). New Material Concerning Jung, Anti-Semitism, and the Nazis. *Journal of Analytical Psychology*, *38*(4), 463–470.

Schirmacher, W. (1983). *Technik und Gelassenheit: Zeitkritik nach Heidegger*. Freiburg: Alber.

Schmitz, H. (1980). *Neue Phänomenologie*. Bonn: Bouvier.

Schmitz, H. (1985). *Aristoteles*. Bonn: Bouvier.

Schmitz, H. (1996). *Husserl und Heidegger*. Bonn: Bouvier.

Schmitz, H. (1999). *Adolf Hitler in der Geschichte*. Bonn: Bouvier.

Schmitz, H. (2005a). *Situationen und Konstellationen: wider die Ideologie totaler Vernetzung* (Originalausg. ed.). Freiburg: Verlag Karl Alber.

Schmitz, H. (2005b). *Situationen und Konstellationen: wider die Ideologie totaler Vernetzung* (Originalausg. ed.). Freiburg: Verlag Karl Alber.

Schmitz, H. (2007). *Freiheit* (Originalausg. ed.). Freiburg: Alber.

Schmitz, H. (2010). *Bewusstsein* (Originalausg. ed.). Freiburg im Breisgau: K. Alber.

Schmitz, H. (2011). *Der Leib*. Berlin and Boston: De Gruyter.

Schmitz, H. (2014a). *Atmosphären* (Originalausgabe. ed.). Freiburg: Verlag Karl Alber.

Schmitz, H. (2014b). *Gibt es die Welt?* (Originalausgabe. ed.). Freiburg: Alber.

Schmitz, H. (2014c). *Phänomenologie der Zeit* (Originalausgabe. ed.). Freiburg: Verlag Karl Alber.

Schmitz, H. (2018). *Wozu Philosophieren?* Freiburg: Verlag Karl Alber.

Schmitz, H., & Grossheim, M. (2008). *Neue Phänomenologie zwischen Praxis und Theorie: Festschrift für Hermann Schmitz* (Originalausg. ed.). Freiburg: Karl Alber.

Sebastian, M. (2000). *Journal 1935–1944: The fascist years*. Chicago: University of Chicago Press.

Stolorow, R., Atwood, G., & Orange, D. (2009). Heidegger's Nazism and the Hypostatization of Being. *International Journal of Psychoanalytic Self Psychology*, *5*:429–450.

Stolorow, R. D. (2007). *Trauma and human existence: Autobiographical, psychoanalytic, and philosophical reflections*. New York: Analytic Press.

Stolorow, R. D. (2011a). *World, affectivity, trauma: Heidegger and post-Cartesian psychoanalysis*. New York: Routledge.

Stolorow, R. D. (2011b). *World, affectivity, trauma: Heidegger and post-Cartesian psychoanalysis*. New York: Routledge.

Stolorow, R. D. (2016). Using Heidegger. *Journal of the American Psychoanalytic Association*, *64*(4), NP12–NP15.

Trawny, P., & Mitchell, A. J. (2015). *Heidegger, die Juden, noch einmal*. Frankfurt am Main: Vittorio Klostermann.

Ulanov, A. B. (1997a). Teaching Jung in a Theological Seminary and a Graduate School of Religion: A Response to David Tacey. *Journal of Analytic Psychology*, *42*(2), 303–311.

Ulanov, A. B. (1997b). Transference, the Transcendent Function, and Transcendence. *Journal of Analytic Psychology*, *42*(1), 119–138.

Weber, M., Gerth, H. H., & Mills, C. W. (2009). *From Max Weber: Essays in sociology*. Milton Park, Abingdon, Oxon and New York: Routledge.

Wolin, R., & Heidegger, M. (1993). *The Heidegger controversy: A critical reader* (1st ed.). Cambridge, MA: MIT Press.

Zhok, A. (2016). The Black Notebooks: Implications for an Assessment of Heidegger's Philosophical Development. *Philosophia*, *44*, 15–31.

Chapter 5

Reading history as an ethical and therapeutic project

Reading saved my life as an exploited child. Now perhaps it may save, or at least grow, my ethical life. The preceding two chapters have illustrated an approach to the philosophy, psychology, and politics of silence and silencing that I will now theorize. While indirect, it possesses pragmatic power, and is available to all literate people. Reading history, especially as written from the perspective of those silenced and violated by history's usual telling,[1] can be an ethical and therapeutic project that makes a difference in the readers and in those around them. Hearing the voices of those drowned out by selfishness, by presumptions of superiority and entitlement, and by sheer historical unconsciousness, can challenge and change presumptions.

This chapter has three main sections: 1) how to read history for ethical hearing; 2) examples of ethical reading; and 3) experiential history for ethical hearing.

Reading history as an ethical and psychoanalytic project[2]

Long before social media exposed racist brutality in the U.S., James Baldwin wrote:

> This is the crime of which I accuse my country and my countrymen, and for which I nor time nor history will ever forgive them, that they have destroyed and are destroying hundreds of thousands of lives, and do not know and do not want to know it.
>
> (Baldwin, 1963, p. 5)

His successors (Coates, 2015) find the vast majority of us today just as mindless as ever. Living in our white bubbles, unafraid that a walk down the street will end in a police confrontation, unworried that entering a shop will get us followed and suspected, or that our very skin constitutes a danger and a problematic signal we can never escape, we whites remain unconscious, a psychoanalyst might say, that the problems of people of color have anything to do with us. Much less do most of us in the U.S. have any insistent sense that the disappearance of the indigenous peoples, whose names we barely know, indicts our possession. This land is my land, we sing enthusiastically.

Lynne Layton (2006) has written extensively and helpfully of what she calls "normative unconscious process," "that aspect of the unconscious that pulls to repeat affect/behavior/cognition patterns that uphold the very social norms that cause psychic distress in the first place" (p. 242). Originating in her studies of gender and sexual identity, and easily expanding to cover racial and ethnic identities, this concept helps to explain experiences, more or less painful, of splits between deeply – though conflictually – absorbed norms of identity and comportment with feelings and values that do not fit the norms. The psychoanalyst attuned to such processes can often open dialogues across these resulting splits, helping to understand the origins of the norms, and to validate the non-normative sensibilities.

In a related vein, talk of "ethical unconsciousness" (Orange, 2017), recently applied extensively to problems of climate justice, refers to splits between what we well-intentioned people may know about various social, economic, and political situations – including those we may reckon dire – and what we actually do about them. Once again, the psychoanalyst asks why, wondering what form of unconsciousness permits us to go about as if our daily lives did not inflict serious damage, indeed jeopardize the existence of the world's poorest people. We allow our politicians to spotlight the so-called "middle class." Somehow, they fail to mention the abjectly poor, the people of color, the aged women, those starving worldwide who make the clothes we then build larger closets to hold. I mean by "ethical unconsciousness" my failure, culturally sustained, to see the faces and to hear the voices of those for whom we are all responsible.[3] The worst, as Baldwin so clearly puts it, is that we do not want to know.

But what if we – or at least some part of us – *do* want to know, to wake up? Listening to prophets like Rev. Dr. Martin Luther King, Jr. can help activate many of us, but we tend to get rid of them, it seems, and cannot replace them easily. Travel writer Rick Steves (2009) suggests that travel can be a political act, reminding us of diversity and richness, allowing us to feel ourselves of somewhat lesser importance. Travel can teach us to treasure diversity, as Steves himself clearly does.[4] Even more, "when we return home, we can put what we've learned – our newly acquired broader perspective – to work as citizens of a great[!] nation confronted with unprecedented challenges. And when we do that, we make travel a political act." (Steves, 2009, Introduction). In a more recent edition, he writes: "Travel challenges truths that we were raised thinking were self-evident and God-given. Leaving home, we learn other people find *different* truths to be "self-evident" (Steves, 2018, p. 3).

Concerned both for those who cannot travel, and for those who return paralyzed by the "challenges" to which he refers, I want to push Steves's idea into another register, considering *reading history as a psychoanalytic and ethical project*. Immediately two questions arise: What kind of history, and what kind of reading? To the first, we may forget the encyclopedic recitation of allegedly perspective-free and context-free "facts" that leave us innocent of the concrete history – of settler colonialism, of chattel slavery, of genocides – into which we are born and from which we continue to profit. As a child, fascinated by other worlds and people, and wondering how things and people traveled from there to here and then to now, I loved to read history, mostly in the form of historical fiction and biography. But I read white history, mainstream history, the history of conquest, heroic pioneers, and saintly missionaries, as I then thought. Only much belatedly did I discover Howard Zinn's mind-bending *A People's History of the United States* (Zinn, 1980) and just recently *An Indigenous People's History of the United States* by Roxanne Dunbar-Ortiz (Dunbar-Ortiz, 2014).[5] Now I am considering history told from the point of view of those on the disadvantaged end of it, complex and terrible stories of people of color throughout the Americas, whether formerly enslaved or refugees from violence or starvation, women's stories – eclipsed, as Adam Knowles (2015) writes, since ancient Greece; those of sexual minorities. Sometimes those disadvantaged no longer live to speak for themselves; still, those who attempt to tell their stories may help us.

So how exactly could reading become an ethical process? Reading as entertainment only, or for data-gathering only, will rarely become ethical, or to speak in psychoanalytic terms, such reading will not challenge our "normative unconscious processes" (Layton, 2004, 2006, p. 238). Though all literature points to otherness and vulnerability, ethical reading means searching out those whose voices tend to remain unheard, listening to their versions of history, making an effort to decenter from our ordinary lives. It wakes us up, surprises us, creates and restores lost links to shared humanity, links broken by racism and hatred, conscious or not.

Such reading may, of course, include thoughtful watching of television and film, a form of the reading recommended here. A colleague listens daily and intentionally to television news, imagining how someone of color would hear whatever is happening or being reported. Similarly, I have been reading history – of Latin America, of chattel slavery, of settler colonialism, of the treatment of Asian Americans – trying to hear the history I learned as conquest and glory as stories of crimes against humanity, from which I continue to live too comfortably. I want to hear Ta-Nehisi Coates (2015) when he tells his son what it means to be white:

> Their new name [white] has no meaning divorced from the machinery of criminal power. The new people were something else before they were white – Catholic, Corsican, Welsh, Mennonite, Jewish . . . it must be said that washing the disparate tribes white, the elevation of the belief in being white, was not achieved through wine-tastings and ice-cream socials, but rather through the pillaging of life, liberty, labor, and land; through the flaying of backs; the chaining of limbs; the strangling of dissidents; the destruction of families; the rape of mothers; the sale of children; and various other acts meant, first and foremost, to deny you and me the right to secure and govern our own bodies.
>
> (pp. 7–8)

A legitimate heir to James Baldwin, Coates teaches a painful but crucial lesson in ethical reading: That the "innocence" involved in calling myself "white" instead of, for example, Irish American, is worse than specious; it is racist, inheriting all the violence of enslavement, lynchings, Jim Crow, and racial profiling. He teaches me to read another history, and to keep on reading it until it really sinks in and begins to change me.

Exposure to the vulnerable face and voice of the other, especially of those others injured by "my people," makes me vulnerable, too, vulnerable to responsibility. This responsibility takes at least two forms. Accused, first, not only by massive historical injustices I may not have created directly – I think of second- and third-generation Germans and Austrians who resent having to hold themselves responsible for Nazi crimes – Coates accuses me of complicity by my very unconsciousness, not to mention my passive bystandership and failure to do anything about the legacy of these crimes. Second, allowing oneself to be affected by prophetic voices like Coates and Baldwin, or by reading detailed histories of slavery or colonialism, may mean a vulnerable accepting of responsible solidarity with others, whoever they may be, but primarily with the most destitute.

So, reading may actually wake me up as my other's keeper. If I am asking like Cain, "what is all that to me?" the reading may do me no good. But "if with all your heart you truly seek him," in my gloss the face of the abandoned and suffering other who bears the trace of the infinite, you shall ever surely find him (apologies to Mendelsohn). Ethical reading desires the other.

Such reading of history may also restore the broken links that maintain ethical unconsciousness. Linking, an important theme in contemporary psychoanalysis (Bion, 1959; Loewald, 2000), means breaking the isolation that keeps the conscious subject unaware of emotional resonances, of personal and cultural history, of the suffering of others. Reading a book like *Open Veins of Latin America* (Galeano, 1973) establishes or restores links to personal and cultural history of crimes obliterating the lives of millions. One can never look at the gold in Baroque Roman Catholic churches in the same way after reading Eduardo Galeano. Nor can one see the transcontinental railroad with innocent eyes after reading Helen Zia's *Asian-American Dreams* (Zia, 2000). Links show up everywhere.

But caution: History can be written or read individualistically, or not. Writing or reading with the assumptions of personal individualism or egoism, where links to others are by chance or choice, leaves us more isolated and judgmental than ever. Assuming land ownership, for example, of land only available by expelling, enslaving, or eliminating indigenous peoples – as in North and South America, and Australia – betrays our commitment to this egoism. We find ourselves unable to resume linking because of a fundamental denial that links to others could exist or matter. What have those people – the colonists, the native peoples, the enslavers – to do with me? This land is my land. In other words, until we call into question the basic assumptions denying solidarity, we cannot begin to read history as an ethical project. We will continue to read the triumphalist versions of history as we have always read them, without noticing anything awry. The splits buried in Layton's normative unconscious processes, often surfacing in psychotherapy or bringing the patient in to see the analyst, have a chance, given the stimulus of ethical reading, to enter dialogue. Ethical unconsciousness, on the other hand, may make the other impossible to perceive as brother or sister. But once we have begun to wonder about these assumptions, if not to overcome them, such reading may take us into sensibilities and conversations we had never before imagined.

Queer theorist Eve Sedgwick (Sedgwick & Frank, 2003), in a hermeneutical tour de force, distinguished between paranoid and reparative reading. Paranoid reading involves the absolute need for certainty, for safety, for above all the assurance that one will never be surprised by anything. Thus, one must know in advance the exact facts of the past and the present so as to predict the future. Anything that looks open, one must immediately close down by reading and interpreting according to models and classifications that yield exact predictions. Reparative reading, on the contrary, depends on vulnerability and allows us to hear unexpected voices. Sedgwick writes:

> To read from a reparative position is to surrender the knowing, anxious, paranoid determination that no horror, however apparently unthinkable shall ever come to the reader *as new*. To a reparatively positioned reader, it can seem realistic and necessary to experience surprise.
>
> (p. 24, emphasis in original)

Clearly, the ethical reading of history which I advocate here relies on reparative reading. And we shall be changed, proclaims Handel's basso. Just how any reading will change us remains a surprise, much like the surprising twists and turns Hans-Georg Gadamer (Gadamer, Weinsheimer, & Marshall, 2004) expected in any conversation worthy of the name. If, however, we find ourselves changed by our reading, more surprises may arrive.

Examples of ethical reading

Let us consider briefly three books as examples for reading history as an ethical project. Two, unfortunately for my agenda, have white authors, but who write in the spirit of reparative reading, complexifying and shifting our usual focus. In a similar white voice writes Douglas A. Blackmon, historian of the post-Civil War period in *Slavery by Another name: The Re-enslavement of Black Americans from the Civil War to World War II* (Blackmon, 2009). For more indigenous historians and historians of color, see Roxanne Dunbar-Ortiz (2014), Ibrahim X. Kendi (2016), and Isabel Wilkerson (2010), among many others.

Wendy Warren

In her meticulously researched book, *New England Bound: Slavery and Colonization in Early America* (Warren, 2016), Wendy Warren brings to life the enslaved African people of seventeenth-century New England, mostly brought from the Caribbean, often exchanged for enslaved indigenous people or other property. She explains that colonists preferred to own the Africans, more docile because of isolation from all family and ties, instead of "Indians" who often fled to tribal homes, and if shipped to the Caribbean sugar plantations, often rebelled or died of suicide.

Using court records above all, Warren allows us to hear the voices of enslaved people and of the colonists who, pious and generous as they believed themselves to be, felt fully entitled not only to the service, but to the ownership and inheritance of enslaved people, almost from the time they landed in New England. She quotes the words of their pleading for their bonds to children, their claims of rape and impregnation by colonists, and the consequent sentences meted out to them: Monetary fines (impossible to pay by people who were owned and owned nothing themselves) and whippings, with numbers of lashes specified. Most often, the woman received the blame for having become pregnant, though it was customary to wait until she had given birth before whipping her. We also hear words of longing in the courts for freedom, giving the lie to the claim that New England slaves were contented with their lot, and for reunion with free blacks who lived in New York.

Warren shows us how intricately slavery, and the slave trade, wove itself without much notice or protest into the economics of the colonial project, even when this venture claimed a religious meaning. She undermines the sense of innocence of many who idealize the early Puritans and Pilgrims, who left England partly as a protest against the remnants of Roman Catholicism in the Anglican Church, and partly to seek wealth. That, in the following century, slaveholding colonists like Jefferson and Washington led the rebellion against English hegemony, setting up a Constitution protecting the slavery system, should come to us as no surprise. It would take longer to see enslaving people as a moral outrage incompatible with the religions they wanted to practice freely. New Englanders like Cotton Mather and John Saffin, she reports, considered ridiculous the position of Samuel Sewall, the judge who had publicly repented his participation in the 1692–1693 Salem witch trials. In 1700, Sewall published a three-page pamphlet, *The Selling of Joseph*, comparing the enslavement of Africans to the biblical crime of Joseph's brothers when they sold him into slavery. Bypassing the argument that some slaveowners eschewed cruelty and violence, Sewall concentrated on commodification: "all Men, as they are Sons of *Adam*, are Coheirs; and have equal Right unto Liberty, and all other outward Comforts of Life . . . .there is no such thing as Slavery" (quoted in Warren, 2016, pp. 222, 228). No amount of money, he believed, could be a fair price for a human life. His critics objected that God had set a hierarchy in which some were naturally masters, and others naturally subjected. Sewall's argument disappeared until the Civil War years, when the slave trade and enslavement had gradually died out in New England. Even Nathanial Hawthorne, sensitive observer of colonial New England and puzzled about the people of color he found there in the pre-Civil War years, believed slavery belonged only to the south.

Warren forces, it seems to me, any of us who read her account carefully to relinquish our innocence about our earliest colonial ancestors. Like contemporary Germans faced every day with the crimes of their grandparents, asking where are the Jews and Roma who once lived among us as our neighbors, we begin to ask, does every single American Indian and person of color I meet carry a history of violence, of genocide, of crimes against humanity perpetrated by people like me, possibly by my own ancestors? Why am I able to live on land in Maine or in California? How did this land come to belong to white people? Did they possess and dominate this land on the backs of black people? Warren's careful research makes me want and dread to know even more.

Frederick Douglass

In a massive and extensively researched new biography (Blight, 2018), *Frederick Douglass: Prophet of Freedom*, we read the story of arguably the most important American of the nineteenth century. Born a slave (c. 1818)[6] in eastern-shore Maryland, probably the son of his mother's owner, this publisher/journalist/public speaker wrote his own autobiography three times: (Douglass, 1845, 1855, 1881). We learn, both from Blight and from Douglass himself, in his writings and countless speeches, of the outrageous indignities and violence in the lives of enslaved people, just as Douglass himself had experienced them. Having learned to read, and having studied rhetoric while still enslaved, Douglass finally escaped to the north, lived for some years as a fugitive slave until others bought his freedom. Blight tells the story of his complicated relationship with famous white abolitionists, while describing his growth into the prophetic voice of liberation he became. Douglass's personal relationships, ongoing financial struggles to support a growing family while on the speech-making circuit, his ever-evolving changes in political philosophy and strategy, culminate in the Civil War years.

Increasingly, his leadership brought him into conflict with Abraham Lincoln, primarily over colonization projects. Emancipation, when it finally came on 1 January 1863, brought Douglass to lead in the rejoicing, and immediately to call for blacks to enroll in the Union Army. Colonization, supported for ten years by Lincoln on the grounds that black and white people could not live together as equals, outraged Douglass. On 14 August 1862, Lincoln had read a written statement to a group of five black pastors:

"You and we are different races. We have between us a broader difference than exists between almost any other two races. Whether it is right or wrong I need not discuss, but this physical difference is a great disadvantage to us both." Blacks and whites mutually "suffer" from each other's presence in the same land, argued the president. For this reason, Lincoln concluded, "We should be separated. . . . But for your race among us there could not be war, although many men engaged on either side do not care for you one way or another." [Blacks, slave or free, were enduring] "the greatest wrong inflicted on any people," [but racial equality of any kind could] never be possible in America. "On this broad continent, not a single man of your race is made the equal of a single man of ours."

(Blight, 2018, p. 371)

Blight continues:

Lincoln beseeched the five black representatives, who must have felt more than a little bewildered, to swallow their wishes for a future in the land of their birth and lead their people to a foreign colony. He did not wish to seem "unkind," but for them to reject his plea to lead in voluntary repatriation would be "an extremely selfish view of the case" and not in the best interest of their race. "It is exceedingly important that we have men at the beginning capable of thinking as white men," he bluntly continued, "and not those who have been systematically oppressed."

(p. 371)

Lincoln concluded, in full racist tones, by claiming that blacks would do best in a "similarity of climate with your native land" (p. 371).

Douglass, who had combatted colonization ideas and schemes as both stupid and inhumane for many years, was horrified. He reprinted in full Lincoln's prepared talk in his newspaper, and editorialized:

Mr. Lincoln assumes the language and arguments of an itinerant Colonization lecturer, showing all his inconsistencies, his pride of race and blood, his contempt for Negroes and his canting hypocrisy. How an honest man could creep into such a character as that implied by this address we are not required to show. [Douglass likened Lincoln's logic to] a horse thief pleading that the existence of the horse is the apology.

(in Blight, 2018, p. 372)

Though some scholars have argued that Lincoln supported colonization to prepare the public to accept emancipation, the racism in this speech remains and remained abhorrent, even if they are right. Even after Douglass's rebuttal, the Lincoln administration next used Postmaster General Montgomery Blair to attempt enlisting Douglass to support colonization on the grounds of "indelible differences . . . made by the Almighty" (in Blight, 2018, p. 376). On 16 September 1862, Douglass wrote a scathing public reply, claiming that all could live "under the same government":

We have readily adapted ourselves to your civilization. We are Americans by birth and education, and have a preference for American institutions as against those of any other country. That we should wish to remain here is natural to us and creditable to you . . . [out of] this terrible baptism of blood and fire through which our nation is passing . . . not as has been most cruelly affirmed, because of the presence of men of color in the land, but by malignant . . . vices, nursed into power . . . at the poisoned breast of slavery, it will come at last . . . purified in its spirit freed from slavery, vastly greater . . . than it ever was before in all the elements of advancing civilization

(in Blight, 218, pp. 376–377)

Nevertheless, Douglass encouraged his black readers to trust Lincoln on his promise of emancipation:

Confide in his word. Abraham Lincoln may be slow, Abraham Lincoln may desire peace even at the price of leaving our terrible sore untouched . . . but Abraham Lincoln is not the man to reconsider, retract and contradict words and purposes solemnly proclaimed over his official signature.

(in Blight, 2018, p. 379)

Some months later, Lincoln invited Douglass, "my friend,"[7] to the White House to help him with recruiting black soldiers from among the newly freed slaves. Though Douglass continued to criticize Lincoln from time to time, challenging all plans to make blacks second-class citizens, he considered Lincoln "honest" and greatly mourned his assassination.

After the war, Douglass moved his family to Washington, DC as soon as he could, continued to travel and lecture, worked in three successive government jobs, and advocated for black civil rights and equality under the law. As ever, he used his prophetic voice and his pen. Horrified by the regressive white supremacy measures and rhetoric of new President Andrew Johnson immediately following the war, Douglass unflinchingly led the fight for full citizenship, including enfranchisement, for the former slaves (males only, of course). Blight's biography shows us this great man without idealizing him. One cannot help wondering how Barack Obama might have written this biography of Douglass, with Lincoln one of his two great inspirations. Reparative reading teaches us to question the voice of the historian, no matter how accomplished, or at least to ask about other possible perspectives.

Michelle Alexander

In our third example, Michelle Alexander (Alexander & West, 2012) tells a story that overlaps the biography of Frederick Douglass and reaches to the Civil Rights era in our country.[8] After the US Supreme Court's *Brown v. Board of Education* decision in 1954 evoked more Jim Crow laws, after the dangerous and inspiring struggles of the 1960s followed by new civil rights legislation, came a massive backlash. Alexander chronicles in detail the war on drugs that became the excuse for incarcerating millions of African Americans, creating the largest prison population in the world and depriving these millions of their right to vote for their whole lives. Left politicians, as sanctimonious as the law-and-order right wing, collaborated to resegregate by imprisonment. Disproportionate sentencing left white-collar criminals effectively free to continue offending, while possession of marijuana could, and often did, provoke many years in prison. Crack cocaine, found in the ghettoes, brought far harsher sentences than powdered cocaine, preferred in the upper classes. The racism in the war on drugs, and the tough-on-crime politics, sat just under the surface, coded, in the normative unconscious, we might say, where anyone with ethical ears could easily hear it. Integration, the white supremacists claimed, causes crime. Those who wanted to be rid of people of color in their communities in the 1990s and early 2000s had an easy and legal way to dispose of them. Three strikes and you're out, advocated former President Bill Clinton. He went on to take money from anti-poverty programs and devote it to building prisons.

Alexander details the pipeline to prison, from walking on the street or driving a car under constant suspicion, through the courts into long, mandatory prison sentences, with the consequent destruction of lives, families, civil rights, futures. People become crime statistics in this story, and the presumption of innocence is largely lost. Worst of all, simply having dark skin made one a suspect, just as today a dark-skinned person who carries a cell phone may be seen as carrying a gun, and be shot by police. There was no way to enforce the war on drugs fairly, nor was this ever the intent.

Here is one example, in Alexander's words:

> Imagine you are Emma Faye Stewart, a thirty-year-old, single African American mother of two who was arrested as part of a drug sweep in Hearne, Texas. All but one of the people arrested were African American. You are innocent. After a week in jail, you have no one to care for your two small children and are eager to get home. Your court-appointed attorney urges you to plead guilty to a drug distribution charge, saying the prosecutor has offered probation. You refuse, steadfastly proclaiming your innocence. Finally, after almost a month in jail, you decide to plead guilty so you can return home to your children. Unwilling to risk a trial and years of imprisonment, you are sentenced to ten years probation and ordered to pay $ 1,000 in fines, as well as court and probation costs. You are also now branded a drug felon. You are no longer eligible for food stamps; you may be discriminated against in employment; you cannot vote for at least twelve years; and you are about to be evicted from public housing. Once homeless, your children will be taken from you and put in foster care.
>
> A judge eventually dismisses all cases against the defendants who did not plead guilty. At trial, the judge finds that the entire sweep was based on the testimony of a single informant who lied to the prosecution. You, however, are still a drug felon, homeless, and desperate to regain custody of your children.
>
> (Alexander & West, 2012, p. 97)

Alexander's book makes challenging reading for any U.S. citizen who wants to feel that racism no longer shapes our public life, our politics, our systems, our attitudes. I thought I knew this story, and I simply did not. Reading it together with Bryan Stevenson's *Just Mercy* (Stevenson, 2014) creates an ethical demand of the type to be studied in our next chapter.

Though rarely found in institute curricula, history also makes good psychoanalytic reading. Perhaps the most prominent theme in contemporary psychoanalytic theorizing, *Nachträglichkeit*, Freud's word for understanding afterwards, points us toward the need to immerse ourselves in history. Whether we need to read Shoah narratives, from Primo Levi to the present, or slave narratives, as Janice Gump (2010) reminds us, we need to be reading history. Otherwise, we treat ourselves and our patients as blank screens or empty petri dishes in a laboratory. Much more, relational psychoanalysis teaches us that we are always implicated in the whole clinical situation, never innocent. Had I been reading Douglas Blackmon's *Slavery by Another Name* (Blackmon, 2009) or Michele Alexander's *The New Jim Crow* (Alexander & West, 2012) when patients of color came to me, I might have been less unconscious and more teachable. I knew I wasn't innocent, but this responsibility has needed to become less abstract for me. Wendy Warren (2016) taught me concretely that I live on stolen land, that I profit every day from genocide and from the enslavement of human beings. Next I will read more of Eduardo Galeano (1973), who never lets me forget the rape of Latin America by the European church into which I was born.

Note

I began to write this before the 2016 election, never imagining that we would find ourselves back in 1933 and 1938, faced with the extreme situations that have already confronted us, as our world is so much smaller and more intricately involved now. The burning of mosques began immediately in January 2017, as did the restrictions on immigration and travel, the challenges to a free press, the destruction of all protections for vulnerable people and our vulnerable climate, and, perhaps worst of all, the extensive undermining of the foundations of a democratic system of government. We need to study history more than ever now. Back then, psychoanalysts either fled, died, or collaborated. Will these be our only possibilities? We may not have much time to find out. But reading history may give us some idea. I recommend it as a psychoanalytic, ethical, and spiritual practice.

Reading Roger Frie[9]

> I pray for the defeat of my country, for I think that is the only possibility of paying for all the suffering that my country has caused in the world
>
> (quoted Visser d'Hooft's conversation with Dietrich Bonhoeffer; Hoffmann, 2011, pp. 119–120)

Roger Frie's courageous and thoughtful book, *Not in My Family: German Memory and the Holocaust* (Frie, 2017), tells of his discovery and coming to grips with his Nazi grandfather's memory.

Neither German nor Jewish, but with a long and serious interest in the period in question, I scarcely know where to begin. Married to a second-generation German American, and having lived the past thirty-some years among Jewish colleagues, patients and friends in New York (beginning with graduate school at Yeshiva University), I do feel myself very much in the middle of these troubles. A beloved cousin of my husband lived in a suburb of Hannover, so I have seen the modern city built on the rubble of the one in which Frie's mother lived through the war. The city now shows none of the destruction, and none of the old beauty. A much-read philosophical influence, Emmanuel Levinas, lived in another suburb of Hannover for five years, 1940–1945, in Fallingbostel, a Nazi forced labor camp. In no way neutral or objective – who can ever be that? – I will try to bring another slant or two to the situation Frie describes.

Immediately after World War II, most German adults said either that they had not known of the massive crimes against humanity perpetrated by the Nazi government and war machine, and had not participated – or if they had, had just followed orders and could not have done otherwise. By the time the *Kriegskinder*, my contemporaries, became adults, they had no idea how to face their parents' silence concerning the whole *Nazizeit*, let alone about their own participation. *Was hast Du in der Nacht getan?* ran the question in their minds until they exploded in violence in the 1960s. Still they found, except in rare instances, no answers, so it is left to the next generation, Roger's and Thomas Kohut's (in his masterful *A German Generation* [Kohut, 2012]), to try to generate understanding and genuine responsibility out of silence, whether defiant or shame-ridden. In most families, it seems, conversation about the war concerns "German suffering" in a discourse where "Germans," by definition, even now do not include Jews, Roma, Sinti, the disabled, or gay people. Germans are people like us. I will return to this problem.

Frie reports a family history similar, perhaps, to many others, terrorized by bombing and the destruction of the family home in Hannover. His beloved grandfather, source of perhaps the future writer's happiest childhood memories, turns out to have been a Nazi, perhaps to have worked on the horrible *Vergeltungs* weapons. Not only must Frie (and his generation) ask himself how this benevolent grandfather, who spoke only of the war to recount so-called German suffering, could also have been a perpetrator. He also asks how his younger self could not have known for so long, when the evidence stared him straight in the face in a familiar photograph. Only when his grandparents were dead did he allow himself to ask and to know. Fortunately, his mother, though she seems not to have fully understood his need to know, has been willing to help him.

If I understand him correctly, Frie himself attributes the knowing and not-knowing to dissociation, to unformulated experience. The kind of dissociation studied by Bromberg and Stern – "not me" – has largely replaced the discourse of repression in contemporary psychoanalysis, and while I believe it does not account for the kinds of dissociation suffered by victims of extreme child abuse and torture, it causes enough trouble. If, as Frie suggests, it allows us to pretend to ourselves that we do not know what some part of us knows very well, and thus to evade responsibility by various strategems ranging from distraction to magical thinking, it can wreak ethical havoc.

Speaking of ethical havoc, I believe we must turn from the psychological origins of the collective and individual silence to the ethical; in other words, to the structural and cultural sources keeping dissociation in place. We noted earlier, as Roger did, that the discourse of "German suffering" does not include the suffering of German Jews, or of other despised categories of human beings stripped of German citizenship, or simply eliminated. Seen as subhumans, they cannot suffer as would people like us. Even after the war, they remain statistics, the six million, abstractions. Our suffering we remember: We were hungry, we were terrified, we lost our sons and our homes. Kohut's (2012) study shows how the elitism of the 1920s German youth movement, producing absolutely committed mid-level Nazis, also produced this ethical blindness.

More than dissociation is going on here: Nazi ideology divided people into those of value, and those to be degraded, used for labor and for the pleasure of cruelty, and eliminated. We cannot expect that, defeated in war, even magnanimously treated by the victors so that they could, as Frie notes, manically rebuild with Marshall Plan money, these perpetrators and bystanders would suddenly turn into people who regard every human being as irreplaceable, as of infinite value and inherent dignity. To place their own wartime suffering, real and traumatic as it was, in the context where it belongs would mean seeing differently – radically differently – from the generation of perpetrators and bystanders who created postwar Germany, the same people who operated the machinery of Nazi war and extermination. Only the top planners were ever brought to trial; the rest, with few exceptions, created the "economic miracle" out of the rubble without any significant change of mind and heart.[10]

Emmanuel Levinas famously wrote that "ethics is an optics" (Levinas, 1969, p. 29). It concerns seeing, and responding to, the face of the other. As Val Vinokur (Vinokur, 2008) has observed, this saying sounds strange from a Jewish phenomenologist known for his Talmudic lectures, for an interpreter of a tradition that proscribes visual images, while placing great emphasis on the auditory. "Hear, O Israel . . ." But, Vinokur explains, in midrashic texts, "hearing, strictly speaking, is still pre-ethical – hearing is simply about being open to the other" (p. 47). The young Levinas seems to have learned – reading Russian literature in his father's bookshop, "above all, Dostoevsky!" (Levinas & Robbins, 2001, p. 28) – to regard the capacity to see (without indifference) poverty and misery as the core of ethics. In other words, this kind of seeing demands doing before hearing (*naase ve nishma*);[11] it interprets by responding first, forming a primary source of meaning.

But the bystander cannot truly see the misery of those being rounded up to be deported, nor their misery on the journey, let alone ask where they are being taken. Primo Levi, one of 18 who returned from a transport of 650, wrote his Auschwitz memoir, he said later, for the Germans:

> Yes, I had written the book in Italian for Italians, for my children, for those who did not know, those who did not want to know, those who were not yet born, those who willing or not had assented to the offense; but its true recipients, those against whom the book was aimed like a gun were they, the Germans. Now the gun was loaded. . . . I would corner them, tie them before a mirror. . . . Not that handful of high-ranking culprits, but them, the people, those I had seen from close up, those from among whom the SS militia were recruited, and also those others, those who had believed, who not believing had kept silent, who did not have the frail courage to look into our eyes, throw us a piece of bread, whisper a human word.
>
> (Levi, 1989, pp. 168–9)

Like Levinas, Primo Levi understood ethics as an optics. Millions "did not have the frail courage to look into our eyes." To see would have been to be obligated, to be responsible. Toward the end of his long odyssey home in October 1945, he observed Germans in their own country:

> We felt we had something to say, enormous things to say, to every single German, and we felt that every German should have something to say to us; we felt an urgent need to settle our accounts, to ask, explain and comment, like chess players at the end of a game. Did "they" know about Auschwitz, about the silent daily massacre, a step away from their doors? If they did, how could they walk about, return home and look at their children, cross the threshold of a church? If they did not, they ought, as a sacred duty, to listen, to learn everything, immediately from us, from me; I felt the tattooed number on my arm, burning like a sore . . .
>
>   . . . everybody should interrogate us, read in our faces who we were, and listen to our tale in humility. But no one looked us in the eyes, no one accepted the challenge; they were deaf, blind and dumb, imprisoned in their ruins, as in a fortress of willful ignorance, still strong, still capable of hatred and contempt, still prisoners of their old tangle of pride and guilt.
>
> (Levi, 1965, pp. 204–5)

"No one looked us in the eyes." For many years after the war, Levi visited Germany on business for his chemical company, perhaps twice a year. Often, he told interviewers, Germans would ask how an Italian came to speak German – this was unusual. "Oh," he replied simply, "I learned in Auschwitz." No one knew what to say next. Or he might be a guest in one of their homes where a child might ask about his tattoo. "Shall I tell her?" he would ask the parents. They hadn't. He found both individual Germans, and Germans generally, without shame, and in his understated style, observed that the industrialists of mass murder (Siemens, Bayer, Krupp) in West Germany continued to prosper:

The crematoria ovens themselves were designed, built, assembled, and tested by a German company Topf of Wiesbaden (it was still in operation in 1975, building crematoria for civilian use, and had not considered the advisability of changing its name).

(Levi, 1989, p. 16)

All over the world in the postwar years, he noted in interviews, the firms that had profited from the Nazi period flourished as millions bought Hitler cars (Volkswagens)[12] and Bayer aspirin. The Germans would never need to think about what they had done. But he did not give up easily; in the preface to the German edition of *If This Is a Man*, he explicitly invited Germans to write to him to help him understand more. In his last book, having received their letters, he considered their justifications and evasions with his usual allergy to hypocrisy and to the slippage of memory. Frie has written about these letters (2016, pp. 191–3).

It might be argued that the recent literature on "German suffering," which as Frie (Frie, 2016) recounts, replays the conversation in families since the war, betrays a deep shamelessness, even now, in the face of public discourse about guilt and responsibility for Germany's crimes. In the Russians who arrived after the Germans had abandoned the camp with the death march, Levi observed:

a confused restraint, which sealed their lips and bound their eyes to the funereal scene. It was that shame we knew so well, the shame that drowned us after the selections, and every time we had to watch, or submit to, some outrage; the shame the Germans did not know, that the just man experiences at another man's crime; the feeling of guilt that such a crime should exist, that it should have been introduced irrevocably into the world of things that exist.

(Levi, 1965, p. 16)

The just among us . . . experienced remorse, shame, suffering, for the misdeeds that others and not they had committed, and in which nevertheless, they felt themselves involved, because they could see that what had happened around them and in their presence, was irrevocable . . . that man, the species man, we in short, are capable of constructing an infinite enormity of pain.

(Levi, 1986, pp. 66–7, trans. in Kleinberg-Levin, 2005, p. 221)

And yet, this kind of shame he believed important, even indispensable. "I command to you (plural) [these words]. Carve/engrave them into your heart, repeat them to your children . . . or may your house be destroyed, illness disable you, and your children turn their faces from you" (my informal translation from Levi [1984, p. 5]). In other words, without this kind of shame, we should be cursed.

How does this sense of moral superiority and the concentration on "our own suffering", isolated from the crimes that evoked it, fit with the public discourse of guilt? Do public apologies absolve us from knowing our personal guilt, or from doing better in the future? I believe these questions belong not only to Germany, though Germany has much to teach us.

How, for example, can we shamelessly speak of building walls against refugees on our southern border in the U.S.? Have we nothing to do with having supported the brutality, during the presidency of Ronald Reagan and after, from which these children and their parents are fleeing? Has our history of slavery, and our white privilege continuously dependent on the existence of a large underclass in this country, nothing to do with why "they" continue to struggle in an ever more radically unequal economy and society? When we insist that poor countries reduce carbon usage before we will, to save our burning planet, have we forgotten that we have contributed far longer and far more than any other nation to the carbon problem? Where is our memory, and where is our needed shame? Not only is there no cure for shame over crimes against humanity; awareness that we belong to a species capable of dehumanizing its fellows to this extent is a shame from which we turn away at the peril of our own further dehumanization.

Experiential history[13] and ethical hearing

Historians and psychoanalysts, each in their own ways, seek unsilencing, truth, and understanding in the past, while we philosophers ask them what it could mean to do this. Already involved in a multidisciplinary task, we find ourselves faced with historical burdens, etymological hints, and psychoanalytic enigmas and intensities interrogating any assumptions we bring to our search for more adequate concepts. Here we take up the idea of experiential history, one crossing disciplinary boundaries, to ask what it may contribute both to understanding the "dark times," as well as to social justice now and ethical hearing in the future.

Signaling a subtle surprise, announcing an enigmatic shift in approach to the historian's work, even sneaking a philosophical question into our imaginations, Thomas A. Kohut (2012) entitled his masterwork *A German Generation: An Experiential History of the Twentieth Century*. Fascinated since childhood with history, but without realizing that this attraction probably led me into psychoanalysis, I had thought we studied history to find facts, to find out what really happened. Seeing Kohut's title, following his narrative and reflections, I remembered that my love of history had included devouring historical fiction, both childhood and adult. Something had led me to wonder what those long-ago people had felt, how they had lived, loved, raged, and died in their own times and places. So, the expression "experiential history" intrigued me. Was this a subdiscipline of professional historians unknown to those of us who had not been reading their professional literature? If so, I am so far unable to find them. Apart from a series of British war videos, I find little reference to this expression apart from citations of Kohut's book. But it may be related to the reparative reading introduced previously.

What, we may ask, would be the natural history of this expression in Western thinking? Kohut tells us first that the 62 interviews, and the use he makes of them, do not serve as witness to historical events. Rather,

The interviewees, in all their subjectivity, are the subject of this book . . . this book is a case study [of the generation that grew up in the Bunds, became mid-level Nazis, and lived to tell their memories]. A particular historical phenomenon is studied historically and in depth not only for its own sake but also with a view to making generalizations that transcend it. . . . An in-depth study of the lives of these sixty-two people, then, enables us to identify and to understand aspects of their experience and response to experience that they shared with generational peers.

(Kohut, 2012, p. 14)

Identifying the case study as a legitimate approach to studying history, to searching for historical truth beyond mere facts, dates, and lists of events or perpetrators, even beyond memorials, trials, and attempts at restorative justice, Kohut borrows from psychoanalysis the narrative, the personal story, the subjective truth, as means to historical understanding. But what is this category called experience that he hopes, like the psychoanalyst he has also been trained to be, to find? And if we can develop a few of its meanings more clearly, then why should it matter to the historian, and, by extension, to all of us? Let us begin with the idea of experience, then return to experiential history.

Experience itself

Experience, as a concept, turns out to have a long story of its own in the Western history of ideas. (Asian and African equivalents are, I am sorry to say, not well known to me.) Recent deconstructionists had good reasons for their rejection of this concept. They objected in particular to claims to absolute authority and concreteness, as in "Experience teaches" or "That's not my experience" (Jay, 2005). Martin Jay, nevertheless, explores its history, especially in its more pluralistic and fluid forms. Beginning with the word's relationships to several European languages, he notes that its root (*periculum*, danger) in Latin connects experience with peril. Experience suggests something about emergence – perhaps sadder and wiser – from extreme circumstances, about having learned from an escape. The experienced person has lost innocence, perhaps, in French (*experience*), in Italian (*esperienza*), and in English. German, famously, gives us two words for experience: *Erlebnis*, lived (*das Leben*, life) experience or personally lived event; and *Erfahrung*, accumulated learning, even practical wisdom. (Book learning, *Bildung*, differing from experience, also gets great reverence.) In *Erfahrung*, we hear both *fahren* (to travel) and *Gefahr* (danger), where the word resonates with the peril we hear in the Romance languages. Both danger and travel may remind us of Odysseus. All these linguistic hints lead us to contrast experience with abstract theorizing, but make us hesitate to absolutize or reify.

Instead, as Jay acknowledges, we might take a clue from Ludwig Wittgenstein's language games (Wittgenstein, 2003), asking how the word is used in various contexts, looking for significances lent by the textures (Figal, 2010) of particular discourses. Tempting as it may be to ask whether Wittgenstein would claim that we mistakenly take our pictures for experience, as Augustine took his picture for the origin of linguistic meaning, we must stay on track and just remember his dictum that the meaning of a word is its use in a context. Then we may be able, perhaps, to claim that experience covers a range of meanings, including its many contexts and their resonating relations with each other. To explore these meanings in their full texture would require a very large book, but let us scan just a few, to get some sense of what Kohut may be picking up when he speaks of "experiential history."

Experience in psychoanalysis

First, once again, we have the psychoanalytic case study. Pioneered by Freud and his earliest followers – if only we could say "collaborators" – this approach to theory construction, also beloved by phenomenologists (Atwood, 2012; Merleau-Ponty & Landes, 2012), forms a contrast, even an opposite approach to the hypothesis-testing, rigidly controlled, statistically analyzed scientific research prevalent in the past century, especially in academic psychology. Though Freud used the *"einzige Krankengeschichte"* (single illness history) heavily in the building of his theories, still, well trained in scientific method and logic, he emphasized repeatedly the limitations of this approach. It is, he wrote (Freud, 1953b) in introducing the Dora story,

> obvious that a single case history, even if it were complete and open to no doubt, cannot provide an answer to *all* the questions arising out of the problem of hysteria. It cannot give an insight into all the types of this disorder, into all the forms of internal structure of the neurosis, into all the possible kinds of relation between the mental and the somatic which are to be found in hysteria. It is not fair to expect from a single case more than it can offer. And anyone who has hitherto been unwilling to believe that a psychosexual etiology holds good generally and without exception for hysteria is scarcely likely to be convinced of the fact by taking stock of a single case history. He would do better to suspend his judgement until his own work has earned him the right to a conviction.
>
> (Freud, 1953b, p. 12)

Notwithstanding Freud's warning to himself and to his readers, the single case history became the gold standard for psychoanalytic writing. It seemed to offer a window through the analyst's experience and interpretation of the patient into the patient's Unconscious motivations for illness manifested in symptoms. As dreams were the "royal road," the *Via Regia*, to the uncon- scious, the case study became the royal road to experience from which the analyst could build theory. But once again, what was this experience? Freud, since his work with Breuer in the 1890s, and even more since his *Interpretation of Dreams*, written in 1897 and issued in

1900 (Freud, 1953a), had exposed a crack in the Western unitary mind, claiming that conscious "experience" showed gaps appearing in dreams, symptoms, slips, and jokes. Reality lay elsewhere, in the dark. The dark realm, full of forbidden wishes, conflicts, and terrors, involved complicated efforts to conceal itself, called defenses. Often these defenses, the denials and evasions of reasonable people, seemed themselves to be experience, until the analyst unmasked them according to the hermeneutics of suspicion (Orange, 2011; Ricoeur, 1970). So, experience, at least that of the patient, became a shape-shifting morass, handed over to the authority of the analyst, the expert. He or she could write a case study, theorizing "on the basis of clinical experience," occasionally remembering Freud's warnings.

Not until Ferenczi, in the late 1920s and early 1930s, listening to his patients' protests, began to suspect that clinical experience emerged from at least two psychological worlds did the one-person case study's authority come into question.[14] As Ferenczi came back from oblivion in the 1980s, just when intersubjectivists (Atwood & Stolorow, 1984; Stolorow, Brandchaft, & Atwood, 1987) began to imagine a field-emergent psychological experience and a relational psychoanalysis (Aron, 1996; Benjamin, 1988; Mitchell, 1988), new forms of writing history emerged in psychoanalysis. Once two (or more) people showed up in "experience," experience itself could not claim unambiguous authority. Now these stories, often called "clinical narratives," even occasionally told from two perspectives (Brickman, 2007; Jacobs, 2007) or from the patient's side (Dimen, 2011), illustrate ever more clearly that we have no access to pure experience, phenomenologists like Husserl and the late William James to the contrary, and developmental researchers to the contrary as well.

Analysts, historians, patients, all of us, we read and elaborate our *Erfahrung*, our endangered and accumulated lives, in relational spatiality and *nachträglich*, backwards and forwards temporally. *Nachträglichkeit* – in particular, Freud's own idea originally – has commanded contemporary attention in many psychoanalytic schools, redefining our sense of sedimented and experiential meanings. As we live forward, our experience develops backwards. I read my own history, and that of my worlds, through ever greater acquaintance with familial violence and secrecy, with slavery and colonialism. Likewise, Kohut and his subjects' experiential history develops *nachträglich*.

Without really defining experience, Kohut's book shows that he has deeply digested the lure and the pitfalls of the psychoanalytic case study. Just as Freud and later psychoanalysts have, he wants to learn from others what goes so profoundly awry that one people can deliberately and methodically destroy another people with whom they have lived for centuries as neighbors. Even more, he wants to know how it becomes possible that people who seem ordinary in their family and daily lives and aspirations can participate in a massacre or do nothing to stop it. Like a good psychoanalyst, he listens carefully to those who were there and can still speak.

But Kohut has left many assumptions of early psychoanalysis behind. Knowing that his own feelings, his own generation, his own legacy as a son of one who fled, position him non-neutrally, he takes seriously what he brings to the table. "I do not particularly like the interviewees," he tells us (Kohut, 2012, p. 16). He continues as follows:

> Although neither of my parents identified themselves as Jewish, both, according to Nazi racial criteria, would probably have been victims of the Final Solution had they been living in territory controlled by Germany during World War II. Although from a German American family, my mother appears racially to have been a quarter Jewish, on her mother's side. And my father was racially wholly Jewish. Indeed, my father escaped the Holocaust only by fleeing Austria in 1939, and four of his five uncles and aunts, as well as cousins, perished in the genocide. In addition to what the interviewees had been in the past. . . . I found their smugness and sense of superiority annoying.
>
> (Kohut, 2012, p. 16)

Kohut worried that his dislike for them may have limited the empathy needed for understanding, for carrying out the task of experiential history he had set himself. Not only do we trust his account more because of his honesty, we also hear his capacity to formulate questions that others without his positioning might not ask. So, perspective not only limits, as it surely does; it also brings to the historian or to the psychoanalyst the opportunity to test hypotheses, knowing they are only hypotheses. Limited perspective, held lightly, fallibilistically, and humbly in a pragmatist spirit (Peirce, 1932, pp. 13–14) can open horizons, as it does for Kohut. If we already know what generalizations we hope to draw from our case study, if we want to validate rather than simply to explore, even if we undertake the study yearning to support our hunches and hypotheses, Kohut's sincere fallibilism can keep us ready to learn something we did not expect. Experience, with its dangers and its unseen future, can still teach us.

Experience in the history of ideas

The word experience, however, has accumulated textural meanings. Here are a few: Humanistic, early hermeneutic, anticipating the phenomenological, and pragmatic. To begin at the dawn of modernity, Michel de Montaigne (1958) considered a human life as what Giorgio Agamben (1993, p. 23) called "an achieved totality of experience." Without defining the word, but clearly opposing the emergent scientific rationalism of his day, his essays portray experience as the path to maturity. In Martin Jay's words,

> More like an unruly life than a logical demonstration, [Montaigne's] "Of Experience" meanders digressively, combining anecdotes and *aperçus* with arguments and quotations, reprising themes and coming at them from different

angles. Its own temporality, rhythmically uneven and irreducible to a unified narrative, duplicates the unsystematic ruminations on time itself to be found in Montaigne's work as a whole. . . . [It] performatively instantiates what it substantively argues.

(Jay, 2005, p. 25)

Already, then, experience, embodied and sensual, messy, aesthetic, and unrepeatable, as Hans-Georg Gadamer (1972, 2004)[15] would later claim, forms a source of learning independent of the scientific demand for method and replicability.

Jumping forward to the Romantic period, we find philosopher, theologian, and ethicist Friedrich Schleiermacher, founder of modern hermeneutics. Immanuel Kant (1793, 1998) had insisted that religion depended on moral and practical reason – it was not theoretical, but originated in the experience of moral obligation. Schleiermacher, as William James (1902) and Rudolf Otto (Otto, 1958; Otto & Dicker, 1931) would do later, mounted a full- throated defense of religious experience as a primary source of truth. Kant had claimed that experience limited in every realm what reason could reach; Schleiermacher treated religious experience (*Erlebnis*), "the feeling of absolute dependence" (Schleiermacher, 1976), as more than a limit, as that which defines and measures religion and theology.[16] Although this kind of experience may seem distant from the "experiential history" we are trying to examine here, we may note that its claim to authority through direct personal intuition, bypassing the claims of logic and reason (and theology), may also be important. Later phenomenological claims of access to the "things themselves," placing the previous structures of reason under the *epoché*, echo this Romantic-era appeal to the claim of experience.

Schleiermacher's biographer Wilhelm Dilthey (1870), was perhaps the first to realize that personal history (or experiential history) shaped theory-building. Dilthey gave us the distinction between the *Naturwissenschaften* (natural sciences) and the *Geisteswissenschaften* (humanities), arguing that the latter provided fully respectable access to truth, and deserved their own place. He further explained the difference between *Erlebnis* (lived experience), the core of his *Lebensphilosophie*, and *Erfahrung*, the accumulated, often social, experience that could live only from *Erlebnis*. For him, *Erlebnis* meant a kind of direct, immediate, description: this suffering is unbearable. Description itself refers both to the context that holds it and to what transcends it. Although Gadamer would later prefer, after extensive examination, *Erfahrung* as dialogical experience, he incorporated much of the immediacy of Dilthey's beloved *Erlebnis*.

From North America came both the transcendentalists (Emerson, 2001) and the pragmatists, their partial heirs. Emerson had written, two years after his five-year-old son's death, a mournful essay entitled "On Experience":

I grieve that grief can teach me nothing, nor carry me one step into real nature. . . . The dearest events are summer-rain, and we the Para coats [raincoats] that shed every drop. Nothing is left us now but death. We look to that with a grim satisfaction, saying, there at least is reality that will not dodge us.

(Emerson, 2001, p. 200)

For Emerson, experience teaches, or it does not. *What* it teaches, or does not, he also seems to call experience. The problem, he thought, was our incapacity to learn, or, perhaps worse, the likelihood that we would die before making use of what we might learn.

Among the pragmatists, like the transcendentalists well educated in European philosophy and Romantic currents, logician Charles Sanders Peirce contributed something more than the pragmatic definition of meaning:

Consider what effects, which might conceivably have practical bearings, we conceive the object of our conception to have. Then the whole of our conception of those effects is the whole of our conception of the object.

(Peirce, 1992, p. 132)

Peirce thus relied on a view of experience as what meaning predicts. Meaning, then, as well as experience, has a cumulative sense, more like *Erfahrung*.

William James, on the contrary, emphasized the variety and plurality of lived experiences, even writing of a pluralistic universe (James, 1977). Resisting the neo-Hegelianism developed in dialogue with the pragmatists by Josiah Royce (1916, 1919), James not only affirmed the value of plurality in religious experience, but also insisted – having learned from cultures beyond the West – that experience itself was variegated and could not be subsumed as the hidden forms of the absolute oneness so dear to idealistic thinkers and to the monists addressed in our last chapter. The search for absolute oneness silences the plurality of voices, the variety of religious experience.

For John Dewey, closer to these Hegelians, experience, both lived and cumulative, formed the ground of all learning (Dewey, 1958, 1963). Nevertheless, schooled by Peirce and James, he had learned to regard experience as an ultimate test, and applied this appeal to experience everywhere, most notably in politics and in educational methods, his greatest area of influence. From Emerson through Dewey, these thinkers took their European intellectual heritage down to earth.

Experience becoming experiential history

From this unforgivably distilled summary, we ask again, what can "experiential history" mean? Clearly Thomas Kohut, born with a mixed intellectual and cultural heritage, writing a history of mid-twentieth-century Europe from a closeness and distance from it, enriched by all the traditions we have sketched and many more, brings an inclusive complexity to his use of "experiential history." Doing history, thinking, feeling, and undergoing history, living as an historian has been his life, as for many others. He knows his work, his craft. My question remains: Why "experiential"? Perhaps, in the service of hearing the voices of those forever silenced, he wants to exclude, or at least bracket, at least for this project, other ways of doing history.

What would "experiential history" require bracketing, or excluding? First, it means dropping a single-perspective view of truth. It means that more than one story can be told, that these plural stories, as James or Gadamer might have thought, bring us closer to understanding truth, if not Truth, about the narrators themselves, and about the times in which they lived. Kohut's attempt to find out from the Nazis themselves, ordinary Nazis whose names no one knows, what they were thinking and feeling, how they became these people, and how they talked to themselves afterwards about their participation, takes *Erlebnis* (or rather, *die Erlebnisse* in the plural), and transforms them into *Erfahrung*, accumulated or collective experience, something from which we can continue to learn.

Such an emphasis on the plurality of experiences has, since Nietzsche, often been mistaken for a claim that there is no truth independent of what we choose to think about it. Instead, we can read Nietzsche's protest, as well as that of his more thoughtful readers, as a dissent from authoritarian views of religion and morality, which are dependent on one-perspective (God's-eye) notions of truth. To write "experiential history," it seems to me, gives no quarter to the truth deniers, but rather provides a richer, if even more painful, account of history, that challenges us in dangerous moments. Getting closer to those who have committed, or assented to, or supported unspeakable crimes contests our own sense of innocence. It reminds us that experience concerns peril, that *Erfahrung* records the sense that we are morally *gefährdet* (endangered).

Shouted down once again by demagogues who want to eliminate those different from the ruling white male class from among us; unable, out of fear, to welcome the stranger, to shelter the refugee; continuously blind to inherited privilege created by historical crimes of settler colonialism and chattel slavery; and thus paralyzed in the face of scientific demands for radical change in our way of life to cope with climate crisis and to protect the world's most vulnerable people, we are once again endangered as were Europeans, and all of us, in the 1930s. Studying the so-called "facts," in isolation from their experiential history, keeps this knowledge abstract and theoretical, partitioned away from our feelings, passions, and convictions. (I have made this argument more extensively elsewhere (Orange, 2017).)

"Experiential history" might disturb and disrupt us. Following the aging Germans' account of their adolescent experiences (*Erlebnisse*), Kohut writes that "The common experience of these [social and historical] circumstances led them to develop a shared generational consciousness [*Erfahrung*] and a shared sense of past, present, and anticipated future" (Kohut, 2012, pp. 10–11). This "shared sense" came to include an elitist and exclusionary sense of Germanness that permitted them to commit and support crimes against humanity in its service. Experiential history means unraveling the cumulative history, now so repulsively recounted, to see what subjective lived experiences tangled together to create such disaster. What Thomas Kohut has done to create experiential history out of heaps of "facts" challenges us to do likewise – to lay bare the sense of privilege that allows us to demonize or to ignore the other.

Seeing this experiential history, we may ask: How is our own time different? Instead of the Jews, Roma, Sinti, homosexuals, and disabled people destroyed by Kohut's "German generation" in their collective superiority and inability to see these others as human, we have other fragile populations who seem not to merit consideration as individuals of equal dignity and worth to our own. Darker skin color, unfamiliar language, unfamiliar religion, unfamiliar sexuality, all place people in categories and quotas, as dangerous migrants, not as fellow human beings, as sisters and brothers. Am I my other's keeper?

But who are these people? Apart from the high-profile crucifixions, we have the sex slavery and rapes and bombed-out children and parents and elders. We have young men from Eritrea who make drawings of excruciating procedures of torture which, allegedly, hundreds are suffering and trying to escape. We have whole regions in severe famine from rapid climate change their own peoples have not created. We white North Americans and Europeans, believing that the lands where we live belong to us, set ourselves above these millions of refugees, building walls and fences. Our experiential history, accumulated from rags-to-riches Horatio Alger stories, creates a narrative saying that good and worthy people do not suffer in these ways. They make it. Experiential history teaches us, as it taught Germans in the 1930s, to despise the weak and to embrace an ideal of strength and masculinity. Avoiding our own vulnerability, we despise others who mirror it back to us. Empathy, as Kohut's book painfully teaches, then extends only to people just like us.

Could experiential history have a different outcome? Can the inherited past avoid the curse of repetition? The lived experiences constituting it would need to include, perhaps, something like what Donald Winnicott (1965) called the capacity for concern. This early developmental relational achievement would then also require an environment that regarded all people as valuable and questioned all forms of bias. Building on children's common obsession with fairness, it could prepare a person to question any preferential treatment, especially that from which the subject profits. In the school years, both teaching about civic courage and modeling inclusiveness could continue to develop these possibilities, even in the face of historical burdens from slavery and discrimination. Teachers could tell stories of the French town of Chambon, or of the Underground Railroad, to let children know that an ethical response to suffering and injustice is actually possible. To those who say this kind of education already exists, I say yes, but it is exceptional. It will require tremendous communal determination, together with relentless self-questioning, to generate a different experiential history.

And yet, truly formidable obstacles stand in the way. Just as injustice thrives on elitism and demagoguery – that is, on the appeal to the desire to belong and to identify with the rich, famous, and powerful – so does an effective turn toward justice require a critical mass. The kind of ethical education described above would need to spread, and to be enriched by the study of what Kohut, toward the end of his book (Kohut, 2012, p. 237ff), calls "historical experience," the fruit of experiential history. We share our human nature, he writes, with the Nazi generation who carried out and enabled the massacre. We have the same need for group belonging, for exclusiveness, the same capacity to dehumanize those different from us.

> We should not count on cultural context to distance us from the Nazis. What separates us from them who carried out the worst horror in modern European history is nothing intrinsic to them or us. What separates us from them is "the grace" of historical experience.
>
> (Kohut, 2012, pp. 240–1)

In other words, if we learn from historical experience, we need not repeat it.

What Kohut calls the "authority" of historical experience means that we cannot escape our history. Whether we are twentieth-century Germans or twenty-first-century whites of European descent, our experiential history determines our possibilities for future undergoing and making of history. We can continue down the current path of racism, indifference, and climate destruction. Or we can draw on the best of our heritage and values to embrace the other of every color, religion, and language, while healing our devastated earth. Which of those possibilities we take up depends, it seems, on whether we study, mourn, and begin to atone for the history into which we are born, so that we can reject the automatic repetition of dehumanizing, and embrace an inclusive humanity. This is reparative reading, reading to hear the voices of the devastated, reading as an ethical and psychotherapeutic project.

Notes

1 *Who Will Write Our History?* This shocking and inspiring film, as well as Gabrielle Schwab's literary work (Schwab, 2010), suggests that writing the history of the oppressed and destroyed constitutes a form of ethical learning and corresponds to the reading suggested in this chapter.
2 This section is based on a conference presentation at the International Association for Psychoanalytic Self Psychology, Vienna, 19 October 2018. Some of this material also came into my "Learning to Hear" workshops at NIP in New York on 2 February 2019 and at the Dallas Society for Psychoanalytic Psychology on 30 March 2019. I am very grateful to the participants in all three groups whose contributions significantly enriched this chapter.
3 This view of responsibility, a radical ethics, I find best articulated in *Otherwise than Being* (Levinas, 1998) and in *The Brothers Karamazov* (Dostoyevsky, Pevear, & Volokhonsky, 1992).
4 Sebastian Luft, in a study of Husserl's natural attitude (Luft, 1998), makes a similar point: "The alien outside our homeworld awakens the 'stranger in us all' . . . we can never go back into our old self-evident knowledge of ourselves and our world" (p. 165).
5 For a Canadian First Peoples' voice, see (Paul, 2000), *We Were Not the Savages*.
6 Birthdates of slaves were rarely recorded.

7 John Stauffer (Stauffer, 2008) tells the story of the remarkable parallels between Douglass and Lincoln – extremely humble beginnings, love for language right down to the same beloved books, and tremendous capacities to grow and change. The story of their unlikely friendship challenges the ordinary hagiography of Lincoln.

8 In two fascinating and related books, historians Douglas A. Blackmon (2009) and Isabel Wilkerson (2010) tell the stories of the re-enslavement of blacks after the Civil War, and of their massive migration to the north and west. Wilkerson's TED talk (www.youtube.com/watch?v=n3qA8DNc2Ss) illustrates Alexander's Jim Crow by citing a state where it was illegal for a black person and a white person to play chess together.

9 An earlier version of this section formed a discussion of a presentation by Frie at Psychology and the Other, Cambridge, MA, 2015.

10 Having dear German friends and knowing significant exceptions to what I am saying, I write this with great sorrow. The first German I came to know well, born just after the war, was amazed (before 9–11 and the Iraq war) that I could easily identify myself as American. "I could never, without terrible shame, look you in the eye, and say that I am German," he told me. Later, he told me his father had been a Nazi and had beaten him mercilessly as a child. Another friend, a distinguished professor in Germany, tells me that his worst misfortune in life has been to be born German. It is a stain that never goes away. One treasures German literature, philosophy, and, above all, music as guilty pleasures.

11 One of Levinas's earliest Talmudic lectures (Levinas, 1990), begins with this text from the Torah, also translated "we will do and we will hear" and goes on to its Talmudic commentaries. Like William James in *The Will to Believe* (James, Burkhardt, Bowers, & Skrupskelis, 1979), Levinas meditates at length on the necessity of commitment before understanding, ethics preceding ontology (see also (Levinas, 1969).

12 With shame, I now realize that the only car I wanted in my youth was a VW beetle. I gave no thought to its origins, nor did I ask who might be profiting from my purchase.

13 An earlier version of this section forms a chapter in "Experiential History: Understanding Backwards" in Roger Frie, ed., *History Flows Through Us: Germany, the Holocaust, and the Importance of Empathy*. London and New York: Routledge (Taylor and Francis Group, 2018, pp. 49–60).

14 Ferenczi, too, questioned the ethics of "using" patients to advance psychoanalytic science (Ferenczi & Dupont, 1988).

15 Aristotle, though in the end he claimed for theoria, the fruit of contemplation, the rank of highest knowing, also wrote that "the unproved assertions and opinions of experienced, old and sagacious people deserve as much attention as those they support by proofs, for they grasp principles through experience" (*Ethics*, 1143b, 10–15).

16 Although many similar terms show up in Schleiermacher's texts, *Erlebnis* itself did not commonly appear, according to Gadamer (2004), until Dilthey's biography of Schleiermacher.

References

Agamben, G. (1993). *Infancy and history: The destruction of experience*. London and New York: Verso.

Alexander, M., & West, C. (2012). *The new Jim Crow: Mass incarceration in the age of colorblindness* (Rev. ed.). New York and Jackson, TN: New Press Perseus Distribution.

Aron, L. (1996). *A meeting of minds: Mutuality in psychoanalysis*. Hillsdale, NJ: Analytic Press.

Atwood, G. E. (2012). *The abyss of madness*. New York, NY: Routledge.

Atwood, G. E., & Stolorow, R. D. (1984). *Structures of subjectivity: Explorations in psychoanalytic phenomenology.* Hillsdale, NJ: Analytic Press.

Baldwin, J. (1963). *The fire next time.* New York: Dial Press.

Benjamin, J. (1988). *The bonds of love: Psychoanalysis, feminism, and the problem of domination.* New York, NY: Pantheon Books.

Bion, W. R. (1959). Attacks on Linking. *International Journal of Psycho-Analysis, 40,* 308–315.

Blackmon, D. A. (2009). *Slavery by another name: The re-enslavement of Black Americans from the Civil War to World War II* (1st Anchor Books ed.). New York: Anchor Books.

Blight, D. W. (2018). *Frederick Douglass: Prophet of freedom* (First Simon & Schuster hardcover ed.). New York: Simon & Schuster.

Brickman, B. (2007). Analytic Transformation of Tragic Trauma and Loss: The Recovery of an Analysis Following the Analyst's Life-Threatening Head Injury. *International Journal of Psychoanalytic Self Psychology, 2,* 383–404.

Coates, T.-N. (2015). *Between the world and me* (1st ed.). New York: Random House.

Dewey, J. (1958). *Experience and nature.* New York, NY: Dover Publications.

Dewey, J. (1963). *Experience and education.* New York, NY: Collier Books.

Dilthey, W. (1870). *Leben Schleiermachers.* Berlin, Germany: G. Reimer.

Dimen, M. (2011). Lapsus Linguae, or a Slip of the Tongue? A Sexual Violation in an Analytic Treatment and Its Personal and Theoretical Aftermath. *Contemporary Psychoanalysis, 47,* 35–79.

Dostoyevsky, F., Pevear, R., & Volokhonsky, L. (1992). *The brothers Karamazov: A novel in four parts with epilogue.* London: Vintage.

Douglass, F. (1845). *Narrative of the life of an American slave.* Boston: Anti-Slavery Office.

Douglass, F. (1855). *My bondage and my freedom.* New York: Miller, Orton & Mulligan.

Douglass, F. (1881). *Life and times of Frederick Douglass.* Hartford, CT: Park Publishing Co.

Dunbar-Ortiz, R. (2014). *An indigenous peoples' history of the United States.* Boston: Beacon Press.

Emerson, R. W. (2001). *Emerson's prose and poetry: Authoritative texts, contexts, criticism.* Ed. J. Porte & S. Morris. New York, NY: W. W. Norton.

Ferenczi, S., & Dupont, J. (1988). *The clinical diary of Sándor Ferenczi.* Cambridge, MA: Harvard University Press.

Figal, G. (2010). *Objectivity: The hermeneutical and philosophy.* Trans. T. D. George. Albany, NY: State University of New York Press.

Freud, S. (1953a). *The interpretation of dreams: The standard edition of the complete psychological works of Sigmund Freud, volume IV (1900).* London, UK: Hogarth Press.

Freud, S. (1953b). *A case of hysteria, three essays on sexuality and other works: The standard edition of the complete psychological works of Sigmund Freud, volume VII (1901–1905).* London, UK: Hogarth Press.

Frie, R. (2017). *Not in my family: German memory and responsibility after the Holocaust.* New York, NY: Oxford University Press.

Gadamer, H.-G. (1972). *Wahrheit und Methode: Grundzüge einer philosophischen Hermeneutik* (3rd, rev. ed.). Tübingen, Germany: Mohr.

Gadamer, H.-G. (2004). *Truth and method* (2nd, rev. ed.). Trans. J. Winsheimer and D. G. Marshall. New York, NY: Continuum.

Gadamer, H.-G., Weinsheimer, J., & Marshall, D. G. (2004). *Truth and method* (2nd, rev. ed.). London and New York: Continuum.

Galeano, E. (1973). *Open veins of Latin America: Five centuries of the pillage of a continent.* New York: Monthly Review Press.

Gump, J. (2010). Reality Matters: The Shadow of Trauma on African American Subjectivity. *Psychoanalytic Psychology, 27*, 42–54.

Hoffmann, P. (2011). *Behind Valkyrie: German resistance to Hitler: Documents.* Montreal: McGill-Queen's University Press.

Jacobs, L. (2007). From the Couch: Trauma and Recovery After Analytic Impingement. *International Journal of Psychoanalytic Self Psychology, 2*, 405–422.

James, W. (1902). *The varieties of religious experience: A study in human nature.* New York, NY: Longmans, Green, and Co.

James, W. (1977). *A pluralistic universe.* Cambridge, MA: Harvard University Press.

James, W., et al. (1979). *The will to believe and other essays in popular philosophy.* Cambridge, MA: Harvard University Press.

Jay, M. (2005). *Songs of experience: Modern American and European variations on a universal theme.* Berkeley, CA: University of California Press.

Kant, I. (1793). *Die Religion innerhalb der Grenzen der bloßen Vernunft.* Königsberg, Prussia: Nicolovius.

Kant, I. (1998). *Religion within the boundaries of mere reason and other writings.* Trans. A. W. Wood & G. Di Giovanni. Cambridge, UK: Cambridge University Press.

Kendi, I. X. (2016). *Stamped from the beginning: The definitive history of racist ideas in America.* New York: Nation Books.

Kleinberg-Levin, D. M. (2005). Persecution: The Self at the heart of metaphysics. In E. Nelson, A. Kapust, & K. Still (Eds.), *Addressing Levinas* (pp. 199–235). Evanston, IL: Northwestern University Press.

Kohut, T. A. (2012). *A German generation: An experiential history of the twentieth century.* New Haven, CT: Yale University Press.

Knowles, A. (2015). A Genealogy of Silence: Chōra and the Placelessness of Greek Women. *Philosophia, 5*, 1–24.

Layton, L. (2004). Relational No More: Defensive Autonomy in Middle-Class Women. *Annual of Psychoanalysis, 32*, 29–42.

Layton, L. (2006). Racial Identities, Racial Enactments, and Normative Unconscious Processes. *Psychoanalytic Quarterly, 75*(1), 237–269.

Levi, P. (1965). *The reawakening (La tregua): A liberated prisoner's long march home through east Europe.* Boston, MA: Little.

Levi, P. (1984). *Se questo è un uomo.* Torino: Einaudi.

Levi, P. (1986). *The reawakening.* New York: Macmillan.

Levi, P. (1989). *The drowned and the saved.* New York: Vintage International.

Levinas, E. (1969). *Totality and infinity; An essay on exteriority.* Pittsburgh, PA: Duquesne University Press.

Levinas, E. (1998). *Otherwise than being, or, beyond essence.* Pittsburgh, PA: Duquesne University Press.

Levinas, E., & Robbins, J. (2001). *Is It righteous to be? Interviews with Emmanuel Lévinas.* Stanford, CA: Stanford University Press.

Loewald, H. W. (2000). *The essential Loewald: Collected papers and monographs.* Hagerstown, MD: University Pub. Group.

Luft, S. (1998). Husserl's Phenomenological Discovery of the Natural Attitude. *Continental Philosophy Review, 31*, 153–170.

Merleau-Ponty, M., & Landes, D. A. (2012). *Phenomenology of perception.* Abingdon, UK: Routledge.

Mitchell, S. A. (1988). *Relational concepts in psychoanalysis: An integration.* Cambridge, MA: Harvard University Press.

Montaigne, M. de (1958). *Complete essays.* Stanford, CA: Stanford University Press.

Orange, D. M. (2011). *The suffering stranger: Hermeneutics for everyday clinical practice.* New York, NY: Routledge.

Orange, D. M. (2017). *Climate crisis, psychoanalysis, and radical ethics.* London, UK: Routledge.

Otto, R. (1958). *The idea of the holy: An inquiry into the non-rational factor in the idea of the divine and its relation to the rational.* New York, NY: Oxford University Press.

Otto, R., & Dicker, E. B. (1931). *The philosophy of religion, based on Kant and Fries.* London, UK: Williams & Norgate Ltd.

Paul, D. N. (2000). *We were not the savages: A Mi'kmaq perspective on the collision between European and native American civilizations* (New 21st-century ed.). Halifax, NS: Fernwood.

Peirce, C. P. (1932). A Fragment. In C. Hartshorne & P. Weiss (Eds.), *Collected papers of Charles Saunders Peirce* (Vol. 1). Cambridge, MA: Belknap.

Peirce, C. P. (1992). *The essential Peirce* (Vol. 1). Bloomington, IN: Indiana University Press.

Ricoeur, P. (1970). *Freud and philosophy: An essay in interpretation.* New Haven, CT: Yale University Press.

Royce, J. (1916). *The hope of the great community.* New York, NY: Macmillan.

Royce, J. (1919). *Lectures on modern idealism.* New Haven, CT: Yale University Press.

Schleiermacher, F. (1976). *The Christian faith.* Philadelphia, PA: Fortress Press.

Schwab, G. (2010). *Haunting legacies: Violent histories and transgenerational trauma.* New York: Columbia University Press.

Sedgwick, E. K., & Frank, A. (2003). *Touching feeling: Affect, pedagogy, performativity.* Durham: Duke University Press.

Stauffer, J. (2008). *Giants: The parallel lives of Frederick Douglass & Abraham Lincoln* (1st ed.). New York: Twelve.

Stevenson, B. (2014). *Just mercy: A story of justice and redemption* (1st ed.). New York: Spiegel & Grau.

Steves, R. (2009). *Rick Steves' travel as a political act.* New York, NY: Nation Books.

Steves, R. (2018). *Travel as a political act: How to leave your baggage behind [spoken word].* New York: Hachette Audio.

Stolorow, R. D., Brandchaft, B., & Atwood, G. E. (1987). *Psychoanalytic treatment: An intersubjective approach.* Hillsdale, NJ: Analytic Press.

Vinokur, V. (2008). *The trace of Judaism: Dostoevsky, Babel, Mandelstam, Levinas.* Evanston, IL: Northwestern University Press.

Warren, W. (2016). *New England bound: Slavery and colonization in early America* (1st ed.). New York: Liveright Publishing Corporation.

Wilkerson, I. (2010). *The warmth of other suns: The epic story of America's great migration* (1st ed.). New York: Random House.

Winnicott, D. W. (1965). *The maturational processes and the facilitating environment.* London, UK: Hogarth Press.

Wittgenstein, L. (2003). *Philosophical investigations: The German text, with a revised English translation by G. E. M. Anscombe* (3rd ed.). Malden, MA: Blackwell.

Zia, H. (2000). *Asian American dreams: The emergence of an American people* (1st ed.). New York: Farrar, Straus and Giroux.

Zinn, H. (1980). *A people's history of the United States.* London and New York: Longman.

Chapter 6

Radical ethics
Beyond moderation

All things in moderation, advised Aristotle.[1] He must have envisioned a philosophical and scholarly world, much like Athens in his time (384–322 B.C.E.) without the triple crises we face today: Climate emergency, extremes of inequality, and white supremacy (Klein, 2019). Today, instead of moderation, much as it has to teach us in the way of practical wisdom, our situation requires a radical ethic. The word 'radical' comes from the Latin *radix*, or root. Apart from its mathematical uses, this word refers to something basic or fundamental, the very root of whatever is at stake. Synonyms include thoroughgoing, thorough, complete, total, entire, absolute, utter, comprehensive, exhaustive, root-and-branch, sweeping, far-reaching, wide-ranging, extensive, profound, drastic, severe, serious, major, desperate, stringent, forceful, rigorous, draconian, revolutionary, reformist.[2] Words like uncompromising, hyperbolic, and prophetic (Heschel, 1962) also come to mind, as well as philosopher Richard Bernstein's title for his book about philosophers reacting to the Shoah, *Radical Evil* (Bernstein, 2002). In my own learning, radical ethics has developed as a commensurate response to the level of evil Bernstein addresses – extreme goodness in the face of extreme threat.

Arguably, we face today the imminent destruction of a livable planet, combined with ever more extreme economic injustice, organized as ever by white supremacists who hold and increase their dominance with the silence-gives-consent of many who may or may not consciously or explicitly hold their racist views. Previous chapters have referenced – especially in the work of Michelle Alexander, Ta-Nehisi Coates, and Bryan Stevenson – recent effects of a long and shameful history, with continuing attempts to appeal to racism while denying it. As a remedy, I have advocated reading the history of people damaged, destroyed, and still seriously disadvantaged by extreme and racist versions of capitalism. These stories help us to see what is happening now, to hear the voices of those silenced by racism, colonialism, sexism, and other forms of hatred.

For inspiration, I have needed to pause my studies of psychoanalytic and even phenomenological intersubjectivity (Orange, 1995, 2008a, 2008b, 2009a, 2009b, 2010b; Orange, Atwood, & Stolorow, 1997; Orange, Stolorow, & Atwood, 1998), though they surely prepared me for radical ethics. This chapter will begin by describing this transition. It will then turn to two philosophers whose radical views emerged from their experiences during the Hitler period.

Where two egos were, there other shall be: from intersubjectivity to ethics in contemporary psychoanalysis

The 1980s were a fascinating time to be joining the psychoanalytic world, especially for those of us trained in philosophy. In North America, Freudian ego psychology, concentrated on the individual "mental apparatus," had worn out its postwar welcome as we were hearing independent voices from object relations innovators in Britain, as well as from interpersonal and self-psychological renegades in New York and Chicago. Jay Greenberg and Stephen Mitchell described this landscape in their *Object Relations in Psychoanalytic Theory* (Greenberg & Mitchell, 1983). This touchstone book became the reference point for all subsequent developments in relational psychoanalysis, now a worldwide alternative to traditional forms of thinking and practice.

Intersubjectivity became an important theme. In the late 1980s, Jessica Benjamin, influenced by Hegel and the Frankfurt School, by Winnicott's developmental thinking, and by feminism, began to articulate intersubjectivity as understood by most relational psychoanalysts today. She has described intersubjectivity as a developmental achievement in which the baby or the patient comes to recognize the subjectivity of the mother or the analyst as equivalent to her or his own (Benjamin, 1988). More recently, she has described failures in intersubjectivity as occurring when one or both people or parties collapse into doer/done to positions (Benjamin, 2018).

Even earlier, however, a more phenomenologically inclined form of intersubjective psychoanalysis appeared in the work of Stolorow, Atwood and Brandchaft (Stolorow, Atwood, & Branchaft, 1994; Stolorow, Brandchaft, & Atwood, 1987), perhaps now best developed by Chris Jaenicke (2008, 2011). Here we find two differently structured subjective worlds in an intersubjective field from the start. Understanding the fundamental bases, organizing principles, or emotional convictions (Orange, 1995) pre-reflectively structuring these worlds forms the bulk of psychoanalytic work for these intersubjectivists, equivalent to making the unconscious conscious. The theoretical and practical news is that this "psychic structure" we now understand as formed, maintained, perceived, and possibly altered within an intersubjective field, in a between. Phenomenological intersubjectivity theory implies a complex contextualist view of development and of pathogenesis, describing the emergence and modification of subjectivity, and defining all these processes as irreducibly relational. As observers and participants, we focus on the evolving psychological field constituted by the interplay between the differently organized experiential worlds of child and caregivers, patient and analyst, and so on. Informally, this means I am always trying not only to describe experience (yours, mine, and ours) in this temporal–relational context, but also to understand in what relational contexts we became the people who participate and experience as we do. (We also found this idea in the work of Thomas Kohut discussed in Chapter 5). No one is innocent, and both parties must be understood if anything is to be understood. Clinical writing changes radically as a result, telling an intertwined story of interwoven experiential worlds as they affect each other and thus change.

In the first years of the twenty-first century, lively debates – perhaps owing something to the different sensibilities of some relationalists and self psychologists – raged about the relative merits of these forms of intersubjectivity in psychoanalysis. Some of us (Orange, 2008a, 2010a) were concerned that mutual recognition intersubjectivists might be setting an agenda for their patients to acknowledge their analysts, whatever the needs of patients might be. With the help of Patchen Markell (2003) I distinguished between the Hegelian mutual recognition that had been fused with a kind of Kantianism by Habermas and Honneth in the Frankfurt school, and another type that seemed to me more suited to psychoanalytic work:

> In German, *kennen* means to know, in the sense of to recognize. *Erkennen* means to recognize, in the sense of to come to a realization of. *Anerkennen* means to recognize, in the sense of to accept, to appreciate, or to acknowledge. This third meaning is used to point to the recognition of someone as something, for example, as father, king, or partner. It illuminates the richness of Benjamin's idea of the recognition that creates another as equally a subject of experience, or better, transforms the mother or analyst from an object of fantasy into a full and equal subject. Still, it seems to me that the simple use of 'recognition' also obscures a whole set of Hegel interpretations masterfully delineated by political theorist Patchen Markell in *Bound by Recognition*. He shows that the "politics of recognition" (Taylor & Gutmann, 1994; Honneth & NetLibrary Inc., 1996) involves a seriously inconsistent appeal to a recognition of already existing identities (in the present instance, subject-status), on the one hand, and to a process of creating the actual from the potential (not-yet-existing) identities (individual or group, as in the politics of multiculturalism), on the other hand. He further argues, to my mind convincingly, that Hegel's master-slave analysis can be read quite differently, if one hears the acknowledgment and acceptance in Hegel's *Anerkennung*. What we acknowledge, in relation to the other, is not primarily the other's identity or status, but rather our own intersubjective vulnerability.[3] This kind of acknowledgment also resonates for me with Ghent's (1990) conception of surrender, which further calls into question the focus on agency with which the politics of recognition is often linked.
>
> (Orange, 2008a, p. 183)

I continued by explaining that expecting the patient to acknowledge the analyst in a scheme of "mutual recognition" understates the essential asymmetry of the clinical situation, where both parties are caught in intersubjective vulnerability, but the therapist or analyst bears outsized responsibility, just as parents do. "To be reduced to having recourse to me is the homelessness or strangeness of the neighbor. It is incumbent upon me" (Levinas, 1981, p. 91). Even Martin Buber (Buber & Buber Agassi, 1999), philosopher of dialogue, had acknowledged that pastors, teachers, and therapists have this special, and often heavy, set of obligations.

Benjamin (2010), as well as others (Ringstrom, 2010; Slavin, 2010), not surprisingly, objected strenuously to my critique, claiming in a careful and extensive response that she had never expected patients to recognize their analysts but rather offered them that developmental opportunity:

> The *chance* – not an imperative "must" but an opportunity; indeed, a transformational process – to see another person as a separate and equivalent center of being can be so relieving, I find it hard to identify with Orange's (2008a) descriptions. When this other can be seen as indeed "someone I don't need to take care of all the time," then mutuality and sharing might actually become possible.
>
> (Benjamin, 2010, p. 247, author's emphasis)

Accepting her account of her own views, I said I was very glad to hear it, as others seemed to have misunderstood her as I had, and were responding to clinical work with this expectation in mind. Patients focused on their own traumatic experience, for example, had sometimes been seen as therapeutic failures, and their therapists as inadequate. Benjamin's clarification was helpful to all.

But much of the energy has now disappeared from these debates, it seems. Why? First, we have, dialogically, attempted to listen to each other, to hear each other's concerns, to give each other the benefit of the doubt, to see what the other is attempting to say that needs to be said and may be missing from our own perspective. Of course, true to the worst legacy of our psychoanalytic history, analysts remain ready to give each other the cold shoulder, to refuse to speak with those with whom they disagree, to describe those with whom they disagree as harmful to patients. We are no saints, and our human frailties limit our prospects in this direction.

Even more, however, our psychoanalytic thinking, either linking the consulting room to its larger context or feeling the intrusion of the "outside" world into clinical work, has been shifting focus. We hear talk of an "ethical turn" in psychoanalysis. The most quickly growing conference – an interdisciplinary gathering of philosophers, psychoanalysts, theologians, and many others – in North America just now is called "Psychology and the Other." Suddenly relationality involves more than two people: It evokes world poverty, racism, economic inequality, climate emergency, and much more. You find Jessica Benjamin deeply involved with injustices to the Palestinians; I have been writing about "suffering strangers" not only in the consulting room, but also those being destroyed by climate crisis and dire poverty. We intersubjectivists have been called out into an ethical turn.

Radical ethics

Given the intersubjectivists' emphasis on the unrepeatable, irreplaceable other, never to be violated by generalizing reductionisms, but to be received and treated dialogically, it was for me a short step into a descriptive phenomenological ethics of responsibility and solidarity. Earlier, I had studied the virtue ethics of Aristotle, as well as normative ethics, the duty ethics of Kant, the cost/benefit ethics of the utilitarians, and the mixed social contract/neo-Kantian social ethics of John Rawls and Jürgen Habermas. These last two have emphasized inclusion and recognition, without exception and preference, as foundational to social ethics. In psychoanalysis, of course, we have Jessica Benjamin's work, attempting to overcome the violence that divides people into perpetrators and victims through mutual recognition.

It seems to me now that even more is at stake. We must ask whether the neo-Kantian ethics of the Frankfurt School, even when fused with Hegelian mutual recognition, has turned out to be adequate either for a psychoanalysis working in a world facing rightist extremism and a climate catastrophe, or for the intimacy of the clinical situation.

Recognition, unfortunately based (in English) on cognition, can be addictive. How much is enough? How much money is enough? Surely, we need something of these goods to survive, or to pursue other ends. When we notice that money or pleasure is not ultimately satisfying, we may ask with Aristotle if it really constitutes an ultimate human purpose, or just a side effect of something good in itself. Maybe we need to ask the same questions about recognition. Perhaps recognition and respect, even when mutual, are not ends in themselves, but effects of justice and ethical life. Judith Butler, writing of "precarious life" (Butler, 2000, 2004), at least hints that another kind of otherness than that available in the Hegelian recognition discourse may be needed for the ethical. She writes:

> A vulnerability must be perceived and recognized in order to come into play
> in an ethical encounter, and there is no guarantee that this will happen . . .
> vulnerability takes on another meaning at the moment it is recognized, and
> recognition wields the power to reconstitute vulnerability . . . norms of rec-
> ognition are essential to the constitution of vulnerability as precondition of
> the "human."
>
> (2004, p. 43)

She goes on to note that she is perhaps offering a "version of Hegel" (p. 44), one, she hopes, that offers a possibility that struggles for recognition may have non-violent outcomes, because they are rooted in something more primary than recognition of the "I" or the "you." She concludes:

> So the question of primary support for primary vulnerability is an ethical one for infant and for the child. But there are broader ethical consequences, from this situation, ones that pertain not only to the adult world but to the sphere of politics and its implicit ethical dimension.
>
> (pp. 45–6)

As Lisa Baraitser (2008) notes, we are now in "another register":

> Self-recognition that relies on recognition by another subject will perhaps always run into difficulties with how to prevent a collapse of alterity due to the colonizing impulse that is inherent not only in "knowing" another but in recognizing too. In contrast, describing the relationship with the Other as an ethical relationship prior to self, a relationship that establishes the subject as a responsible subject before being a subject at all.
>
> (p. 102)

We hear in Baraitser echoes of Emmanuel Levinas, philosopher/prophet of asymmetrical responsibility. For me, Levinas addressed my own besetting sins – evasion and indifference; that is, bystandership. Hearing, in his reading of Dostoevsky and of the Hebrew scriptures, the right answer to Cain's insolent question, "Am I my brother's keeper?" he contested Western philosophy on every form of egoism. Claiming that ethics is an optics, he challenged us to see human suffering without turning away. A five-year Nazi labor camp survivor who lost all his Lithuanian family, he wrote:

> . . . that face facing me, in its expression – in its mortality – summons me, demands me, requires me as if the invisible death faced by the face of the other – pure alterity, separate, somehow, from any whole – were "my business." [As if I were, always already, my brother's and sister's keeper.] As if, unknown by the other whom already, in the nakedness of its face, it [the invisible death faced by the other] concerns, it "regarded me" before its confrontation with me, before being the death that stares me, myself, in the face. The death of the other man puts me on the spot, calls me into question, as if I, by my possible indifference, became the accomplice of that death, invisible to the other who is exposed to it; and as if, even before being condemned to it myself, I had to answer for that death of the other, and not leave the other alone to his deathly solitude. It is precisely in that recalling of me to my responsibility by the face that summons me, that demands me, that requires me – it is in that calling into question – that the other is my neighbor.
>
> (Levinas, 1999, pp. 24–5)

The miserable other *interpellates* (calls me out), traumatizing me, taking me hostage, calling me to subjection, to substitution (Levinas, 1981), to the only kind of meaningful suffering, that taken on for the sake of the other. Levinas used "interpellate" in its precise philosophical meaning of "to bring into being or give identity to," as well as "to command." Precisely in responding to the command that the other's suffering imposes on me I am brought to subjectivity, constituted as subject, in his view. No masochism is here, no pleasure in this suffering.

Nor am I allowed to ask whether the other owes me. When asked this question, Levinas answered:

> Perhaps, but that is his affair. One of the fundamental themes of Totality and Infinity . . . .is that the intersubjective relation is a non-symmetrical relation . . . In this sense, I am responsible for the other without waiting for reciprocity, were I to die for it. Reciprocity is his affair.
>
> (Levinas & Nemo, 1997, p. 98)

Danish phenomenologist Løgstrup (1971) – similarly wrote of an ethical demand – silent, radical, one-sided, and impossible – based on what he considered a basic fact:

> The other person must to such a degree be dependent upon me that what I do and say in the relationship between us – I alone and nobody else, here and now and not at some other time or in some other manner – is of decisive importance. If my relation to the other person is the place where my relation to God is determined, then it must at the same time be the place where that person's existence is so totally at stake that to fail him is to fail him irreparably.
>
> (Løgstup, 1997, p. 5)

The ethical demand was one-sided because it can claim nothing in return. If, as Løgstrup took as axiomatic, my life is a gift, I have nothing to which I am entitled. I possess nothing that I have not received and cannot, as he said, make counterdemands.

> A person is a debtor not because he or she has committed some wrong but simply because he or she exists and has received his or her life as a gift. The demand that he or she take care of the other person's life is rooted in the very fact of his or her indebtedness for all the different potentialities he or she has him or herself received: intelligence, speech, love, and many others.
>
> (Løgstup, 1997, p. 116)[4]

Entitlement and ego disappear in both thinkers, as does reciprocity.

But, of course, no one can live up to the infinite demand, the endless responsibility – so, like Dostoevsky, I am forever guilty for all, before all. Daily the unexpected stranger comes before me, welcomed into the queue before me, helped up the subway steps by thousands of unexpectedly courteous New York-ers and out of the floods by heroic Houstonians, allowed into the expressway lane. She need not prove her documented status if she needs help. Then when her face appears as a public assistance recipient, I will know how to vote. When someone calls her a "dirty Jew," I will know to say that I'm Jewish too, or to hide my neighbor from ICE (US Immigration and Customs Enforcement). Though the ethic of responsibility – framed in response to extreme situations, and full of trau-matic memory – often sounds extreme, it grounds itself in everyday proximity to those unexpected interpellations, situations that ethically call us out.

Robert Bernasconi (2012) draws special attention to this radical ethics, based on *Totality and Infinity*'s (Levinas, 1979) demand coming from the naked and vulnerable face of the other, holding me to an impossibly burdensome responsibility.[5] He suggests that this discourse, including what I have quoted previously, needs to be read in the context of Levinas's whole work, especially the ordinarily neglected last third of *Totality and Infinity*. While I cannot consider, or even summarize, his entire argument here, the fecundity (productivity, fruitfulness, richness, fertility) emphasis struck me as especially important for psychoanalysts bewildered by radical ethics.[6] We turn to this now.

Levinas, Bernasconi tells us, saw philosophy itself as the quest for transcen-dence. In a short YouTube video interview,[7] he kept repeating, "La sortie du soi, la sortie du soi." But to where does this self-absorbed self, with its place in the sun, exit? To transcendence, to the other, to non-indifference, to the infinite, to else-where, beyond self, via fecundity. Fecundity, neglected – also by me – because equated here with paternity until maternity appears in *Otherwise than Being* (Levinas, 1998), offers the only escape from infinite guilt and responsibility. In Bernasconi's words, "Levinas opened the way to a form of responsibility where the emphasis is not on the past, but where there is still time to be for the Other in a future that is not mine" (Bernasconi, 2012, p. 266). Biological fecundity gives way to giving life in other ways, addressing poverty and hunger, making peace.

Therefore, while fecundity seems a matter for the young, it is indispensable for later years. Psychoanalysts might consider bringing Erik Erikson back into our conversations, interrogating his rich writings on the generativity of middle life,[8] in which the ever-developing person provides a stable environment for the next generation. The climate emergency, of course, makes such generativity and fecun-dity urgent. So far, we elders have instead left a carbon and methane-poisoned planet to the young; now at least we could prioritize their lives enough to help them limit the damage.

Simon Critchley (2007) comments that infinite responsibility to the other cre-ates what Levinas liked to call "the curvature of intersubjective space" (Levinas, 1969, p. 291) in which the other always occupies the upper point, perhaps another reference to Levinasian "transcendence." Similarly, Judith Butler hears the ethi-cal call in the affirmation of the precarious, the vulnerable, and the traumatized:

if they [the unnamable and ungrievable lives] do not appear in their precari-ousness and their destruction, we will not be moved. We will not return to a sense of ethical outrage that is distinctively for an Other, in the name of an Other. We cannot, under contemporary conditions of representation, hear the agonized cry or be compelled or commanded by the face.

(Butler, 2004, p. 150)

She worries that our ethical subjectivity becomes systematically occluded by media manipulation.

The ethical constitution of subjectivity

Suppose we grant to developmental and intersubjective psychoanalysts that subjectivity, or a sense of selfhood, originally emerges – absent significant developmental trauma – from the harmonious interpenetrating mixup (Balint, 1979); maternal care (Winnicott, 1965); self-selfobject relatedness (Kohut, 1977); primordial density (Loewald, 1980); the intersubjective field (Stolorow et al., 1987); or relationality (Mitchell, 2000). The daily work of psychotherapists involves understanding and responding to those many in our world whose early and later trauma and other trouble brings them to our door.

But what constitutes our own subjectivity, our own moral center or *hegimonikon*, as the ancient Greeks and Romans would have called it? Where do we hear the voice of the *daimon*, of conscience, of responsibility? Butler, in a lecture at the Nobel Museum in Sweden (Museum, 2011) easily available on YouTube, suggests that the precarious face of the suffering other faces us daily on television, in our newspapers, and on our handheld devices, infinitely close and infinitely distant.

How does one respond? Some join Doctors Without Borders, surely a life without recognition. In 1939, theologian Dietrich Bonhoeffer returned to Germany to rejoin other German Christians in the plot against Hitler's life instead of remaining safe in New York, as colleagues advised him to do. He spent much of the war in prison and was hanged before its end. Witold Pilecki, as we now know from his newly available account (Pilecki, 2012), volunteered to be a prisoner in Auschwitz, where he remained for three years, attempting to organize resistance and to communicate to the outside world about the nature of the place. He tried to keep his name unknown to protect others. He was tortured, tried, and executed by the communist government of Poland in March 1948. Likewise, many journalists have died in their recent effort to tell the stories of oppression and violence.[9]

But many serve humbly, and scarcely know themselves that they simply do what they must. A colleague objects to thinking of herself as ethical as she faithfully accompanies and cares for dying friends while continuing all of her own work. But her very subjectivity – whatever that may be – emerges in this response to the other, I am claiming. In similar fashion, my current neighbors are welcoming some of the few released from our wretched neighboring immigration prisons, asking all of us for clothes and bits of work they can do. I am grateful for the following words from French theorist Gilles Deleuze:

To say something in one's own name is very strange, for it is not at all when we consider ourselves as selves, persons, or subjects that we speak in our own name. On the contrary, an individual acquires a true proper name as the result of the most severe operations of depersonalization, when he opens himself to the multiplicities that pervade him and the intensities which run through his whole being.

(*quoted in* Baraitser, 2008, p. 86)

So, to begin with, we must never expect to be recognized in our own name. Multiplicities run me through. Moreover, as Dostoevsky understood once he had been to Siberia, morality is no abstraction. The other – possibly ugly, disgusting, demanding, and grotesque, at least in need of my care – is my sister or brother. The colicky infant who can give me nothing requires me to respond. Radical responsibility replaces recognition in the world of the ethical. Recognition, sought as an end in itself, may collapse into the world social contract philosopher Thomas Hobbes and Brooke (2017, p. 43) believed natural to humans: Solitary, poor, nasty, brutish and short. When recognition arrives by chance, it seems to me a gift to be humbly received and passed on to others.

Subjectivity constituted by response to the other will look quite unpretentious. Years ago, as a young graduate student in philosophy and a stranger in New York, I was a guest for some weeks at a convent while I looked for a place to stay near the university where I would be studying. Remarkably, it took me two weeks to find out which of the sisters was the local superior. Her attitude of service to the others made her indistinguishable from the rest. She also worked for many years as a contemporary Freudian psychoanalyst, and became an important influence on my decision to study psychology and psychoanalysis.

To serve the other, without much recognition, without self-promotion, is to allow ourselves to be commanded (interpellated), and thus brought into being, every day – both at home and far away. Many will call this an impossible life, and surely for any one of us, on any given day, it has its limits. Granted, but we see simple, extraordinary goodness around us every day, dependent on a capacity for ethical hearing nourished by reparative reading.

Voices of radical ethics

What may I do? What must I do? What must I never do? And why or why not? Ethics, usually taught as a calculus of justice or risk and reward, in the rationalistic, individualistic, and thoroughly Western voices of Kant and the utilitarians, claims an indispensable place in ordinary human life, whatever that may be: Promises, contracts, even medical triage. In a distinctly secondary place, we have descriptive ethics, from Aristotle to Paul Woodruff (Woodruff, 2014), teaching us to ask what makes a human character good, and what in human life is worth pursuing. Intuition ethics, with a long British history and now resurrected in social psychologist Jonathan Haidt's *The Righteous Mind* (Haidt, 2012), explains why people hold moral positions for which they can give no grounds except that that they feel so convinced. Some behaviors evoke disgust and extreme disapproval, even when we cannot explain why. Arguably, however, we once again live in times where all these normal ethics fail us. Radical ethics – our topic here – attempts to meet the challenges of what Hannah Arendt (1968) described as the "dark times," those times, no, rather, *these times* when everything is at stake; when, for example, human life has no value whatever to our controlling economic systems and when our planetary home will soon be uninhabitable. In these times, the voices of those most in need have been silenced, and those responsible seem uninterested in their plight. Radical ethics, as the ancient prophets knew, orients everyday life but becomes crucial in emergencies.

Further, as Paul Roazen reminded us, we psychoanalysts need always to live in the space of ethical questions:

> The problem of ethics itself . . . is one which has traditionally been difficult to establish securely as a legitimate subject within psychoanalysis. Yet Freud . . . has been flourishing in countries like France where psychoanalysis has been kept closely allied to philosophy. Freud's effort to demarcate psychoanalytic psychology from ethical thought was taken literally in America, thus not absorbing the full implications of all Freud's writings, which certainly included an explicit moral component. The future of psychoanalysis may depend on the extent to which the political, social, and strictly philosophic sides of psychoanalysis continue to be explored. Such an enterprise should make it less likely that clinical practices become rigidified.
>
> (Roazen, 2002, p. 55)

Still, even accepting Roazen's admonitions and mine (Orange, 2010c), the voices of radical – usually phenomenological – ethics sound strange. Can one be both a philosopher and a prophet? Most philosophers would immediately say no, and, I think, most prophets would say no, perhaps more slowly. Though we may have learned the relational ethic of Martin Buber long ago, many of us know a truly radical ethical voice primarily or only in the work of phenomenologist and Talmudist Emmanuel Levinas. Thanks to his fellow survivor of totalitarianism and theorist of liquid modernity, Zygmunt Bauman (lost to us in 2017 after a prolific and challenging old age), as well as to Levinas scholar Simon Critchley (Critchley, 2007), I have been discovering a second border-crosser who often upset rigorous disciplinarians both in theology and philosophy: the Danish Lutheran philosopher of ethics Løgstrup. (Less radical than Løgstrup and Levinas, Bernhard Waldenfels considers the phenomenology of the alien). We will take these three in turn, considering what each contributes to our story about hearing the silenced. We will then examine attempts, fully well-intentioned, to tame these fiercely challenging voices, and ask whether such projects amount to silencing the prophets by downsizing the message so that we then can ignore their reproaches.

Knud Ejler Løgstrup[10]

Zygmunt Bauman (2007) tells of his mid-1980s sabbatical in Newfoundland before he wrote *Postmodern Ethics* (Bauman, 1993). "Ethical philosophy of the modern era," he believed, "could not but reflect the legislative and order-building ambition, the defining trait of modernity" (2007, p. 114). Searching the library shelves, having previously found only Emmanuel Levinas to challenge traditional rationalistic ethics, he had nearly given up when he came upon a probably unread copy of Løgstrup's *The Ethical Demand* (Løgstrup, 1997) in English translation, where, he recounts, he found his lost time compensated many times over. Now he could counter the calculus of philosophers who thought like Stephen Toulmin's (1958) so-called moral person. For both Bauman and Løgstrup this righteous fellow was a "dreadful person" who would return John's book just because everyone must return what is borrowed. This "moral person," a good Kantian universalizer, "cares not two pins about John but is merely concerned with his own fidelity to his promises so that the social order may be preserved" (Løgstrup, 2007, p. 104). Such conventional ethics, he said, was "morality's way of being immoral" (p. 103).

Perhaps the most important Danish philosopher since Søren Kierkegaard, Løgstrup was born in 1905 and lived through the Nazi occupation of Denmark, taught philosophy and theology at Aarhus University, and died in 1981. His magnum opus, translated into English as *The Ethical Demand*, claims that the impossible command to love one's neighbor, as heard in Christianity, need not be linked to institutional religion or dogma, but instead must be understood humanly as *silent*, *radical*, *one-sided*, and *impossible*. He believed that the basic phenomenological fact of human trust in each other, absent abuse of this trust, means that our lives come to us as a gift and that we have a fundamental duty to take care of each other. As quoted in a previous section in reference to utter vulnerability:

> The other person must to such a degree be dependent upon me that what I do and say in the relationship between us – I alone and nobody else, here and now and not at some other time or in some other manner – is of decisive importance. If my relation to the other person is the place where my relation to God is determined, then it must at the same time be the place where that person's existence is so totally at stake that to fail him is to fail him irreparably.
>
> (Løgstrup, 1997, p. 5)

Immediately, we hear an unusual voice: Clear, straightforward, uncompromising, without philosophical or theological jargon. And yet, this clarity carries an implicating[11] message. The other is at our mercy. Let us look more closely.

He called the ethical demand silent because it comes to us without words in two senses. Unspoken but implicit in all conversation, the other's dependence on me means I must not mistreat or abandon this raw vulnerability. "Regardless of how varied the communication between persons may be," he wrote, "it always involves the risk of one person daring to lay himself or herself open to the other in the hope of a response" (p. 17). "There is self-surrender in all forms of communication," (p. 8). Our vulnerability to the other generates pre-emptive shame, keeping the ethical demand unspoken:

> It must at all costs never become apparent to the other person, and preferably not even to ourselves, that it is a matter of disappointed expectation, because though we have been exposed we are at pains not to admit it. We would much rather admit blemishes and weaknesses, mistakes and stupidities than admit to our having laid ourselves open.
>
> (p. 11)

The silent demand, though it commands response, does not specify its content, but leaves each of us to work that out. Like the humanitarians to whom nurse-educator Jean Watson (2005) recommends both Løgstrup and Levinas, the recipient of the demand must find its content in the context. An ethical response, one that takes care of the vulnerability of the other, differs depending on the age of the child, the illness and capacities of the patient, the resources of the surrounding world, and the precarity Judith Butler's recent work (2004, 2010) foregrounds. The demand remains silent on its content, but does not permit or exonerate bystanding.

Though the ethical demand remains silent and pervasively implicit, still Løgstrup insists on its radicality, not in words and actions but in the demand itself. This ethics requires that what I do and say in relation to the other be done unselfishly, for the sake of the other:

> The demand, precisely because it is unspoken, is radical. This is true even though the thing to be done in any particular situation may be very insignificant. Why is this? Because the person confronted by the unspoken demand must him or herself determine how he or she is to take care of the other person's life. If what he or she does is to result in something of real value to the other person, he or she must think and act unselfishly.
>
> (Løgstrup, 1997, p. 44)

> The radicality of the demand consists, further, in the fact that it asks me to take care of the other person's life not only when to do so strengthens me but also when it is very unpleasant, because it intrudes disturbingly into my own existence. And this is not all. Even in distrust the other person is still delivered over into my hands. Even my enemy is to a large degree dependent upon me and upon the manner in which I respond to him or her.
>
> (p. 45)

Finally, he concludes, as if he had studied Levinas on the ethical constitution of subjectivity: "the demand has the effect of making the person to whom the demand is directed a singular person. Ethically speaking the demand isolates him or her" (p. 45). I respond, therefore I am. In Patrick Stokes's (Stokes, 2016) words:

> Against the reflective tendencies of contemporary ethics, and the forms of "character building" subject formation that it endorses, this stream offers a very different account of moral psychology, one that decenters the individual agent and emphasizes purgation and surrender rather than habituation and will – a path of upbuilding as demolition.
>
> (p. 142)

Radical ethics replaces the normalizing of everyday character building and habit formation with self-diremption, self-emptying to make room for the other.

Løgstrup notes that we are not required to "turn ourselves inside out . . . to abandon all spiritual reticence" (Løgstrup, 1997, p. 16). Rather, we must protect the life of the other who has been delivered over into our hands. Løgstrup cautions that our responsibility for the other does not mean taking over the responsibility for the other's own responsibilities. He further cautions that mistaking radical responsibility for limitlessness can easily lead us to encroach on the other in the name of taking care. The radicality of the demand may require us to do less-than-radical actions.

Besides being silent and radical, the demand is one-sided, asymmetrical, because it can claim nothing in return. If, as Løgstrup took as axiomatic, my life is a gift, I have nothing to which I am entitled. I possess nothing that I have not received and cannot, as he said, make counterdemands.

> A person is a debtor not because he or she has committed some wrong but simply because he or she exists and has received his or her life as a gift. The demand that he or she take care of the other person's life is rooted in the very fact of his or her indebtedness for all the different potentialities he or she has him or herself received: intelligence, speech, love, and many others.
>
> (p. 116)

Some will object, Løgstrup knew, to characterizing life as a gift, especially in the face of suffering and death, loss and despair. But, he concludes, "the thing that makes us dispute that life is a gift is not death or suffering, it is our own will to be worshiped and feel our own power" (p. 122). By characterizing life as gift, he seems to mean unearned, and thus not grounding any sense of entitlement or priority of my life over that of the other. Quite the contrary. He notes, however, that suffering becomes bearable only if others support life as gift. I am reminded of Levinas's description in *Totality and Infinity* (Levinas, 1979) of the non-demanding caress.

One-sidedness, the demand's third trait, shows up most clearly when the other feels less like a gift and more like a nuisance:

> When . . . does the one-sided demand address us? . . . It is when we regard him or her as something entirely other than a gift because he or she is a bother

and an inconvenience to us. The demand that we nevertheless take care of his or her life is therefore directed to us on the presupposition that our own life has been given to us as a gift.

(p. 127)

Through the demand we are . . . asked whether we intend to make ourselves masters of our own life to the point of deciding for ourselves who shall and who shall not be a part of it, or whether we will accept our life as a gift in order to use it for taking care of the other person's life.

(pp. 127–8)

So the question of reciprocity, what does the other owe to me, receives the same answer from Løgstrup as from Levinas: That is his affair (Levinas & Nemo, 1985, p. 98). My only concern is that the other comes first. The common or divergent sources of their convictions on this one-sidedness or asymmetry would make a larger study than I can undertake here. Both equally opposed any social contract ethics based on reciprocity or mutual recognition.

And last, the demand is impossible or unfulfillable because it so seems to contradict our acquired selfishness. The demand is further impossible because we can never know whether we have truly acted unselfishly. The demand does not tell us *how* we are to take care of the other – sometimes, the other would seem to prefer to be left in the rubble – but that we must take care. Nor can we know if we have done enough. Løgstrup acknowledges that the demand sometimes involves us in knotty problems of thinking we know better, like a parent, what is good for the other, but insists that these problems cannot allow us to become bystanders. The good Samaritan is Løgstrup's model. The ethical demand does not prescribe what exactly we who observe injustice should do; it requires that we respond and leaves us all the problems of practical wisdom (Fink & Stern, 2017). The needs are infinite, and we are not. We thus live divided between the demand and our possibilities.[12]

Though his emphasis on trust could seem to place Løgstrup among the promise-keeping Kantians, his ethics utterly transcends a calculus of what we owe to each other, based on any kind of social contract.[13] He described instead rather a radical vulnerability into which we are born, and in which we live. Trust, he wrote, "is essential to every conversation. In conversation as such we deliver ourselves over into the hand of another" (Løgstrup, 1997, p. 14). He continues:

What happens is that simply in addressing the other, irrespective of the importance of the content of what we say, a certain note is struck through which we, as it were, step out of ourselves in order to exist in the speech relationship. For this reason the point of the demand – though unarticulated – is that the speaker is accepted as the note struck by the speaker's address is accepted. For a person inadvertently or even intentionally not to hear the note in what we say, therefore, means that it is we ourselves who are being ignored, provided it is we ourselves who dared to make the overture. That all speech takes place in such fundamental trust is evident in the fact that the most casual comment takes on a false note if one believes that it is not accepted in the sense that it is intended.

(p. 15)

Parenthetically, we might note that misunderstandings and ruptures, therapeutic and in intimate relationships, occur when the other feels some important nuance unheard, and trust breached. The silent demand is to protect trust, the pre-condition for everything.

It might be tempting to think that Løgstrup denies moral complexity and the difficulty inherent in some situations. What he contests, I believe, is substituting endless deliberation and calculation for ethical response. In radical ethics, the commitment to respond to the other comes before, and structures, Aristotelian *phronesis* (practical wisdom). Again, Stokes: "moral deliberation . . . a sort of phronetic practical reason that only comes into play once one has already *implicitly* and non-reflectively committed oneself to meeting the ethical demand" (Stokes, 2016, p. 145). Wisdom and prudence cannot serve as excuses for doing nothing, for leaving the stranger to die alone in the ditch. We are first responders (ambiguity intended). Although to my knowledge, philosopher and psychoanalyst Anne Dufourmantelle (Dufourmantelle, 2011; Dufourmantelle, Payne, Sallé, & Malabou, 2018) did not cite Løgstrup, he would surely have recognized her response to the ethical demand when she gave her life without hesitation to save two drowning children.

Løgstrup's ethical philosophy – like that of Emmanuel Levinas, with whom he begs to be compared – mostly emerged from his reflections on the behavior of bystanders and of courageous people during the Nazi period. He wrote of the differences in ethical decision required in Norway and Denmark during World War II. In Denmark, he thought, the presence of a government that persisted between the people and the Nazis meant time for deliberation. In Norway, with nothing but Nazi government, people constantly faced radical choices where protecting the vulnerable meant immediate risk of death or concentration camps for themselves or their families. This meant, Løgstrup thought, that their previous patterns of response to the ethical demand would probably predominate in their choice to collaborate, resist, or protect the lives of vulnerable others. "There is a psychic maturity," he wrote, "which can make the direction of many an instant decision a foregone conclusion. Even where much is at stake, a person need not therefore necessarily be in doubt about what he or she will do" (Løgstrup, 1997, p. 150). Although we may, in our present moment, still have time to deliberate, to "sleep on it," I find it useful to realize that every choice I make may be preparing a direction for fiercer challenges. Løgstrup himself, by the way, involved himself in much more active and dangerous resistance to the Nazi occupiers than many of his Danish colleagues were willing to do.

Two further aspects of Løgstrup's thinking help to make his radicality clear. First, he raged – as much as his reserved philosophical voice would let him – against Kierkegaard, dearly beloved ancestor of so many of us who grew up in the 1960s and 1970s with existentialism. In his view, Kierkegaard, putting away Regina Olsen and his love for her, focused much too much on his own purity of heart. (Others, of course, may view Kierkegaard differently, or view these two as much closer). In Løgstrup's view, ethics has little to do with how holy and pure the individual can become. Instead, ethics means hearing the moans of the stranger in the ditch or begging on the street as addressed to me.

Further, in the years after his most famous book, Løgstrup wrote of what he called the "sovereign expressions of life" (Løgstrup, 2007, p. 50ff.). This odd-sounding phrase refers to qualities of relatedness (he might have said character traits) like sincerity, trust, and mercy, characterizing response to the ethical demand, but contrasting with obsessive and self-enclosed phenomena, including betrayal, jealousy and envy (Løgstrup, 2007). He called these life expressions "sovereign" because they make the putative agent into the exact opposite. They rule. Stokes (2016) explains:

> Trusting someone . . . is not so much something I *do* as something I *let happen*, because trust arises in a situation where I experience it as an external force that should be allowed to have its way in a given situation, and to which I am currently acting as an impediment. As a result, we are not to *employ* trust, mercy, or sincerity, but must instead *give in*to their impetus; we don't use these expressions, we simply get out of their way.
>
> (p. 143, emphasis in original)[14]

Much of Løgstrup's later work involved describing these contrasts, so neglected, he thought, by Kierkegaard, and by conventional moral philosophy.

Knud Løgstrup and Emmanuel Levinas

Emmanuel Levinas, born in Lithuania in 1906, student and early admirer of Heidegger, came to mount an ethical and phenomenological critique of what he called "totalizing," every form of reducing people to things or categories, a tendency he found both violent and endemic to the Western tradition (Levinas, 1979). From the time Hitler came to power, with Heidegger enthusiastically endorsing him, Levinas contrasted this murderous totalizing with response and responsibility toward infinity and transcendence, to the face of the other, commanding me, accusing me. Presentiment and memory of the Nazi horror, he wrote, haunted all his work. In his second great book (Levinas, 1981), substitution, the other's life before mine, the other's death of more concern than mine, takes center stage. Ethical saying – *hineni* (me here, yes) – replaces the objectifying, categorizing "said," now treating the naked and vulnerable other as of ultimate value. The face of the other now bears the trace of the infinite, and only in the other can the infinite be found and heard.

So how do these two thinkers of radical ethics compare and contrast? Rooted in religion, Lutheran (Stern, 2017) and Jewish, respectively, both intended to work as phenomenologists but picked up different strains. Influenced by Bergson, Husserl and Heidegger, both lived at the same times in Strasbourg – where Levinas was teaching when Løgstrup arrived as a student – and Freiburg (both Husserl and Heidegger were there in the early 1930s), though they seem never to have met. Where Levinas developed his phenomenology by inverting Husserlian intentionality – the other faces and accuses me – Løgstrup studied with Hans Lipps in Göttingen, absorbing the Heideggerian being-in-the-world conviction, but following this being into ethical relatedness. Our very situatedness with others creates the ethical demand. Heideggerian thrownness became for Løgstrup basic trust, only destroyed by betrayal and trauma. Løgstrup, though neither novelist nor poet, often illustrated his ethical concepts with relational stories, creating a type of narrative phenomenology:

> At four o'clock in the morning there is an insistent ring at the door. When the woman descends the secret police are outside, demanding that she open up. Once inside, they ask for her husband. They are informed that, as it happens, he is not at home but away on business. One of the two men, the subordinate, heavily armed, ugly as sin, and looking capable of every kind of brutality, starts searching the house. The other, possessed of an engaging manner, all amiability and courtesy, is talking to the woman meanwhile and assuring her that the visit is of no consequence, merely a routine procedure. The woman acts obligingly, appearing surprised – a composed and polished performance. She is perfectly aware that his charming insistence on the insignificance of their visit is aimed solely at getting her to talk, and is not taken in by anything that he says. She knows that from the least unconsidered remark ammunition will be forged for use against her husband and herself. In spite of that – and this is probably the oddest part of the whole business – she needs constantly to rein in an inclination to talk to the man as to another human being, as though he might be drawn from his destructive enterprise to properly human perceptions and good sense. Unremittingly, she must keep a cool head. Why? What manifests itself in that inclination? Nothing other than the elemental and definitive peculiarity attaching to all speech qua spontaneous expression of life: its openness. To speak is to speak openly.
>
> (2007, pp. 83–4)

Here, we have a good sample of phenomenological description in Løgstrup's hands. The basic trust exerts an almost instinctual hold. He justified his view of the ethical demand and of the sovereign expressions of life on grounds of experiences with which the reader or hearer could easily identify.

Levinas, directly Heidegger's student, but even earlier a translator and student of Husserl, found another phenomenological voice:

> The self is a sub-jectum: it is under the weight of the universe . . . the unity of the universe is not what my gaze embraces in its unity of apperception, but what is incumbent upon me from all sides, regards me, is my affair.
>
> (Levinas, 1981, p. 89)

Here we find a prophetic voice challenging the whole philosophical tradition. The first-person perspective so beloved by phenomenologists finds itself no longer agentic, no longer the agentic constructor of experience, but subject as subjected, under the weight of incumbency, obligated from all sides, "more passive than all passivity" (Levinas, 1998, p. 14). Because Levinas (1906–1995) outlived Løg-strup (1905–1981) into the digital age, we have an additional access to his distinctive voice in the form of interviews from his later years easily accessible to all of us. We can hear him repeat the importance of returning to texts, and like a mantra: "*la sortie du soi, la sortie du soi*" (the exit from self). Each thinker describes in his own idiom a radical ethical demand, of responsibility to care for the vulnerable other. Phenomenologists both, both thinkers challenge what Critchley names the "autonomy orthodoxy" of Western moral theory, and both describe ethical experience rather than justifying ethical choices. Both, in addition, share a Judeo-Christian sensibility shaping their preference for the poor and the abandoned ones. (The expression "Judeo-Christian" can, of course, seriously mislead). Phenomenology gives both thinkers a secular language, one might say, for communicating their radical ethics in human terms.

Raised in an intellectual strain of Judaism in Kovno, Lithuania, and ever allergic to more mystical forms, then profoundly educated in Russian literature in exile in Ukraine in his *Gymnasium* years, and in phenomenology in Europe with Husserl and Heidegger, Levinas emerged from five years in captivity during the war to study Talmud with the famous Chouchani, also the teacher of Elie Wiesel. Headmaster of a Jewish school (ENIO) in Paris, Levinas gave weekly Rashi commentaries and produced Talmudic commentaries, published with a different publisher from his philosophical work. These, as well as his explicitly philosophical works, show a fascinating interdisciplinary voice, with a strong resistance to theologizing.

The Danish Lutheran Løgstrup, for his part, began his best-known work, *The Ethical Demand*, by framing its purpose as making the basic message of Jesus – love thy neighbor – accessible in human terms. Simon Critchley (2007) hears Løgstrup throughout glossing Matthew 5:43–7, from the Sermon on the Mount:

> You have heard that it was said, "You shall love your neighbor and hate your enemy." But I say to you, Love your enemies and pray for those who persecute you, so that you may be sons of your Father who is in heaven; for he

makes his sun rise on the evil and on the good, and sends rain on the just and on the unjust. For if you love those who love you, what reward have you? Do not even the tax collectors do the same? And if you salute only your brethren, what more are you doing than others? Do not even the Gentiles do the same?

How many times should I forgive my brother? Seventy times seven. A radical, one-sided, and unfulfillable demand, like the Levinasian ethic, this inordinate, excessive demand seems to echo "be perfect, as your heavenly Father is perfect" (Matthew 5:48).

But Løgstrup did not quote these words. Educated in theology and philosophy, he, like Levinas, avoided theologizing, preferring description and narrative of ethical experience. He knew we could not be perfect, and relied on his Lutheran faith to believe that we are always already forgiven. "The Christian message does not solely take into account what a person actually is, but also takes into account what a person is in light of the message: a forgiven human being" (Løgstrup, 2007, p. 32). The demand is impossible: It requires of forgiven sinners that we be perfectly good. Faith provides him not content, but context.

As Hans Fink and Alisdair MacIntyre write in their introduction to *The Ethical Demand*:

> Løgstrup did indeed take the ethical demand to be that which was commanded by Jesus when he repeated the injunction of Leviticus to love our neighbor as ourselves. But for Løgstrup . . . the ethical demand is not laid upon Christians rather than non-Christians. There is not Christian morality *and* secular morality. There is only human morality.
>
> (Løgstrup, 1997, pp. xxxvii–xxxviii)

He saw people living out their acceptance of the ethical demand in the present and struggling with it. Levinas would speak of a split in subjectivity, with the demand originating in the immemorial past, a demand to which I am always inadequate, thus torn apart by it. In Judith Butler's straightforward words, "Let's face it. We're undone by each other. And if we're not, we're missing something" (Butler, 2004, p. 23).

For both thinkers, Western religious sensibility grounded and shaped what they came to understand as the human ethical relation. How much either would be able to engage in interfaith dialogues beyond their partially shared traditions remains, for me, an open question. Both profoundly challenged the individualism underlying Western ontologies, colonialism, and other forms of reductive and murderous violence. Løgstrup substituted trust, Levinas solidarity. Both seem close to Buddhist compassion and to African *Ubuntu*, though to my knowledge, neither mentioned these ideas.

A striking similarity between these two thinkers, absent from other major moral philosophers, is one-sidedness (Løgstrup) or asymmetry (Levinas). The ethical demand is on me, not you. This stupefying, excessive, exorbitant quality defies the logic of justification. Only stories demonstrate its possibility, and even reasonableness. But I must mention that in his last years, Levinas tended to call these examples of the ethical response holiness.[15] Løgstrup, more reserved, thought they simply demonstrated true humanity.

Despite the striking parallels, we find in Løgstrup an emphasis on human interdependence underpinning his constant talk of basic trust, for him, a phenomenological fundamental that finds no exact equivalent in Levinas, for whom an anarchic responsibility refuses all appeal to something foundational. But do they differ so much? Both stress one-sidedness and asymmetry, but the vulnerability of Løgstrup's speaker, and the nakedness of the face of Levinas's widow, orphan, and stranger share a common fragility and impose a common demand. You shall not turn away, you shall not remain indifferent, you shall not murder me with your categories, you shall not leave me to die alone. To my ears, these messages from a Lutheran and a Jewish phenomenologist sound equally demanding; others, lacking such voices, must turn to practical philosophers like Dorothy Day, whom both Løgstrup and Levinas would have very well understood.

Bernhard Waldenfels

Probably the most important German phenomenologist of the past 50 years, Bernhard Waldenfels (1934–) studied with Paul Ricoeur and Maurice Merleau-Ponty. He has extensively studied Husserl, in particular rethinking the core idea or "*shibboleth*" of phenomenology, i.e. intentionality. In this reworking, he has made extensive use of French phenomenologists, especially Merleau-Ponty, Foucault, and Levinas.

Waldenfels formulates intentionality as the grasping of "something *as* something." This we accomplish not actively, as in classical intentionality (to think is to think something, to want is to want something, etc.), but rather by pathos. In other words, we are affected by something, taken by it, called by it. Attention happens when something occurs to us, when we are struck by something, he believes. He writes:

> Behind intentional acts, there appear events that overcome or happen to us. Those events belong neither to a first-person perspective as subjective acts that we perform, nor to the third-person perspective . . . from the very beginning I am involved, but not under the title of a responsible author or agent.
>
> (Waldenfels, 2011, p. 46)

Like the *moi* in Levinas, more passive than all passivity, Waldenfels finds subjectivity sub-jected generally. We might say he creates, on purpose or not, the conceptual context for the ethical receptivity and responsivity he and Levinas both describe.

Waldenfels defines the human as a creature who responds. He often cites philosopher and communication theorist Paul Watzlawick (1968, p. 32), who liked to say, "*Man kann nicht nicht kommunizieren*" (one cannot not answer). In other words, even a refusal to respond is a response, as playwright Robert Bolt's Cromwell explained to Thomas More's jury:

> Gentlemen of the Jury, there are many kinds of silence. Consider first the silence of a man when he is dead. Let us say we go into the room where is lying: . . . What do we hear? Silence. What does it betoken, this silence? Nothing. This is silence, pure and simple. But consider another case. Suppose I were to draw a dagger from my sleeve and make to kill the prisoner with it, and suppose their lordships there, instead of crying out for me to stop or crying out for help to stop me, maintained their silence. That would betoken! So silence, can, according to circumstances, speak.
>
> (Bolt, 1962, p. 151)

Thomas More, of course, insisted that his silence said nothing in this case.

Undoing normalization: why we need radical ethics

When the suffering of others becomes routine, turning into "collateral damage" in wars or in the name of economic progress, the voices of the vulnerable go silent, forgotten, dissociated. Many have observed that normalizing is a response to those who seem far away and thus unrelated to us. Though it can form a useful defense to our own suffering ("so it goes"), as a reaction to others' pain and loss, normalizing can shock the sufferer in its cruelty. A form of blaming the victim, normalizing suggests that expressing distress, even in the face of devastating losses and traumatic violence, amounts to self-pity. Buck up, after all! No pain, no gain.

Normalizing, of course, may intend to serve solidarity and compassion, and can even do so. In the face of shame, humiliation, and self-blame, one sometimes helps by acknowledging one's common humanity: "We eldest children are often held responsible for . . . ." "We who have been raped tend to feel . . . ." Such normalizing helps only if it does not erase difference and personal experience, if it stays close to the other without taking a know-it-all (*Besserwisser)* attitude. Asked how she could have risked her life in Cambodia to save a mother trying to nurse an already dead baby, Lane Gerber's patient told him (Gerber, 2018): "When people hear each other's pain and talk together, then the suffering calls to them and reminds them that they have different stories, yet they are all people" (p. 401). Non-indifference allows suffering to call out to us, to command us.

More often, however, normalizing reduces the other to the same (Levinas, 1979). Losing the capacity to see the homeless ones nearby or to hear the suffering of the climate refugees on television, we normalize their suffering. Gerber (2018) addresses professionals:

> What fears do we as clinicians have in straying from the path of a non-seeing normality due to the necessities of maintaining our façade of professional

respectability and staying on insurance panels? Isn't the medical model and the demand for evidence-based therapy in many ways an unethical view of human existence, given the political suffering all around us?

(p. 405)

These are hard but necessary questions, similar to those that keep us quiet about the climate emergency, already causing traumatic dislocations and violence to the world's most vulnerable, while we professional normalizers find ourselves unable to see, hear, or speak the devastation all around us. Robert Jay Lifton (Lifton, 2017) calls our posture "malignant normality." Its opposite is vulnerability to others' suffering, a sense of ethical responsibility that places the other first. We need to tune up our ethical hearing.

Notes

1 An early version of this thought is attributed to Greek historian Hesiod (700 B.C.E.).
2 Antonyms include superficial, trivial, ignorable. I might add gradualist, moderationist.
3 Though I was not the first to use the expression "intersubjective vulnerability" (Ipp, 2006; Sussillo, 2005) (Pizer & Pizer, 2006), and have no idea whether I unconsciously borrowed it, the concept became important in my transition to radical ethics, where I found this idea front and center in the work of both Løgstrup and Levinas. Lewis Aron (Aron, 2016) has been an important kindred spirit for me in this emphasis.
4 For an extensive and thought-provoking consideration of this basic idea in Løgstrup, see Reinders (2007).
5 This kind of infinite responsibility tends to worry psychoanalysts, who may call it masochism. See (Orange, 2016)
6 I use "radical ethics" precisely to avoid attributing to Levinas, or to Levinas throughout his writings, what he and others have brought me to think. As Bernasconi notes, and I too had noticed, in his later years, Levinas spoke more often of "holiness."
7 www.youtube.com/watch?v=Zvnk6moRmEA
8 Erikson thought this stage extended only to age 65, when old age and the stage of ego integrity began. Today, I know people clearly involved in generativity well into their 90s.
9 John L. Roberts (Roberts, 2018) writes of "traumatic ethics."
10 An earlier and shorter version of this section formed a lecture at Psychology and the Other, Cambridge, MA, 2017.
11 I write "implicating" rather than "implied" here because Løgstrup seems to mean, as does Levinas, that the other's vulnerability accuses me, implicates me.
12 It is tempting here to enter a discourse about sacrifice, so fiercely and convincingly challenged by Biblical scholars Joanna Dewey (Dewey, 2011) and Nancy Jay (Jay, 1992), who link sacrifice to paternalism and the silencing of women. Løgstrup's examples and concepts concern, instead, service and care, tasks he does not consign to women.
13 Patrick Stokes (Stokes, 2016) writes of the need for an alternative to Kantian ethics, and to what Stokes calls "the remorselessly calculative character of utilitarianism" (p. 140), the two most prominent forms of rationalistic ethics (142).
14 In a similar vein, Kees van Kooten Niekerk writes: "They [the sovereign expressions of life] are spontaneous modes of response that benefit other persons, or enhance communication with them, and they are sovereign insofar as they precede, or break through, our selfishness and express themselves in our lives. They dethrone our sovereign selves, so to speak" (Niekerk, 1999, p. 424).

15 Compare the attitude of Sigmund Freud, in his notes to the Freud-Fließ correspondence: "'Saintliness' is something based on the fact that, for the sake of the larger community, human beings have sacrificed some of their freedom to indulge in sexual perversions" (Freud, 1985, pp. 209).

References

Arendt, H. (1968). *Men in dark times*. New York: Harcourt.

Aron, L. (2016). Mutual Vulnerability: An Ethic of Clinical Practice. In D. Goodman & E. Severson (Eds.), *The ethical turn: Otherness and subjectivity in contemporary psychoanalysis* (pp. 19–41). London and New York: Routledge.

Balint, M. (1979). *The basic fault: Therapeutic aspects of regression*. New York: Brunner/Mazel.

Baraitser, L. (2008). Mum's the Word: Intersubjectivity, Alterity, and the Maternal Subject. *Studies in Gender and Sexuality, 9*, 86–110.

Bauman, Z. (1993). *Postmodern ethics*. Cambridge, MA: Blackwell Publishers.

Bauman, Z. (2007). The Liquid Modern Adventures of "the Sovereign Expressions of Life." In S. Andersen & K. V. K. Niekerk (Eds.), *Concern for the other: Perspectives on the ethics of K.E. L?gstrup*. Notre Dame, IN: University of Notre Dame Press.

Benjamin, J. (1988). *The bonds of love: Psychoanalysis, feminism, and the problem of domination* (1st ed.). New York: Pantheon Books.

Benjamin, J. (2010). Can We Recognize Each Other? Response to Donna Orange. *International Journal of Psychoanalytic Self Psychology, 5*, 244–256.

Benjamin, J. (2018). *Beyond doer and done to: Recognition theory, intersubjectivity and the third*. London and New York: Routledge, Taylor & Francis Group.

Bernasconi, R. (2012). Levinas's Ethical Critique of Levinasian Ethics. In S. Davidson & D. Perpich. *Totality and Infinity at 50* (pp. 253–269). Pittsburgh: Duquesne University Press.

Bernstein, R. J. (2002). *Radical evil: A philosophical interrogation*. Cambridge, UK and Malden, MA: Polity Press and Blackwell.

Bolt, R. (1962). *A man for all seasons: A play in two acts*. New York: Random House.

Buber, M., & Buber Agassi, J. (1999). *Martin Buber on psychology and psychotherapy: Essays, letters, and dialogue*. New York: Syracuse University Press.

Butler, J. (2000). Longing for Recognition. *Studies in Gender and Sexuality, 1*(3), 271–290.

Butler, J. (2004). *Precarious life: The powers of mourning and violence*. London and New York: Verso.

Butler, J. (2010). *Frames of war: When is life grievable?* (Pbk. ed.). London and New York: Verso.

Critchley, S. (2007). *Infinitely demanding: Ethics of commitment, politics of resistance*. London and New York: Verso.

Dewey, J. (2011). Sacrifice No More. *Biblical Theology Bulliten, 41*, 1–8.

Dufourmantelle, A. (2011). *Éloge du risque*. Paris: Payot.

Dufourmantelle, A., Payne, K., Sallé, V., & Malabou, C. (2018). *Power of gentleness: Meditations on the risk of living* (1st ed.). New York: Fordham University Press.

Erikson, E. H. (1974). *Dimensions of a new identity*. New York: Norton.

Fink, H., & Stern, R. (2017). *What is ethically demanded? K. E. Løgstrup's philosophy of moral life*. Notre Dame: University of Notre Dame Press.

Freud, S., et al. (1985). *The complete letters of Sigmund Freud to Wilhelm Fliess, 1887-1904.* Cambridge, MA: Belknap Press of Harvard University Press.

Gerber, L. (2018). Hidden Injuries: Stories of Social Class, Politics, and the Face of the Other. *Psychoanalysis, Self, and Context, 13*(4), 398–408.

Ghent, E. (1990). Masochism, Submission, Surrender: Masochism as a Perversion of Surrender. *Contemporary Psychoanalysis, 26,* 108–136.

Greenberg, J. R., & Mitchell, S. A. (1983). *Object relations in psychoanalytic theory.* Cambridge, MA: Harvard University Press.

Haidt, J. (2012). *The righteous mind: Why good people are divided by politics and religion* (1st ed.). New York: Pantheon Books.

Heschel, A. J. (1962). *The prophets* (1st ed.). New York: Harper & Row.

Hobbes, T., & Brooke, C. (2017). *Leviathan.* Harmondsworth, Middlesex: Penguin Books.

Honneth, A., & NetLibrary Inc. (1996). *The struggle for recognition the moral grammar of social conflicts studies in contemporary German social thought* (1st ed., p. xxi, 215 p.). Retrieved from www.columbia.edu/cgi-bin/cul/resolve?clio4243368.

Ipp, H. R. (2006). The Dialectics of Analytic Disclosure: Discussion of Barbara Pizer's Paper. *Contemporary Psychoanalysis, 42*(1), 47–53.

Jaenicke, C. (2008). *The risk of relatedness: Intersubjectivity theory in clinical practice.* Lanham: Jason Aronson.

Jaenicke, C. (2011). *Change in psychoanalysis: An analyst's reflections on the therapeutic relationship.* New York: Routledge and Taylor & Francis Group.

Jay, N. B. (1992). *Throughout your generations forever: Sacrifice, religion, and paternity.* Chicago: University of Chicago Press.

Klein, N. (2019). The Battle Lines Have Been Drawn on the Green New Deal. *The Intercept* (February 13). Retrieved from https://theintercept.com/2019/02/13/green-new-deal-proposal/.

Kohut, H. (1977). *The restoration of the self.* New York: International Universities Press.

Levinas, E. (1979). *Totality and infinity: An essay on exteriority.* The Hague and Boston Hingham, MA: M. Nijhoff Publishers and Distribution for the U.S. and Canada and Kluwer Boston.

Levinas, E. (1998). *Otherwise than being, or, beyond essence.* Pittsburgh, PA: Duquesne University Press.

Levinas, E. (1999). *Alterity and transcendence.* New York: Columbia University Press.

Levinas, E., & Nemo, P. (1985). *Ethics and infinity* (1st ed.). Pittsburgh: Duquesne University Press.

Lifton, R. J. (2017). *The climate swerve: Reflections on mind, hope, and survival.* New York: New Press.

Loewald, H. W. (1980). *Papers on psychoanalysis.* New Haven, CT: Yale University Press.

Løgstrup, K. E. (1997). *The ethical demand.* Notre Dame, IN: University of Notre Dame Press.

Løgstrup, K. E. (2007). *Beyond the ethical demand* (English language ed.). Notre Dame, IN: University of Notre Dame Press.

Markell, P. (2003). *Bound by recognition.* Princeton, NJ: Princeton University Press.

Mitchell, S. A. (2000). *Relationality: From attachment to intersubjectivity.* Hillsdale, NJ: Analytic Press.

Museum, N. (Producer). (2011). Judith Butler: Precarious Life: The Obligations of Proximity. Retrieved from www.youtube.com/watch?v=KJT69AQtDtg.

Niekerk, K. (1999). Review Article on Knud Ejler Løgstrup: The Ethical Demand. *Ethical Theory and Moral Practice*, *2*, 415–426.

Orange, D. M. (1995). *Emotional understanding: Studies in psychoanalytic epistemology.* New York: Guilford Press.

Orange, D. M. (2008a). Recognition as: Intersubjective Vulnerability in the Psychoanalytic Dialogue. *International Journal of Psychoanalytic Self Psychology*, *3*, 178–194.

Orange, D. M. (2008b). Whose Shame Is It Anyway? Lifeworlds of Humiliation and Systems of Restoration. *Contemporary Psychoanalysis*, *44*, 83–100.

Orange, D. M. (2009a). Intersubjective Systems Theory: A Fallibilist's Journey. In N. VanDerHeide & W. Coburn (Eds.), *Self and systems: Explorations in contemporary self psychology* (pp. 237–248). Boston: Blackwell.

Orange, D. M. (2009b). Kohut Memorial Lecture: Attitudes, Values and Intersubjective Vulnerability. *International Journal of Psychoanalytic Self Psychology*, *4*, 235–253.

Orange, D. M. (2010a). Revisiting Mutual Recognition: Responding to Ringstrom, Benjamin, and Slavin. *International Journal of Psychoanalytic Self Psychology*, *5*, 293–306.

Orange, D. M. (2010b). Recognition as: Intersubjective Vulnerability in the Psychoanalytic Dialogue. *International Journal of Psychoanalysis Self Psychology*, *5*(3), 227–243.

Orange, D. M. (2010c). *Thinking for clinicians: Philosophical resources for contemporary psychoanalysis and the humanistic psychotherapies.* New York: Routledge.

Orange, D. M. (2016). *Nourishing the inner life of clinicians and humanitarians: The ethical turn in psychoanalysis.* London and New York: Routledge.

Orange, D. M., Atwood, G. E., & Stolorow, R. D. (1997). *Working intersubjectively: Contextualism in psychoanalytic practice.* Hillsdale, NJ: Analytic Press.

Orange, D. M., Stolorow, R. D., & Atwood, G. E. (1998). Hermeneutics, Intersubjectivity Theory, and Psychoanalysis. *Journal of the American Psychoanalytic Association*, *46*(2), 568–571.

Pilecki, W. (2012). *The Auschwitz volunteer: Beyond bravery* (1st ed.). Los Angeles, CA: Aquila Polonica Pub.

Pizer, B., & Pizer, S. A. (2006). "The Gift of an Apple or the Twist of an Arm": Negotiation in Couples and Couple Therapy. *Psychoanalytic Dialogues*, *16*(1), 71–92.

Reinders, H. (2007). Donum or Datum? K.E. Løgstrup's Religious Account of the Gift of Life. In S. Anderson & K. Niekerk (Eds.), *Concern for the other: Perspectives on the ethics of K.E. Løgstrup* (pp. 177–206). Notre Dame, IN: University of Notre Dame Press.

Ringstrom, P. A. (2010). Commentary on Donna Orange's, "Recognition as: Intersubjective Vulnerability in the Psychoanalytic Dialogue". *International Journal of Psychoanalysis Self Psychology*, *5*(3), 257–273.

Roazen, P. (2002). The Problem of Silence: Training Analyses. *International Forum of Psychoanalysis*, *11*(1), 73–77.

Roberts, J. L. (2018). *Trauma and the ontology of the modern subject: Historical studies in philosophy, psychology, and psychoanalysis* (p. 1 online resource). London and New York: Routledge, Taylor & Francis Group.

Slavin, M. (2010). On Recognizing the Psychoanalytic Perspective of the Other: A Discussion of "Recognition as: Intersubjective Vulnerability in the Psychoanalytic Dialogue," by Donna Orange. *International Journal of Psychoanalytic Self Psychology*, *5*, 274–292.

Stern, R. H. (2017). Freedom from the Self: Luther and Løgstrup on Sin as "Incurvatus in Se". Retrieved from www.reformation500.uk/userfiles/files/Robert%20Stern%20Symposium%20%20St%20Margaret%27s.pdf.

Stokes, P. (2016). The Problem of Spontaneous Goodness: From Kierkegaard to Løgstrup (via Zwangzi and Eckhart). *Contintental Philosophy Review*, *49*, 139–159.

Stolorow, R. D., Atwood, G. E., & Branchaft, B. (1994). *The intersubjective perspective.* Northvale, NJ: J. Aronson.

Stolorow, R. D., Brandchaft, B., & Atwood, G. E. (1987). *Psychoanalytic treatment: An intersubjective approach.* Hillsdale, NJ: Analytic Press.

Sussillo, M. V. (2005). Good Grief: What Becomes of the Lost Relationship: Reply to Commentaries. *Psychoanalytic Dialogues*, *15*(4), 559–566.

Taylor, C., & Gutmann, A. (1994). *Multiculturalism: Examining the politics of recognition.* Princeton, NJ: Princeton University Press.

Toulmin, S. (1958). *The uses of argument.* Cambridge: Cambridge University Press.

Waldenfels, B. (2011). *Phenomenology of the alien: Basic concepts.* Evanston, IL: Northwestern University Press.

Watson, J. (2005). *Caring science as sacred science* (1st ed.). Philadelphia: F.A. Davis Co.

Watzlawick, P., et al. (1968). *Pragmatics of human communication: A study of interactional patterns, pathologies, and paradoxes.* London: Faber.

Winnicott, D. W. (1965). *The maturational processes and the facilitating environment: Studies in the theory of emotional development.* New York: International Universities Press.

Woodruff, P. (2014). *Reverence: Renewing a forgotten virtue* (2nd ed.). New Nork, NY: Oxford University Press.

Chapter 7

Ethical hearing
Demand and enigma

This final chapter is dedicated in gratitude to the memory of Lewis Aron, theorist of mutual vulnerability and practitioner of relational inclusiveness in a spirit inherited from those who recite: "Hear, O Israel . . ."

Psychoanalysis, like other cultural forms, tends to silence dissenting voices. Beginning with Freud's "that is not psychoanalysis!", we find those who think otherwise relegated to the shadows, marginalized, disparaged, even cast out and excommunicated. Though more patients have joined the ranks of the treatable, many of their therapists and analysts share an allergy to developmental concerns, and thus to vulnerability, the very core of the ethical. Even the creation of relational psychoanalysis has not mitigated this tendency, though two new books (Aron, Grand, & Slochower, 2018a, 2018b) from within this school are mounting a challenge to some of the more dogmatic tendencies in relational psychoanalysis. My contribution to the second of these volumes appears in condensed form here, as it leads us into our closing considerations on silence, hearing, and radical ethics.

Unsilencing vulnerability in contemporary psychoanalysis

Nothing, William James loved to remind us, is so practical as a good theory. But our theories, as his friend Charles Sanders Peirce taught relentlessly,[1] need holding lightly as they always need correcting. The "contrite fallibilism" in which the pragmatists believed serves us well as we study the history of psychoanalysis, including the shorter history of relational approaches. It comes with a robust optimism that we can always learn more, both from our patients and from each other, within a community of scholars that embraces those who speak many languages, and who teach in ways we may not initially appreciate, verbally and nonverbally. In our attempts to improve our theories, we may make false steps, but we can try again.

Here I will describe two related aspects of the theorizing of leading relational theorists Stephen Mitchell (1946–2000) and Philip Bromberg (1931–), suggest where I believe residual problems lie, and suggest a tentative solution using resources from my two disciplines of philosophy and psychoanalysis.

When Stephen Mitchell died, he had just completed a decade of intensive study of the work of Hans Loewald, his favorite psychoanalytic writer. Their rereading of Freud shows not only in the first two chapters of *Relationality* (Mitchell, 2000), but in its entire developmental cast. Mitchell, author of the disparaging phrase "developmental tilt" (Mitchell, 1984), had reversed himself, seeming no longer concerned about infantilizing patients, and now – with Loewald, Bowlby, and Winnicott – envisioned psychoanalysis itself as a developmental process. What has become of Mitchell's reversal since his death? Perhaps the clinical thinking of Jody Davies, with her receptivity to the younger voices of the patient, as well as the Winnicottian work of Slochower and Ogden, have taken up this reversal. The wildly popular turn to "multiple self-state" talk, however, I regard as ambiguous and problematical. While it advances our sense of the complexity of experience and replaces simple talk of regression, it may also occlude a developmental sensibility like that possessed in common by Loewald, Winnicott, and Kohut, all voices needed within the relational chorus.

I will further suggest that this shared developmental sensibility, toward which Mitchell was firmly turning in his last years and which has faded again since we lost him, is a foundational element of the "ethical turn" in psychoanalysis, being written about by Cushman (2007), Layton (2009), Leary (2000), Baraitser (2008) and others. Psychoanalysis as process of mourning and integration relates closely to moral integrity, courage, and the embrace of vulnerability, personal and intersubjective.

In this context, I will mention the disdain for an ethic of care in some relational circles, as well as the exclusionary "not relational enough" and "that's not psychoanalysis" attitudes that betray the anti-developmental tilt.

In other words, my essay will advocate compassion for the vulnerable and suffering child within our patients and ourselves, as well as toward the burning world within which we are all living and dying.

Mitchell: the influence of Loewald and the developmental turn

Like most analysts trained in the interpersonalist tradition, the young Stephen Mitchell lost no love on developmentalists like D.W. Winnicott and Heinz Kohut. Though the critique began in his revolutionary book with Jay Greenberg (Greenberg & Mitchell, 1983), Mitchell published his now famous paper (Mitchell, 1984) on "developmental tilt," making his objections much clearer, just a few months later. By "developmental tilt," he meant "accommodative strategy" (in the book, "mixed-model"); that is, keeping drive theory and the Oedipus complex intact, but installing object relations earlier and deeper.[2] For him, primary practitioners of this approach now included Klein, Balint, Mahler, Guntrip, Winnicott, and Kohut. These theorists, he believed, saw relational needs as infantile and regressive. Their practice, in the younger Mitchell's view, tended to see patients as passive victims of early deprivation, and analysts as all-good providers. In Mitchell's view, the more consistent theorists he preferred – Fairbairn, Sullivan, and Bowlby – understood relational needs, and even more mature dependency needs, as simply human. Unfortunately, he thought, their theorizing lost all the elegance and complexity of Freudian theory and tradition. In 1984, prior to the full development of his own relational perspective, Mitchell simply laid out this drawback with great clarity; he did not yet suggest his alternative concept.

In the next years, Mitchell's important books (Mitchell, 1988, 1993, 1997) developed the *relational matrix* as the theoretical and clinical basis of what was coming to be called relational psychoanalysis. In 1987 he defined it thus:

> The relational model rests on the premise that the repetitive patterns within human experience are not derived, as in the drive model, from a pursuit of secret pleasures (nor, as in Freud's post 1920 understanding, from the automatic workings of the death instinct), but from a pervasive tendency to preserve the continuity, connections, familiarity of one's personal world. There is a powerful need to preserve an abiding sense of oneself as associated with, positioned in terms of, related to, a matrix of other people, both in terms of actual transactions as well as internal presences. The basic relational configurations have, by definition, three dimensions – the self, the other, and the space between them. There is no "object" in a psychologically meaningful sense without some particular sense of oneself in relation to it. There is no "self", in a psychologically meaningful sense, in isolation, outside a matrix of relations with others. Neither the self nor the object are meaningful dynamic concepts without presupposing some sense of psychical space in which they interact, in which they do things with or to each other. These dimensions are interwoven in a subtle fashion, knitting together the analysand's subjective experience and psychological world.
>
> (Mitchell, 1987, p. 403)

The word matrix appears twice here: "a matrix of other people" and "a matrix of relations with others," as if the matrix were always contemporary. But earlier, in discussions of Kohut, Mitchell had used the expression "maternal-child matrix" (Mitchell, 1979) and of Winnicott, "infant/mother matrix" (Mitchell, 1983). So, his capacity to absorb the profoundly developmental psychoanalysis of Hans Loewald, and to identify his relational matrix with Loewald's "primordial density," should not surprise us.

Arguably, what has developed since in contemporary psychoanalysis – whether it uses this language or not – stands in relation to this idea of the relational matrix.[3] Easy to reference is the work of those who write of thirdness in one form or another (Aron, 2006; Benjamin, 2004; Gerson, 2009; Knoblauch, 1999; Muller, 1999; Ogden, 1994), though clearly these authors differ widely in their use of the term. (None of these authors, however, to my ears, gives thirdness the profound developmental cast that Mitchell's matrix had by the end of his life). In addition, pervasive assumptions of mutual engagement, involvement, and responsibility in analysis owe their origin to Mitchell's relational matrix. His invisible influence may pervade us as insistently as does Freud's.

His pioneering voice, however, may mask his quieter path as a devoted and scholarly student of the history of psychoanalysis, one that emerged clearly in his *Relationality*, a book that appeared so close to his death that most of us never had the opportunity to engage him in conversation about the changes in his thinking that it signaled. He devoted the first two chapters of this book to the work of Hans Loewald, whose work he had been reading and rereading for more than a decade (Mitchell, 2004, p. 828) with great "joy." He told us that Loewald had become "my favorite psychoanalytic writer." Who was this Loewald, and who was he to Mitchell?

Loewald gathered up the brilliant fragments of Freud's thinking – pieces Freud had left lying around as he inventively confronted new clinical and theoretical conundrums – and used what he learned from Heidegger to weave them into a whole.[4] Loewald (2000, p. 186) saw us always trying to refind our original unitary experience, our "primordial density" – the same one Winnicott studied as "no such thing as an infant" – from which we later differentiate as we become ourselves in relation to others. (Balint would have called it the "harmonious interpenetrating mixup" [Balint, 1960, p. 39]). Loewald reinterpreted drive theory much as contemporary evolutionary biology does, not as a theory of struggle, but as Eros (Lear, 1998), a striving to refind the original oneness. Instincts for him emerge from the integration of infant and environment. Basic concepts in psychoanalytic theory lose their strangeness in Loewald's hands – in part because he read and thought in Freud's German, and constantly attempted to escape what we might call the standardized edition. "Cathexis" becomes organizing activity, bonding, sometimes even love. "Primary process" becomes the richness of our ongoing access to our earliest and embodied mother-infant experience, constantly alternating with the differentiated, more organized and linguistic life. "Secondary" in Loewald's view gains the connotation of secondary as coming later in the process of psychological organization and integration of experience. "Primary process" completely loses its shamefulness and becomes the rich resource of imaginative, cultural, and even, perhaps, transcendent life. A close reader of Freud who never left the American Psychoanalytic Association and never founded a school of thought, Loewald recognized the baby-watchers and Winnicott as his kindred spirits.

No wonder. As a phenomenologist, Loewald had profoundly rethought temporality. Past, present, and future interpenetrate so much that he could welcome primary process as the source of our creativity and of religious life. (He repeatedly expressed regret that Freud could see so little constructive use for religion).

How did Loewald accomplish all this rethinking? *Nachträglich*; that is, backwards. He took a late text of Freud, from *Civilization and Its Discontents*, and used it to read everything that came before, as if to say, "Here is the deeper meaning in Freud that he would have developed, if he had had time." Freud wrote:

An infant at the breast does not as yet distinguish his ego from the external world as the source of the sensations flowing in upon him. He gradually learns to do so, in response to various promptings. . . . In this way, then, the ego detaches itself from the external world. Or, to put it more correctly, originally the ego includes everything, later it separates off an external world from itself.

(Freud & Strachey, 2005, pp. 66–8)

This text in hand, Loewald relationalized Freud and argued in his most famous paper (Loewald, 1960) that the therapeutic power of psychoanalysis resulted from the relational, i.e. transferential, transformation of old miseries. The analyst, far from a detached and distant mirror, makes himself available to the patient for the ego-developmental process of transference, of which Loewald wrote:

Without such transference – of the intensity of the unconscious, of the infantile ways of experiencing life which have no language and little organization, but the indestructibility and power of the origins of life – to the preconscious and to present-day life and contemporary objects – without such transference, or to the extent to which such transference miscarries, human life becomes sterile and an empty shell. On the other hand, the unconscious needs present-day external reality (objects) and present-day psychic reality (the preconscious) for its own continuity, lest it be condemned to live the shadow-life of ghosts or to destroy life.

(Loewald, 2000, p. 250)

The most famous passage in this paper, so important to Mitchell that he named his paper on Loewald (Mitchell, 1998) after it, is always worth rereading:

The transference neurosis, in the technical sense of the establishment and resolution of it in the analytic process, is due to the blood of recognition which the patient's unconscious is given to taste – so that the old ghosts may reawaken to life. Those who know ghosts tell us that they long to be released from their ghost-life and led to rest as ancestors. As ancestors they live forth in the present generation, while as ghosts they are compelled to haunt the present generation with their shadow-life. Transference is pathological in so far as the unconscious is a crowd of ghosts [my favorite definition of unconsciousness], and this is the beginning of the transference neurosis in analysis: ghosts of the unconscious, imprisoned by defenses but haunting the patient in the dark of his defenses and symptoms, are allowed to taste blood, are let loose. In the daylight of analysis the ghosts of the unconscious are laid and led to rest as ancestors whose power is taken over and transformed into the newer intensity of present life, of the secondary process and contemporary objects.

(Loewald, 2000, pp. 248–9)

First, like the infant researchers, particularly Daniel Stern (Stern, 1985), Loewald believed that we organize and heal ourselves through "internalization," especially in the areas that Freudians speak about in the region of superego development. No longer compelled like an automaton, the growing child or adult has made moral values her or his own: "A sense of self begins to emerge with increasing internalization, leading to the development of a sense of self-responsibility with the formation of the superego and the shouldering of guilt" (Loewald, 1985, p. 437). In analysis, he believed, the work of mourning indispensibly linked up with resuming the processes of internalization.

> The relinquishment of external objects and their internalization involves a process of separation, of loss and of restitution in many ways similar to mourning. During analysis, problems of separation and mourning come to the fore in a specific way at times of interruption and most particularly in the terminal phases of treatment.
>
> (Loewald, 2007, p. 1114)

Mourning internalizes what must be relinquished, and integrates a personal life, a moral life, as he would later say.

Now, in the 1990s, in addition to Sullivan and Fairbairn, Mitchell had found a third (after Sullivan and Fairbairn) proto-relational theorist, one who had become his "favorite psychoanalytic writer." Loewald had linked all the disparate experiences with which analysts and patients struggle with the original oneness, and understood the analytic process itself as linking. Mitchell elegantly condensed Loewald's account of psychopathology as the primal density lost:

> in Loewald's view, psychopathology, most broadly conceived, represents an imbalance between the centrifugal and centripetal forces of mind. In psychosis, the primal density undermines the capacity to make adaptive, normative distinctions between inside and outside, self and other, actuality and fantasy, past and present. In neurosis or, Loewald occasionally suggests, the normative adaptation to our scientistic, hypertechnologized world, the constituents of mind have drifted too far apart from their original dense unity: Inside and outside become separate, impermeable domains; self and other are experienced in isolation from each other; actuality is disconnected from fantasy; and the past has become remote from a shallow, passionless present.
>
> (Mitchell, 1998, p. 826)[5]

Mitchell, restored to continuity with Freud by his immersion in Loewald, began to study attachment theory seriously, and to read Winnicott with an ear for "the core of the individual in a solitary privacy" (Mitchell, 2000, p. 87), for a similar sense of an individual's development, as well as for the differences regarding illusion and fantasy. As had Ferenczi before him in "Child Analysis in the Analysis of Adults" (Ferenczi, 1931), Mitchell and his relational psychoanalysis could now unsilence a developmental sensibility in our work, along with the younger voices of our patients. Let us now consider how a clinical theory may silence ethical hearing by denying its very possibility.

Bromberg on multiple self-states: hearing both parts and center

Even before Greenberg and Mitchell (1983) shook the world for so many of us – or rather, gave us a way to think about our doubts and hopes – Philip Bromberg was writing about regression (1979) – a subversive activity for an interpersonalist. While corresponding, as we now know, with the radical Merton Gill (Bromberg, 2011), he surfaced a developmental question, whether considered classically or from an object relations point of view. At this early juncture, Bromberg seems to have seen regression as indicating almost precisely the developmental view of psychoanalysis that I am attributing to Loewald and to the later Mitchell:

> But regardless of how "deep" the regression is, I am suggesting that regression in the sense that I am using it here, is not a concept limited to analytic patients having severe ego impairment, but is a fundamental component to psychoanalysis in general, and the interpersonal approach in particular. The ego (or self) in order to grow, must voluntarily allow itself to become less than intact – to regress. Empirically, this is one way of defining regression in the service of the ego.
>
> (Bromberg, 1979, p. 653)[6]

Trained at the William Alanson White institute, Mitchell and Bromberg in the late 1970s and early 1980s were working their way toward integration of psychoanalytic perspectives from similar beginnings. Bromberg later writes (Bromberg, 2013) of his affection for Mitchell, and we may assume, Mitchell's for him. Adrienne Harris writes of this period:

> One of the fascinating puzzles for me has been the sea change in Mitchell in reapproaching problems of development and early experience, that is, his move away, at the end of his life, from the antidevelopmental tilt of his first relational work. I see now that Bromberg's work on regression was part of the preamble to those shifts in Mitchell. Certainly later on, the reemergence of Bowlby and attachment theory played a role in changes in Mitchell's preoccupations, but what Bromberg was doing, we can see, was crucial for his own work, but I also believe contributed to shifts in Mitchell's as well.
>
> (Harris, 2011, p. 242)

Like most readers of Mitchell's last work, Harris here either misses or ignores his "favorite psychoanalytic writer," Loewald.[7] Still, she makes a fascinating suggestion: The possibility that Bromberg planted something in his conversations with Mitchell, something that Mitchell early on could not take up but later did with a vengeance, and something that Bromberg himself later downplayed in favor of the less developmental concept of dissociation. Whether she would see in her own idea what I do, I cannot say, but nonetheless, I find it fruitful for tracing what seems to have occurred.

Beyond popular, multiple self-state theory (Bromberg, 1991, 1994, 1996) has become axiomatic in contemporary relational psychoanalysis and beyond, in disciplines like religious studies (Cooper-White, 2007). In an amazing metaphor, Bromberg imagines different, dissociated regions in the patient to which the analyst gains passports. The basic experience to which this theory refers, described originally by Harry Stack Sullivan (1926, pp. 1–15), rejects and dissociates particular emotions, motivations, actions, or traumatic residues. Bromberg explains the goal for such treatment:

> Optimal mental functioning consists in a person's being able to access multiple self-states conflictually, and psychoanalytic treatment must provide a favorable context for facilitating internal communication between disjunctive states that are kept sequestered from each other dissociatively.
>
> (Bromberg, 2009, p. 350)

Writers of clinical and applied psychoanalysis have used this concept routinely in recent years, e.g. (Bass, 2002; Chefetz, 2003; Davies, 1996; Harris, 1996; Hirsch, 1997; Yerushalmi, 2001), without much attention to what may be lost, or to their corollary assumption that such talk implies that no central, organizing, or responsible personality exists. Yet Bromberg himself spoke, at least in the early years of this theory, quite otherwise:

> We count on the existence in the patient of a cohesive core personality that feels to us and to the patient more or less like the same person regardless of moment-to-moment shifts in self-state, alterations in mental functioning, or even the unanticipated emergence of dissociated phenomena that Sullivan (1953) calls "not-me" experience.
>
> (Bromberg, 1991, p. 403)

Matters become confusing, both phenomenologically and clinically, when extreme splits occur – with amnesia, as those who work clinically with survivors of torture and combat, extreme child abuse, genocides, and the like, can attest. Are we still speaking of the multiple self-states these writers so easily attribute to all of us? Where is the unifying personality when the spouse and children say, "I don't know him anymore"? What about the patient who returns the next day and remembers nothing whatever of the previous day's session in which she had relived a gang rape? Who is the patient, and who bears responsibility for what this patient promises, and does, and says? All these questions arise when we imagine that there exists, or does not exist, a central personality. In addition, of course, Bromberg and those he has inspired have developed extremely useful reflections on the intersubjective processes involved in many forms of dissociation, especially those we see in clinical work.

But we must note that these questions lie in different realms of discourse: 1) the philosophical and the ethical disputes about human identity that John Riker (2013) reviews for us, and that Charles Taylor laid out so masterfully in his *Sources of the Self* (Taylor, 1989); 2) the speculative (metapsychological) questions about what lies behind the clinical phenomena – a unitary totality or prime mover, a cluster of self-states, or both, an emergent personality organization, and so on; and 3) the experiential clinical phenomena themselves, as describable from both sides. Our difficulties, I think, lie in our failure to distinguish these.

Distinctions, however, are the stock in trade of philosophers, so here we go. Let us look first at dissociation, a word used at least since Pierre Janet. In current psychoanalysis, it has come to have a cluster of meanings that Ludwig Wittgenstein would have described as "family resemblance."[8] From full amnesia after an auto accident, to loss of memory while traveling because preoccupied with another problem, to rejection of aspects of one's emotional life as "not-me" – all these phenomena and more are being named dissociation. Multiple self-state theory, I would suggest, falls into a logical trap when it argues from a cluster of dissociative phenomena that have only a "family resemblance" with each other as if we could attribute this concept to everybody. The theory then seems to imply that humans cannot, *and should not*, strive for good-enough personality integration. This mode of clinical thinking tends to suggest that dialogue with ourselves cannot lead to some sense that "this is what *I* believe," and "these things are important to *me*." We will return to the ethical problems generated by this "cannot."

Secondly, let us turn to the evidence adduced for multiple self-state theory. Bromberg writes:

> There is now abundant evidence that the psyche does not start as an integrated whole, but is nonunitary in origin – a mental structure that begins and continues as a multiplicity of self-states that maturationally attain a feeling of coherence which overrides the awareness of discontinuity (Bromberg, 1993, p. 162). This leads to the experience of a cohesive sense of personal identity and the necessary illusion of being "one self."
>
> (Bromberg, 1994, p. 521)

And what, exactly, is this "abundant evidence"? He continues:

> For psychoanalysts, this view of the mind has been supported by psycho-analytically oriented infant studies such as those by Emde, Gaensbaure, and

Harmon (1976), Sander (1977), Stern (1985), Wolff (1987), and Beebe and Lachmann (1992), but the most direct support has come from nonanalytic empirical research into normal and pathological adult mental functioning – research representing a wide range of disciplines and research centers.

(p. 521)

He then goes on to cite the studies by Frank Putnam (Putnam, 1988) of extreme dissociation that would now be diagnosed as dissociative identity disorder and complex post-traumatic stress disorders, and argues from these that mind is essentially multiple and self-experience illusory.

The argument for contemporaneous multiplicity persuades because it establishes continuity between extreme psychopathology and everyday human experiences, just as Freud did when he invented psychoanalysis. Dramatic and traumatic suffering draw closer to our ordinary struggles. "We are all more simply human than otherwise." (Sullivan & Mullahy, 1948, p. 16). But in this case, we may need to hear the voice of Wittgenstein reminding us that the king in chess and the king of England function quite differently, though they share the same name. Not only dissociation may be a matter of family resemblances, but so may experiences of multiplicity generally.

Further, the "abundant evidence" from developmental studies for mind as multiple concurrent self-states, and mental health defined as the capacity to "stand in the spaces" between them, needs a close look. Unfortunately, Daniel Stern and Lou Sander are no longer with us, but we can consult their work. Stern's[9] classic work (1985) entirely concerns the human development of a sense of self, and to my reading, contains no hint that, at that time, he would have agreed that humans should give up on the project of personal integration. Yes, he differs with Winnicott and Loewald on the original oneness, but like them, pictures a human being always in search of integration. His later, more phenomenological work, on the developmental impact of the present-moment encounter and on the vitality affects, as well as his leadership of the attachment-focused Boston Process of Change Study Group, complexifies but does not abandon his earlier work.

Lou Sander, giant of infant research, worked, as does Bromberg, from the perspective of nonlinear self-organizing systems and complexity theories. For Sander, these theories best explained what he saw in development about identity emerging from recognition (Sander, 1995), and well accorded with what he had learned from Winnicott:

> I know of no better description of a process of recognition than that of the process Winnicott (1972) describes. He describes, and illustrates with many case examples, the interactive process between therapist and child that goes on as each alternates drawings in the game he calls "squiggles." Winnicott details the drawings by which each embellishes the squiggle of the other, within the context of Winnicott's observations, to bring them both to a moment of

shared awareness as the child becomes aware that another is aware of what the child is aware within. This is a moment of specificity in recognition that Winnicott called the "sacred moment" – a "moment of meeting" that involves a new coherence in the child's experiencing of both its inner and its outer worlds of awareness. The consultations Winnicott describes were often single diagnostic sessions, but if the "sacred moment" of being "known" was reached, there ensued a change in the child's self-regulatory organization that endured over many years, even from that single experience. Recurrence of such moments provides the conditions within which one comes to "know" oneself as one is "known." With recurrence and the brain's inherent construction of expectancy, it is a small step to Erikson's (1950) definition of identity as an "accrued confidence that inner sameness and continuity are matched by the sameness and continuity of one's meaning for others.

(p. 228)

Gradually, both Winnicott and Sander believed that, in good-enough developmental conditions, a sense of a "true self" – as contrasted with the "false self" of compliance – would prevail.

Where Bromberg generalizes from his observations "the normal nonlinearity of the human mind" (Bromberg, 1996, p. 529), and believes that clinically "what is required is that the multiple realities being held by different self-states find opportunity for linkage" (p. 543), Sander finds a lifelong relational search for Eriksonian identity. It seems a stretch to cite his thinking as evidence for Bromberg's views.

Beatrice Beebe and Frank Lachmann's thinking, closely related to that of Stern and Sander, similarly describes the development of coherence and incoherence of self-experience depending on the infant's relational situation. In contrast to multiple self-state theory, Lachmann draws a clinical theory that presumes:

a process model of self as singular, striving for integration, and temporally continuous. This self is never static, but is constantly being updated in interactions that require the regulation of affects, arousal, and perceptions in a context, and with a background, of responsive, contingent, mutual regulation. Shifting in different contexts, the integrated self can prioritize experiences, embrace a range of conflicts, and tolerate disparate affect states.

(Lachmann, 1996, p. 610)

Clearly Lachmann, like Stern and Sander, finds in infant research "abundant evidence" for complex self-experience always in process of integration, but he would reject the uses to which Bromberg and other adherents of multiple self-state theory are putting his work. (Actually, I believe Bromberg finds kinship with these infant researchers not because they provide evidence for multiple-self-state theory, but because he himself never really abandoned a developmental perspective; e.g. [Bromberg 1998, p. 90]).

Problems with multiple self-state theory

Beyond the weaknesses in the arguments adduced to support this theory, I believe it has serious inherent problems: 1) it returns relational psychoanalysis, even if unintentionally, to its early anti-developmental tilt; 2) it evades the problems of human finitude and mourning; and, worst of all, 3) it fails to ground and support ethical subjectivity. These are serious charges, so let us fill them out.

First, with important exceptions (Bass, 2009; Davies, 2009; Grand, 2010; Orange, 2011; Slochower, 2013),[10] it seems to me that relational psychoanalysis has largely returned to the anti-developmental tilt of the late 1980s, and forgotten the radical move of Mitchell's last years. Adopting a developmental tilt with Winnicott, Loewald, Kohut, Bowlby, Fairbairn, and the Mitchell of his last years, means seeing the analytic process itself as a developmental process. In the words of Heinrich Racker:

> I close this section on the analyst's internal position by saying that the patient can only be expected to accept the re-experiencing of childhood if the analyst is prepared to accept fully his new paternity, to admit fully affection for his new children, and to struggle for a new and better childhood, "calling upon all the available mental forces" (S. Freud, 1917). His task consists ideally in a constant and lively interest and continuous empathy with the patient's psychological happenings, in a metapsychological analysis of every mental expression and movement, his principal attention and energy being directed towards understanding the transference (towards the always present "new childhood") and overcoming its pathological aspects by means of adequate interpretations.
>
> (Racker, 1968, p. 33)

It seems safe to say that contemporary psychoanalysis (Mitchell-inspired relationalists, relational self-psychologists, contemporary Freudians, and others) generally agrees with Racker, though developmentalists' attitudes may be diversely expressed. Analysts begin to write of "analytic love" (Shaw, 2003), and to remember Sándor Ferenczi not only for experiments in mutual analysis, but for his unsilencing and full-throated advocacy of the child in the adult patient (Ferenczi, 1931, 1949). But backlash comes: At times, multiple self-state theory seems associated with a firm rejection of the ethics of care in psychoanalysis. Recently in New York, a prominent interpersonalist/relationalist author proclaimed: "I care for my children; I do not care for my patients!"

Multiple self-state theory, too, recognizes that many patients dissociate[11] – i.e., split themselves – to cope with relational trauma, often of developmental origin, very often transgenerationally transmitted. Indeed, in the service of unsilencing and liberation, the theory intends to explain how patients and analysts evoke and catalyze each other's splits. The theory's combined adherence to nonlinear temporality, combined with the here-and-now doctrine inherited from interpersonalist psychoanalysis, however, makes it difficult to see the analytic process itself as developmental. If development requires a linear concept of time – as it does not for Stern, Sander, Beebe and Lachmann, or Loewald – this theory can aim at no more than standing in the spaces (Bromberg, 1996) between one's self-states.

Moreover, as Rich Chefetz asks (Chefetz & Bromberg, 2004), and I wonder, especially reading Sue Grand (Grand, 2000), whether such "standing between" takes the extreme traumatic states of the soul-murdered (Shengold, 1989) or the drowned (Levi, 1988) seriously enough. Whether we work with perpetrators as Grand and other colleagues do, or with victims of malignant narcissists (Shaw, 2014) who believe themselves benevolent but treat us cruelly, questions of responsibility arise that stretch multiple self-state theory.

But what if development – as Stern, Sander, Beebe, and Lachmann all believed with Thelen and Smith's classic (Thelen & Smith, 1996) – is itself nonlinear and complex? What if the *Nachträglichkeit* left to us by Freud, and so widely studied today (Birksted-Breen, 2003; Dahl, 2010) can now be understood as intersubjective *Nachträglichkeit*, without complete loss of the search for personal integration and ethical integrity that seems so fragile in today's world? This topic deserves more development than space allows here.

Second, mourning and the recognition of finitude (Hoffman, 2000; Stolorow, 2007) require of each of us more integration than simply letting the self-states co-exist. Mourning means realizing that people and places and aspects of myself are actually and irretrievably lost, saving and treasuring what I can, and letting go of the rest. Freud began to teach us about this; Loewald and Mitchell continued. Accepting finitude, both death and vulnerability, means that someone knows that the many "not-mes", including those generated in early years (Ferenczi, 1949) and often silenced both by ourselves and others, belong to a someone who will not go on forever, and meanwhile has ever more limited capacities and future, even while expanding in other respects.

Third, how can one who stands in the spaces – the idealized outcome of much contemporary relational psychoanalysis – take an ethical stand against injustice? Even contemporary psychanalysts bear the legacy of those who claimed not to know what the Nazi regime or the Pinochet regime were doing. Likewise we psychoanalysts, like many of our fellow citizens, live in a comfortable bubble of "multiple self-states" that I call double-consciousness (Orange, 2017), knowing and not knowing that we are destroying both our earth and even sooner, our poorest brothers and sisters. A theory that valorizes maintaining split consciousness, and ridicules the search for personal integrity and integrated selfhood, just because we often feel "of two minds," may fail crucial tests of civic courage. I doubt that colleagues who speak glibly of multiple self-states have truly thought through the ethical and political implications of this theory.

Yet ever more, we hear voices within relational psychoanalysis crying for social justice – for those marginalized by gender and sexual orientation, by poverty and race, by exclusion of every kind. We feel more and more called to see and hear those others to whom our privileged position keeps us blind and deaf, and to perceive our own implication in their plight. Does preference for dissociation over developmental sensibility evade this ethical sensibility? If we cannot hear the voices of the children within ourselves and each other, to which developmental psychoanalysis attunes us, how will we hear the cries of the hungry and destitute? What does the struggle for development of personal ethics involve? Easily, I can watch and listen as the parts of myself, called "self-states," debate the pros and cons of a political problem, and of my potential involvement. But when do I say: "Here I stand, I can do no other"? How does self-state theory account for the righteous Gentiles, honored at Yad Vashem, who risked everything to protect their Jewish neighbors? How does it understand the clarity of a Nelson Mandela, who remained in prison for several extra years rather than to compromise the full political equality of his people? How does it describe my activist neighbor, who goes to prison for protesting the U.S. government's treatment of undocumented immigrants, or the psychologist who confronts the involvement of other psychologists in torture?

No one would argue that one needs a fully unitary sense of self, much less a linear stage theory of development, to do these things; on the contrary, we define moral and civic courage by reference to the capacity to face down our fears for the sake of something that centrally matters to us. Now perhaps we come closer to the heart of the problem. "Self" eludes definition, as does "identity," many philosophers and psychologists would agree, though in daily life, we Westerners use these concepts constantly and informally. Probably we need them for our implicit moral discourse.[12] When a patient tells me that he or she has no self, or no sense of self, I sometimes ask, "What really matters to you?" or "What do you most care about?" After some time, if the answers come out, I will say, "Well, that's what it is to be yourself, to be someone who has a strong sense of what matters to you. We can build on that, and see what else there is, and what else troubles you."

If, however, the answer comes that at times he seems to care for those in his life, and at other moments behaves as if they didn't exist or matter, and has no idea why, then do I conclude that he has multiple selves, or instead, that he (the speaker) is concerned about something seriously awry in his life for which he is seeking help? One of my first patients came to me because she found that someone was taking notes in her classes in her handwriting, but she had no memory of having attended these classes. I did not conclude that she had multiple selves, but understood that she (the patient) was someone seeking to live as one person. She did not want to be multiple selves, but an integrated person. She wanted to be sure that she could be responsible for everything that was done in her name.

Who is the patient in multiple self-state theory? Are there several, and several analysts? If an analyst holds the assumptions of this theory, what becomes of the patient who arrives seeking greater personal integration and ethical integrity? Will she be persuaded to abandon her search? To return to our earlier question, can great personal courage emerge from this kind of thinking and treatment? Am I, as patient or analyst, to be satisfied with standing in the spaces between my self-state in which I live in the entitlement of white privilege and one which hears the voices of Maya Angelou and Rev. Dr. Martin Luther King, Jr.? Must I not struggle beyond standing in the spaces?

Let us consider, for example, Hans and Sophie Scholl. These student members of the White Rose resistance, killed in München in 1943, embodied the empathy and serenity that Heinz Kohut attributed to a fully integrated value system. A recent film, *Sophie Scholl: The Final Days* (2005), based on newly discovered documents, convinced me of the rightness of Kohut's view of these students. Here is Sophie's last dream: After she had been aroused from her sleep to face the day of her execution, she told the following dream to her cellmate. In the dream, she said,

> "it was a sunny day, and I carried a child, dressed in a long white garment, to be baptized. The path to the church led up a steep mountain; but I held the child firmly and securely. Suddenly there was a crevasse gaping in front of me. I had barely enough time to deposit the child on the far side of it, which I managed to do safely – then I fell into the depth." After Sophie had told her dream she immediately explained its meaning to her companion. The child, she said, is our leading idea. It will live on and make its way to fulfillment despite obstacles.
>
> (Kohut 1985, p. 21)

He reports further: "She went to her execution without a trace of fear" (p. 21). (Winnicott's description of the good-enough conditions necessary for the developmental capacity for concern [Winnicott, 1965] support Kohut's views here, I think).

It seems to me that Kohut's emphasis on civil courage as manifestation of robust selfhood makes clear the ethical implications of my concern here. Without making any metaphysical claims for self or identity, it seems important to express concern for the evasive potential in a clinical theory that suggests giving up on personal integration and integrity. Oh, well, I can always say, my other self-state did it, or didn't let me do it. Bromberg himself provides a wonderful personal example of this process in his story (Bromberg, 1996) about the homeless man outside his window and the two coffee cups. His inner dialogue, probably familiar to all of us who have lived in urban settings, includes a reflection on the clinical relevance of this situation, and like most such reflections, is cut short. "Saved by the buzz!" We are left with the decentered self, allowed to evade the ethical question. Courage waits for another day. Of course, one might object, clinicians need all their courage just to face another day of sessions. True, but do our theories support a belief in ultimate courage? Do they prepare us to act, as the pragmatists taught, or only to stand in the spaces between alternatives and self-states?

Bromberg's most recent published statement (Bromberg, 2013), in honor of Stephen Mitchell, actually expresses an integrated return to his earlier views of psychoanalysis as developmental process, toward cohesive selfhood. Using Winnicott, he writes of the transformation of fantasy into imagination:

> For a person who is "imagining," the state of affairs is different; the person is experiencing the self as it now exists, *projected into the future*. Because the

self being imagined is the same self that is doing the imagining, the person as he is *now* has the capacity to act into a future that is real to him *because the future that is imagined in the here-and-now is itself real.*

(pp. 12–13, emphasis in original)

Here we have psychoanalysis as a developmental process, creating a continuous sense of self that acts, not content to stand in the spaces. We must earnestly hope that the many users and quoters of multiple self-state theory will hear Philip Bromberg now. Like him and like Stephen Mitchell, we may find the courage to hold our theories lightly.

We turn next to an ethical self, constituted by the capacity to hear, to turn a resonating ear toward the suffering other.

Ethical hearing

We have seen that ethical hearing has a demand character. Both Løgstrup and Levinas believed that it imposes on the hearer more than an invitation or even a call. Rather it reaches from vulnerability to vulnerability, requiring response even though the content of the response may vary with the situation. One can refuse the demand, but at great cost:

> the human speaker can remain silent, can refuse to be exposed in sincerity (Levinas Interview in [Kearney & Ricoeur, 1984, p. 79] . . . this ability to keep silent, to withhold oneself, is the ability to be political. Man can give himself in saying to the point of poetry – or he can withdraw into the non-saying of lies.

(Kearney & Ricoeur, 1984, p. 80)

Even when the face of the other lies face-down in the ditch, we hear the cry for help and hesitate only long enough to choose a wise-enough form of care. But we also ask, and by implication, face a further question: Whose suffering counts? Judith Butler, challenging us with her "which lives are grievable," challenges us to learn ethical hearing. It does not depend on physical proximity or on cultural similarity. Teaching us to ask whose suffering matters, she writes:

> we confront a certain rift or schism that recurs at the heart of contemporary politics. If certain lives are deemed worth living, protecting, and grieving and others not, then this way of differentiating lives cannot be understood as a problem of identity or even of the subject. It is rather a question of how power forms the field in which subjects become possible at all or, rather, how they become impossible. And this involves a critical practice of thinking that refuses to take for granted that framework of identitarian struggle which assumes that subjects already exist, that they occupy a common public space, and that their differences might be reconciled if only we had the right tools

for bringing them together. The matter is, in my view, more dire and requires a kind of analysis capable of calling into question the framework that silences the question of who counts as a "who" – in other words, the forcible action of the norm on circumscribing a grievable life.

(Butler, 2009, p. 173)

As we can see, Butler's early postmodernist gender work has evolved into an intense concern with ethical deafness, and the individualist presuppositions supporting it. She has become a prophetic voice for radical ethics in the twenty-first century, while still writing like a philosopher. In the spirit of the radical ethics introduced in the previous chapter, she writes:

Precariousness implies living socially, that is the fact that one's life is always in some sense in the hands of the other. It implies exposure both to those we know and to those we do not know; a dependency on people we know, or barely know, or know not at all. Reciprocally, it implies being impinged upon by the exposure and dependency of others, most of whom remain anonymous. These are not necessarily relations of love or even of care, but constitute obligations toward others, most of whom we cannot name and do not know, and who may or may not bear traits of familiarity to an established sense of who "we" are. In the interest of speaking in common parlance, we could say that "we" have such obligations to "others" and presume that we know who "we" are in such an instance.

(Butler, 2009, p. 14)

Does, for example, the suffering of millions of climate refugees from an increasingly desertified Africa count? Does the suffering of indigenous populations the U.S. government confined to reservations, then criticizes for their inability to live like the colonists, does this suffering matter? Does the suffering of oppressed and vastly underpaid workers in Asia who make cheap clothing for compulsive consumers whose closets already need experts to sort them, does this suffering matter? Grievability, Butler writes, "is a presupposition for the life that matters" (Butler, 2009, p. 14). My neighbors who think about these matters, even if they have not read Butler, often say when tempted to complain, "But this is a first-world problem!" They are learning to hear, realizing that our own privilege most often underlies ethical deafness.

Hearing as learned and unlearned

Answers to Butler's questions depend on learning, a learning so basic that we might call it an *ethical a priori*. This concept, originally from Max Scheler (Scheler, 1972) and his friend theologian Ernst Troeltsch (Troeltsch, 1977, 1992), means that we consider our responses to others and to political situations on the basis of tightly held assumptions. These presuppositions involve, primarily, hierarchies of value determining what and whom we consider of greater and lesser importance. Scheler thought Kant's universalizing categorical imperative to be inadequate, because it bypassed the singularity of the ethical person, whose system of values comes into play in every ethical situation. Scheler believed that the most basic value system – ascending from pleasure to utility to vitality, culture, and holiness – was objectively given to experience, and imposed an "ought."

Bringing a psychoanalytic lens to the ethical a priori, we might consider how it comes into existence for persons and groups. Recent work on intergenerational transmission of trauma could expand to conceptualize inheritance of presuppositions and values. Such transmission might come quite clearly and directly: "You have to be taught to hate and fear . . . you have to be carefully taught." Don't play with those non-Catholics, they will lead you into sin. Other forms are childhood games like cowboys and Indians, and popular songs learned in childhood. We had no idea of the history and continued white supremacy embedded in songs like "Dixie," as we sang them cheerfully. Less direct forms of transmission come from parental example. Whom did my parents consider worth knowing and worth respecting? Whom did they avoid or implicitly judge? Parental silences, considered at more length in an earlier chapter, form another source of inherited ethical unconsciousness, or of an ethical a priori.

This a priori also resembles the prereflective unconsciousness studied by psychoanalytic contextualists and phenomenologists (Atwood & Stolorow, 2014; Stolorow, Atwood, & Branchaft, 1994), as well as by relational/cultural thinkers (Cushman, 2019) (Layton, 2006). This learned ethical a priori, closely resembling Lynne Layton's "normative unconscious," shapes one's response to every situation. Invisible to the one who inherits it, this basic attitude – one I have elsewhere described in detail as a superiority complex – is often excruciatingly obvious to others, those excluded from full humanity in the eyes of the "superior" ones. This ethical a priori – or we might better say, unethical a priori – thus deafens the normatively unconscious ones to the agonies suffered by these others. Many examples have appeared in earlier chapters.

Dialogue is indispensable to awareness of the ethical a priori – psychoanalysts might say to making the normative unconscious conscious. This cannot happen in a vacuum, but requires exposure and listening to excluded others. Unfortunately, the very structures and systems hiding the humanity of the other prevent such dialogue. Here are some examples.

1   Systems of white privilege perpetuate the very "separate but equal" segregation the U.S. Supreme Court debunked and outlawed in 1954. Public education has become the only possibility for most children of color, and avoided by striving white families. This makes children unlikely to meet, study, talk, and play with those of other classes, races, and cultures.
2   Resistance among the privileged to learning languages keeps whites separated from others who speak Spanish, Asian languages, or the many languages of

the climate refugees. This systemic racism makes demagogic hate and fear easier to spread.

3   Many of us born during or since World War II, even if we do not number ourselves among the affluent, have grown up with conveniences that we take for granted: Petroleum-hungry cars, packaged food, clothes dryers, air travel, and so on and on. What happens to our planetary home, to other species, and to its poorest and most vulnerable people, we have not, until recently, thought to ask.

4   Living in single-family homes on land we bought or inherited, we in the U.S. and a few other places imagine that we belong there, and that more compact, efficient multi-housing constitutes an intolerable loss. This means we cannot face up to the history of our own countries, where the land was stolen from indigenous people and distributed to whites via land-grants. It also contributes to urban sprawl, and leads to industrialized farming, including industrial-style meat and poultry production. We were born into these privileges, deafened to their results, and therefore find it impossible to imagine life in the compact cities found in Europe, Japan, and other multi-housing cultures. Manifest Destiny (borrowed by Hitler as *Lebensraum)* tells us that all this space is our birthright, creating a form of ethical a priori.

Why repeat these obvious and well-known instances? When deprived of an a priori privilege, many people become resentful and prey to demagogues, nationalism, and racist and sexist cults. Inability to recognize our unjustified privilege just because it has been ours longer than we can remember makes us anxious and vulnerable to those who say this privilege belongs to us, and that we must fight for it. These cultural assumptions, treated as religious – multiply and fill the earth – lead to a further assumption that anyone who question must be a dangerous Marxist radical.

So, relearning to hear requires effort. It brings discomfort, worry, even insomnia, as Emmanuel Levinas wrote:

> I have described ethical responsibility as *insomnia* or *wakefulness* precisely because it is a perpetual duty of vigilance and effort which can never slumber. Ontology as a state of affairs can afford sleep. But love cannot sleep, can never be peaceful or permanent. Love is the incessant watching over of the other; it can never be satisfied or contented with bourgeois ideal love as domestic comfort or the mutual possession of two people living out an *égoisme-à-deux.*
>
> (Levinas quoted in Kearney & Ricoeur, 1984, p. 81)

Nor is ethical responsibility masochism, as both Simone Drichel (2019) and I (2019) have explained in detail. In her superb "Emmanuel Levinas and the 'Specter of Masochism': A Cross-Disciplinary Confusion of Tongues," Levinas scholar Simone Drichel takes up my cryptic challenge (Orange, 2016) to read Emmanuel

Ghent's work (1990) as an antidote to psychoanalysts' misunderstandings of Levinasian responsibility as masochistic. Not only does she do in depth the work to which I alluded, but she develops an elegant account based on D.W. Winnicott, citing his desire to turn us invulnerable ones into sufferers. From there her return to Emmanuel Levinas, with his challenging language, becomes actually graceful. Having already linked masochism to narcissism as means of coping with psychological trauma, she can now invoke Levinas as he linked philosophical egoism with narcissism. She makes her "cross-disciplinary" turn clear, but the connections clear as well, creating a model for those of us who want to contribute across disciplines and discourses.

To begin, masochism, as we psychoanalysts inherited the term from Freud (1924) and as ordinary language adopted it, has commonly held a cluster (Wittgenstein, 1973) of meanings, all pejorative – a desire to suffer for neurotic reasons, a compulsive need to be good or helpful, self-absorption in one's suffering, the seeking and enjoyment of suffering, even disavowed sadism. In my earlier work (Orange, 2016), I traced a number of efforts by Freudians and interpersonalists to seek the origins of so-called masochistic phenomena in developmental and relational experiences. Drichel has enriched and deepened this approach, reading Winnicott and Ghent so closely that she might be a psychoanalyst.

In addition, she picks up a kind of ethical incapacity, an inability to live turned toward the other. (For me this ethical incapacity comes in part from the inherited privilege I am calling an ethical a priori). Drichel, following Paul Marcus (2008, 2010), calls it "ethical impairment" (Drichel, 2017, p. 122); Dan Shaw, in his study of the malignant and traumatic narcissism characteristic of cult leaders, names it a compromised "capacity for intersubjective relatedness" (Shaw, 2014, p. 3). One of my favorite titles in Winnicott, by contrast, is "The Development of the Capacity for Concern" (Winnicott, 1965, pp. 73–82), where he described this capacity as relationally engendered between mother and baby, after the infant has profited from the period of primary maternal preoccupation. Concern, he wrote, "refers to the fact that the individual *cares*, or *minds*, and both feels and accepts responsibility" (p. 73). In opposition to the Kleinian view of primary and inborn aggression, the putative bedrock of everything, Winnicott believed that lying, stealing, and other antisocial behavior resulted from never having received such concern, and thus not being able to feel that one could actually hurt the other whom one also needed and could also both hate and love. In other words, Drichel believes, with Claire Elise Katz (2013), that ethical capacity, the self-turned-toward-the-other, is not a given, but must be developed through education, inclusively understood.

Extreme early trauma, in all the forms with which we clinicians are familiar, absent needed witness and support, can, of course, isolate the child and prevent developing any sense of responsibility for others. Without the "developmental second chance" (Orange, 1995) provided by the devoted[13] psychoanalyst or some similar experience, then survival, and perhaps revenge, become all that matters. Later trauma, from genocides, torture, natural disasters, unexpected losses, and so on, may or may not remove ethical capacity, depending on what kind of subjectivity was organized earlier and what kind of "empathic milieu" (Ornstein, 2003, 2007; Stolorow, 2011) became available after the devastation. "Recovery" would then involve recovery of ethical capacity established earlier, not a repair of the losses and wounds.

Turning now to Levinas, his language of trauma, of persecution, and of a summons to responsibility that never ends, does tend to upset people, including many thoughtful clinicians who already feel themselves challenged to their limits. As Drichel (2019) points out, trauma has a different meaning here, more like interruption, or rather, like a pre-primordial invasion by otherness. I never did – and never will – belong to myself but am for the other before even meeting her. This radical language, however, follows from a set of philosophical "inversions." Drichel picks up this typical word of Levinas when she quotes him in conversation with Philippe Nemo:

> whatever the motivation which explains this inversion, the analysis of the face such as I have just made, with the mastery of the Other and his poverty, with my submission and my wealth, is primary. It is the presupposed in all human relationships. If it were not that, we would not even say, before an open door, "After you, sir!" It is an original "After you, sir!" that I have tried to describe.
>
> (Lévinas & Nemo, 1985, p. 89)

The inversion in question is "the presupposed," the sense that the other, without question, comes first. Philosophically speaking, it inverts the egoism of Hobbes, of Hegel, and of Heidegger. It replaces autonomy, agency, and authenticity, with sincerity and vulnerability. Not only does the naked face of the other take priority, the self (*le soi*) becomes vulnerable, naked, and emptied of ego. "*La sortie du soi*" (the exit from self), Levinas often repeated in conversation. Unlike the disciplines of the Zen Buddhist and others, we find here no concentration on becoming pure, but rather exactly a turn away from this endeavor, a turn toward the other. Language, Levinas wrote, can dominate, reduce, and classify, or it can speak to the unrepeatable individual, inverting Western (and Heideggerian) ontology. "Proximity, is *by itself* a signification. . . . The orientation of the subject upon the object has become a proximity, the intentional has become ethical. . . . It indicates a reversal of the subjectivity" (Levinas, 1987, p. 116, emphasis in original). Proximity, of course, destroys the distance needed for naming, classifying, and other forms of violence.

The masochist, unfortunately, needs the therapist's help because she suffers from concentration on self, from the fusion of narcissism and suffering that Drichel analyzes. Temporarily, therapy for such trouble may involve more focus on the patient's invulnerable egoism, but once accompanied, once truly witnessed, it may turn into usable suffering, the kind Levinas contrasted with "useless suffering" (Levinas, 1988) in his essay by this name. In this short piece addressing physical suffering, mental agony, and the genocides of the twentieth century, he claimed that suffering itself is absurd, "for nothing," and that theodicy, any scandalous attempt to justify another's pain collapses into Nietzsche's "death of God." "The justification of the neighbor's pain," he wrote, "is certainly the source of all immorality" (Levinas, 1988, p. 163). (He might well have said the same of clinicians who believe our patients want to suffer, or that clinicians who are willing to extend themselves to stand by them are masochists). Instead, he believed, the only useful suffering occurs as what he had named *substitution* (Levinas, 1981). The meaningless "for nothing" suffering undergoes another inversion:

> a radical difference develops between suffering in the Other, which for me is unpardonable and solicits me and calls me, and suffering in me, my own adventure of suffering, whose constitutional or congenital uselessness can take on a meaning, the only meaning to which suffering is susceptible, in becoming a suffering for the suffering – be it inexorable – of someone else.
>
> (1988, p. 159)

We may remember the recent story of French policeman Arnaud Beltrame, who offered himself as hostage replacement and died for it. Nothing we have learned about this man suggests that he had an addiction to suffering; rather, he reminds me of Robert Bernasconi's essay "What is the Question to which 'Substitution' is the Answer?" (Bernasconi, 2002). If I understand rightly, the question is whether useful suffering, sacrifice, is actually possible, whether human beings can actually both feel and respond to the ethical summons of the other's suffering. The concept of substitution says, yes, it is possible, and no, it is not masochism, but ethics. Substitution, inverting all familiar orders, places the other where the Western ego has lived. Instead of Freud's "*Wo es war, soll ich werden*" (where id was, there ego shall become), we have: Where ego was, there the other is already. Solidarity comes first. Ethics, the sensibility and vulnerability before all thinking, no longer has time to calculate whether anything will be reciprocated.

Social contracts, as envisioned by Hobbes and Locke, and enshrined in liberal democracies, make no sense when the other's life is at stake. Generalizability, the crown jewel of Kantian ethics both original and more contemporary, also disappears in this radical ethics. The summons is addressed to me, accused, more than all the others, according to Dostoevsky (Dostoyevsky, Pevear, & Volokhonsky, 1992). There is no time for a moral calculus.

Meanwhile, this inversion inverts phenomenology's beloved intentionality (MacEvoy, 1996), so that the directionality runs not from the subject to what it perceives or knows, but from the other to what evokes subjectivity, vulnerable sensibility, a responsible and responsive subjectivity.[14] Where Heidegger's Being-in-the-World (Heidegger, 1962) was thought to have obliterated the subject-object distinction, Levinas, seeing that ethics also disappeared, returned to Husserl, but upended him. The me, no longer to be spoken in the nominative case as the subject does not begin there, is accused and in the accusative, affected by the other, "more passive than all passivity" (Lâevinas, Peperzak, Critchley, & Bernasconi, 1996, p. 121), a creature. The subject is subjected to the other. This is still phenomenology, but a new kind, an inverted kind, requiring new eyes and new ears. Levinas famously claimed that "ethics is an optics" (Levinas, 1969, p. 29), but in his later writings, we also hear the cries of the poor and hungry, to whose suffering we must not deafen ourselves. "Dasein in Heidegger is never hungry" (Levinas, 1979, p. 134), Levinas noted, implying the ethical emptiness of Heideggerian worldedness.[15] I remember the photographs of very well-fed Germans brought to see the piles of emaciated corpses in Bergen-Belsen in 1945. Reminding me of Leibniz's windowless monads, Drichel notes that this is "a violently egological anti-relational relationality" (p. 23). The dominant and monadic ego can neither hear nor see the other.

So, we are perhaps speaking of a double and truly radical inversion: The phenomenological, where the other affects and creates subjectivity, standing traditional epistemology and phenomenology on its head; and the ethical, turning toward the other. Probably the two are so closely intertwined that it might be impossible to say which is more basic. In Levinas's view, the consequences reach everywhere, reaching from ordinary courtesy, through a life filled with and shaped by the conviction that the "the widow, the orphan, and the stranger" are my sister and brother, ending in what he called substitution. Granted that any and all of what I have called radical ethics – also found in Knud Løgstrup (Løgstrup, 1997) – demands rejection of the typical Western gospel of "healthy" self-development, self-reliance, and even self-promotion. A turn toward the other is bound to be seen as pathological, or at least as strange. People who live quietly, unobtrusively, in the service of others, just do not make sense in a self-promoting world. They must be abnormal.

Finally, to embrace vulnerability, as Drichel, Winnicott, Ghent, and Levinas do, inverts Western humanism, brings it down from its egoist high horse to a place where it can speak of unspeakable suffering, of tenderness and compassion, of the caress. No longer will we describe those who work in service of others as masochists, but as devoted public servants. No longer will we imagine clinical success as the building of a strong and self-sufficient ego, but as the turning of invulnerability, just as Winnicott told us, into the capability to suffer. Bringing our own readiness to suffer, our "relational vulnerability" (Drichel, 2019, p. 3ff.) to our not-yet-ready-to-suffer patients, we invert knowing into proximity. Though Levinas would surely not have used this term, I (Orange, 2008, p. 178) have sometimes called this form of emotional availability "intersubjective vulnerability" and consider it indispensable to good clinical work

The radical passivity found in the ethics of demand and responsibility could seem to resemble Buddhist beliefs about suffering.[16] Life is simply hard, they say, and the sooner we realize this, the less we will continue to expect an easy life (Itsuki, 2001). Sometimes the river is clear, (then wash your treasures); other times the river is muddy (then wash your feet), goes an old Chinese verse (p. 54). These beliefs may help us survive the unbearable, and deserve admiration for that. But radical ethics is something else. When I inflict suffering, or tolerate it in others who flee persecution or starve from famine or both, it is not to be accepted. It is senseless and absurd (Levinas, 1988), as explained previously. Only my own suffering, accepted for the sake of reducing misery for the other, makes any sense. This acceptance, sometimes as extreme as Beltrame's, Levinas called substitution.

Substitution

Perhaps the most radical thought in radical ethics, unremarked by many readers of Levinas though mentioned previously in passing, substitution challenges the egoistic ethical a priori, a presumption that always puts the speaking subject first. The speaker, as Waldenfels and Hans-Georg Gadamer would also say, responds to a call whose hearing/responding creates the speaker as subject. Instead of cutting in line or leaving the other to die alone, substitution puts the other first. More than empathy, it requires me actively to imagine myself in the other's trouble, in exile, homeless, hungry, a second or third-class citizen. As passivity, it requires me to undergo the trouble in the other's place. It refuses to let me walk away, or to sleep well.

What can this possibly mean? Levinas explained at length in *Otherwise than Being* (1981), as well as in his previous essay entitled "Substitution." Easier to read, here is his formulation in interviews collected as *Is It Righteous to Be?* (Lévinas and Robbins, 2001)

> For me, the notion of substitution is tied to the notion of responsibility. To substitute oneself does not amount to putting oneself in the place of the other man in order to feel what he feels; it does not involve becoming the other nor, if he be destitute and desperate, the courage of such a trial. Rather, substitution entails bringing comfort by associating ourselves with the essential weakness and finitude of the other; it is to bear his weight while sacrificing one's interestedness and complacency-in-being, which then turn into responsibility for the other. In human existence, there is, as it were, interrupting or surpassing the vocation of being, another vocation: that of the other.
>
> (p. 228)

Substitution does not mean joining the stranger in the ditch in the Good Samaritan story, but it also does not allow looking away in indifference, or just passing by. It does mean that the other's suffering, that of my sister or brother, "entails bringing comfort by associating ourselves with the essential weakness and finitude of the other." Substitution means bearing the weight of the other while giving up self-absorption: "He ain't heavy, he's my brother." For clinicians and other humanitarians, substitution may seem absurd as it may seem to destroy the clinical distance and detachment needed to remain helpful. It brings up again the question of masochism discussed previously. If one treats every patient as a brother or sister whose suffering must be borne, how does the clinician survive to work tomorrow?[17] But let us listen further:

> All of the culture of the humans seems to me to be oriented by this new "plot," in which the in-itself of a being persisting in its being is surpassed in the gratuity of being outside-of-oneself, for the other, in the act of sacrifice or the possibility of sacrifice, in holiness.
>
> (p. 228)

Sacrifice and holiness? The first suggests returning the clinician and humanitarian to the traditional woman's role, and would seem to risk losing all the gains of the feminist movement. On the contrary, Levinas meant to suggest here, I think, that when self-absorbed "persistence in being" gives way, or is inverted into, being for the other, secular life is made holy, the root meaning of sacrifice. Substitution, looking like sacrifice in the common meaning of the word, turns suffering into suffering for the other, making it holy.

Some will object that we are no longer talking phenomenology, but rather religion. True, but not a particular religion. Though we can think of people whose lives of "sacrifice" for others seem motivated without specific religious beliefs – Nelson Mandela, perhaps – all ethical examples, small and large, involve belief in something beyond the individual. Rev. Dr. Martin Luther King, Jr., for example, and many who accompanied him in his struggle, had religious motivation. Still, no one needed specific religious beliefs to join his struggle, to risk violence and imprisonment for others. Other examples include the white helmets of Syria, and Doctors Without Borders. Substitution may be holy without being religious. (A fuller treatment of secular holiness would lead us too far astray and is probably beyond my competence).

But it resembles the "spontaneous goodness" of which Australian philosopher Patrick Stokes (Stokes, 2016) writes in contrasting the radical ethic of Knud Løgstrup with all forms of calculation and deliberation, with rationalist ethics. Such spontaneous goodness, in my view, results from upending what we have been so carefully taught, and from relearning ethical hearing.

Notes

1 Peirce wrote: "no matter how far science goes, those inferences which are uppermost in the mind of the investigator are very uncertain. They are on probation. They must have a fair trial and not be condemned till proved false beyond all reasonable doubt; and the moment that proof is reached, the investigator must be ready to abandon them without the slightest tenderness toward them. Thus, the scientific inquirer has to be always ready at a moment to abandon summarily all the theories to the study of which he has been devoting perhaps many years." (1998, p. 25).

2 Here I borrow from my discussion of Greenberg and Mitchell's view of Kohut (Orange, 2013).

3 It would be more than unjust to ignore the use by Thomas Ogden (Ogden, 1986) of *matrix*. His use of it suggests its etymological reference to the mother, and particularly

refers to Winnicott. I do not know whether Mitchell and Ogden arrived at their uses of this word independently, but suspect that their uses may have influenced each other.

4 This section expands paragraphs on Loewald in (Orange, 2016).

5 In a posthumously published discussion, Lewis Aron, who worked closely with Mitchell during this period, emphasizes the Loewald-Mitchell connection (Aron, 2019).

6 A similar reverence for needed regressive process, of course, shows up in Ferenczi (Ferenczi, 1931; Ferenczi & Dupont, 1988), so enormously important in contemporary psychoanalysis, as well as in the creative confrontations with evil in the work of Sue Grand (Grand, 2000, 2010), where perpetrators and sufferers re-engage, strangely.

7 Why Loewald himself has been so ignored is another question, addressed by Lawrence Friedman (Friedman, 2008). Harris and Suchet (Harris & Suchet, 2002) clearly note this influence in their review of *Relationality* (Mitchell, 2000) as does (Harris, 2011).

8 Replacing univocal concepts that apply in the same way to everything they cover, and replacing categories to which people or things simply belong or not, he reminded us that in families, some members have similar eyes, other have similar noses, chins or hair. These features, he thought, allow us to recognize people as related even when no two of them have all the same features in common. He thought concepts, whether of colors or of theories, similarly overlapped. "We see a complicated network of similarities overlapping and criss-crossing: sometimes overall similarities, sometimes similarities of detail" (Wittgenstein, 2003, p. 27, paragraph 66).

9 Interesting to note is that the expression "self-state" became prominent in Heinz Kohut's work (1984) on self-state dreams, and was then picked up by Stern and Sander in their developmental studies. They considered the work of psychoanalysis to concern the transformation of self-states.

10 I ask forgiveness if I should have cited others; these are examples.

11 One of my most seriously "dissociative" patients repeatedly objected to me that "dissociation" is a misnomer; one rather *associates*, under the right relational conditions, to the traumatic past.

12 Postmodernism has been in question, not to say demise, in recent years, precisely because of the ethical problems of its intellectual giants: Heidegger, Paul de Man, and perhaps even Derrida. So, it is not surprising that a psychoanalysis dependent on postmodern ideas might also founder on ethical shoals. It may embrace difference, but not know how to stand up against totalitarians.

13 "Devoted" characterized absolutely needed maternal care in Winnicott (Winnicott, 1975); he often implied that a similar type of care must characterize psychoanalysis with the most fragile patients.

14 Proximity, Levinas writes, "indicates a reversal of the subjectivity which is *open upon* beings and always in some measure represents them to itself, positing them and taking them to be such or such . . . into a subjectivity which enters *into contact* with a singularity, excluding identification in the ideal, excluding thematization and representation, – an absolute singularity, as such unrepresentable" ("Language and Proximity" in Levinas [1987], p. 116, emphasis in original). MacEvoy argues, quite convincingly, that this reversal occurs because proximity to the other overwhelms, thwarts the ego.

15 The context was his reading of Heidegger as isolating the implement from enjoyment and satisfaction. Levinas went on to say: "Food can be interpreted as an implement only in a world of exploitation" (p. 134), marking his critique as relational.

16 In the words of history of religions scholar Donald A. Braue: "The hard life, suffering, is caused by ignorant craving, perhaps the craving for self-identity. At its core, Buddhism rejects any notion of the self, so central in Western thought" (personal communication, 25 March 2019).

17 This question I tried to begin addressing in (Orange, 2016, p. 51380).

References

Aron, L. (2006). Analytic Impasse and the Third: Clinical Implications of Intersubjectivity Theory. *International Journal of Psychoanalysis, 87*, 349–368.

Aron, L. (2019). Discussion of "Bread and Roses: Empathy and Recognition". *Psychoanalytic Dialogues, 29*, 92–102.

Aron, L., Grand, S., & Slochower, J. A. (2018a). *De-idealizing relational theory: A critique from within*. Abingdon, Oxon and New York, NY: Routledge.

Aron, L., Grand, S., & Slochower, J. A. (2018b). *Decentering relational theory: A comparative critique*. Abingdon, Oxon and New York, NY: Routledge.

Atwood, G. E., & Stolorow, R. D. (2014). *Structures of subjectivity: Explorations in psychoanalytic phenomenology and contextualism* (2nd ed.). London and New York: Routledge and Taylor & Francis Group.

Balint, M. (1960). Primary Narcissism and Primary Love. *Psychoanalytic Quarterly, 29*, 6–43.

Balint, M. (1992). *The basic fault: Therapeutic aspects of regression*. Evanston, IL: Northwestern University Press.

Baraitser, L. (2008). Mum's the Word: Intersubjectivity, Alterity, and the Maternal Subject. *Studies in Gender and Sexuality, 9*, 86–110.

Bass, A. (2009). The As-If Patient and the As-If Analyst. *Psychanalytic Quarterly, 76*, 365–386.

Bass, G. (2002). Something Is Happening Here. *Psychoanalytic Dialogues, 12*(5), 809–826.

Beebe, B., & Lachmann, F. M. (2001). *Infant research and adult treatment: A dyadic systems approach*. Hillsdale, NJ: Analytic Press.

Benjamin, J. (2004). Beyond Doer and Done to: An Intersubjective View of Thirdness. *Psychoanalytic Quarterly, 73*, 5–46.

Bernasconi, R. (2002). What Is the Question to Which "Substitution" Is the Answer? In S. Critchley & R. Bernasconi (Eds.), *The Cambridge companion to Levinas* (pp. 234–251). Cambridge, UK: Cambridge University Press.

Birksted-Breen, D. (2003). Time and the Après-Coup. *International Journal of Psychoanalysis, 84*, 1501–1515.

Bromberg, P. M. (1979). Interpersonal Psychoanalysis and Regression. *Contemporary Psychoanalysis, 15*, 647–655.

Bromberg, P. M. (1991). On Knowing One's Patient Inside Out: The Aesthetics of Unconscious Communication. *Psychoanalytic Dialogues, 1*(4), 399–422.

Bromberg, P. M. (1994). "Speak! That I May See You": Some Reflections on Dissociation, Reality, and Psychoanalytic Listening. *Psychoanalytic Dialogues, 4*(4), 517–547.

Bromberg, P. M. (1996). Standing in the Spaces: The Multiplicity of Self and the Psychoanalytic Relationship. *Contemporary Psychoanalysis, 32*, 509–535.

Bromberg, P. M. (1998). *Standing in the spaces: Essays on clinical process, trauma, and dissociation*. Hillsdale, NJ: Analytic Press.

Bromberg, P. M. (2009). Truth, Human Relatedness, and the Analytic Process: An Interpersonal/Relational Perspective. *International Journal of Psychoanalysis, 90*, 3347–3361.

Bromberg, P. M. (2011). The Gill/Bromberg Correspondence. *Psychoanalytic Dialogues, 21*(3), 243–252.

Bromberg, P. M. (2013). Hidden in Plain Sight: Thoughts on Imagination and the Lived Unconscious. *Psychoanalytic Dialogues, 23*(1), 1–14.

Butler, J. (2009). *Frames of war: When is life grievable?* London and New York: Verso.

Chefetz, R. (2003). Healing Haunted Hearts: Toward a Model for Integrating Subjectivity, Commentary on Papers by Philip Bromberg and Gerald Stechler. *Psychoanalytic Dialogues, 13*, 727–742.

Chefetz, R., & Bromberg, P. (2004). Talking with "Me" and "Not-Me": A Dialogue. *Contemporary Psychoanalysis, 40*, 409–464.

Cooper-White, P. (2007). *Many voices: Pastoral psychotherapy in relational and theological perspective.* Minneapolis, MN: Fortress Press.

Cushman, P. (2007). A Burning World, an Absent God: Midrash, Hermeneutics, and Relational Psychoanalysis. *Contemporary Psychoanalysis, 43*, 47–88.

Cushman, P. (2019). *Travels with the self: Interpreting psychology as cultural history.* New York: Routledge.

Dahl, G. (2010). Nachträglichkeit, Wiederholungszwang, Symbolisierung: Zur psychoanalytischen Deutung von primärprozesshaften Szenen. *Psyche Zeitung für Psychoanalyse, 64*, 385–407.

Davies, J. (2009). Love Never Ends Well: Termination as the Fate of an Illusion: Commentary on Papers by Jill Salberg and Sue Grand. *Psychoanalytic Dialogues, 19*, 734–743.

Davies, J. M. (1996). Linking the "Pre-Analytic" With the Postclassical: Integration, Dissociation, and the Multiplicity of Unconscious Process. *Contemporary Psychoanalysis, 32*, 553–576.

Dostoyevsky, F., Pevear, R., & Volokhonsky, L. (1992). *The brothers Karamazov: A novel in four parts with epilogue.* London: Vintage.

Drichel, S. (2017). On Narcissism and "Ethical Impairment": A Discussion of Gregory Rizzolo's "Alterity, Masochism, and Ethical Desire: A Kohutian Perspective on Levinas' Ethics of Responsibility for the Other. *Psychonal. Self Cxt., 12*(2), 122–130.

Drichel, S. (2019). Emmanuel Levinas and the "Specter of Masochism": A Cross-Disciplinary Confusion of Tongues. *Psychoanalysis, Self, and Context, 14*(1), 3–22.

Ferenczi, S. (1931). Child-Analysis in the Analysis of Adults. *International Journal of Psycho-Analysis, 12*, 468–482.

Ferenczi, S. (1949). Confusion of the Tongues Between the Adults and the Child (The Language of Tenderness and of Passion). *International Journal of Psycho-Analysis, 30*, 225–230.

Ferenczi, S., & Dupont, J. (1988). *The clinical diary of Sándor Ferenczi.* Cambridge, MA: Harvard University Press.

Freud, S. (1917). Introductory Lectures on Psycho-Analysis: 27th and 28th Lectures. In *Standard edition* (Vol. 16–17). London: Hogarth.

Freud, S. (1924). The Economic Problem of Masochism. In *The standard edition of the complete psychological works of Sigmund Freud* (Vol. 19 (1923–1925), pp. 155–170). London: Hogarth.

Freud, S., & Strachey, J. (2005). *Civilization and its discontents.* New York: Norton.

Friedman, L. (2008). Loewald. *Journal of the American Psychoanalytic Association, 56*, 1105–1115.

Gerson, S. (2009). When the Third Is Dead: Memory, Mourning, and Witnessing in the Aftermath of the Holocaust. *International Journal of Psychoanalysis, 90*, 1341–1357.

Ghent, E. (1990). Masochism, Submission, Surrender: Masochism as a Perversion of Surrender. *Contemporary Psychoanalysis, 26*, 108–136.

Grand, S. (2000). *The reproduction of evil: A clinical and cultural perpsective.* Hillsdale, NJ: Analytic Press.

Grand, S. (2010). *The hero in the mirror: From fear to fortitude.* New York: Routledge.

Greenberg, J. R., & Mitchell, S. A. (1983). *Object relations in psychoanalytic theory.* Cambridge, MA: Harvard University Press.

Harris, A. (1996). The Conceptual Power of Multiplicity. *Contemporary Psychoanalysis, 32,* 537–552.

Harris, A. (2011). The Relational Tradition: Landscape and Canon. *Journal of the American Psychanalytic Association, 59,* 701–735.

Harris, A., & Suchet, M. (2002). Relationality: From Attachment to Intersubjectivity. Stephen A. Mitchell. Hillsdale, NJ: Analytic Press, 2000. xvii & 173 pp. $39.95. *American Imago, 59,* 102–111.

Hirsch, I. (1997). The Widening of the Concept of Dissociation. *Journal of the American Academy of Psychoanalysis, 25*(4), 603–615.

Hoffman, I. Z. (2000). At Death's Door. *Psychoanalytic Dialogues, 10*(6), 823–846.

Itsuki, H. (2001). *Tariki: Embracing despair, discovering peace.* Tokyo and New York: Kodansha.

Katz, C. E. (2013). *Levinas and the crisis of humanism.* Bloomington: Indiana University Press.

Kearney, R., & Ricoeur, P. (1984). *Dialogues with contemporary continental thinkers: The phenomenological heritage: Paul Ricoeur, Emmanuel Levinas, Herbert Marcuse, Stanislas Breton, Jacques Derrida.* Manchester, UK and Dover, NH: Manchester University Press.

Knoblauch, S. H. (1999). The Third, Minding and Affecting. *Psychoanalytic Dialogues, 9*(1), 41–51.

Kohut, H., et al. (1984). *How does analysis cure?* Chicago: University of Chicago Press.

Kohut, H. (1985). On Courage. In C. Strozier & E. Kohut (Eds.), *Self psychology and the humanities* (pp. 5–50). New York: Norton.

Lachmann, F. M. (1996). How Many Selves Make a Person? *Contemporary Psychoanalysis, 32,* 595–614.

Lâevinas, E., Peperzak, A. T., Critchley, S., & Bernasconi, R. (1996). *Emmanuel Levinas: Basic philosophical writings.* Bloomington: Indiana University Press.

Layton, L. (2006). Racial Identities, Racial Enactments, and Normative Unconscious Processes. *Psychoanalytic Quarterly, 75,* 237–269.

Layton, L. (2009). Who's Responsible? Our Mutual Implication in Each Other's Suffering. *Psychoanalytic Dialogues, 19,* 105–120.

Lear, J. (1998). *Love and its place in nature: A philosophical interpretation of Freudian psychoanalysis.* New Haven, CT: Yale University Press.

Leary, K. (2000). Racial Enactments in Dynamic Treatment. *Psychoanalytic Dialogues, 10*(4), 639–653.

Levi, P. (1988). *The drowned and the saved.* New York: Summit Books.

Levinas, E. (1969). *Totality and infinity: An essay on exteriority.* Pittsburgh: Duquesne University Press.

Levinas, E. (1979). *Totality and infinity: An essay on exteriority.* The Hague and Boston Hingham, MA: M. Nijhoff Publishers and Distribution for the U.S. and Canada and Kluwer Boston.

Levinas, E. (1981). *Otherwise than being: Or, beyond essence.* Hague and Boston Hingham, MA: M. Nijhoff and Distributors for the U.S. and Canada and Kluwer Boston.

Levinas, E. (1987). *Collected philosophical papers.* Dordrecht, The Netherlands and Boston Hingham, MA, USA: Nijhoff and Distributors for the United States and Canada and Kluwer Academic.

Levinas, E. (1988). Useless Suffering. In R. Bernasconi & D. Wood (Eds.), *The provocation of Levinas: Rethinking the other* (pp. xii, pp. 157–167, 194 p.). London and New York: Routledge.

Levinas, E., & Nemo, P. (1985). *Ethics and infinity* (1st ed.). Pittsburgh: Duquesne University Press.

Lévinas, E. and Robbins, J. (2001). *Is it righteous to be? Interviews with Emmanuel Lévinas*. Stanford, CA: Stanford University Press.

Loewald, H. W. (1960). On the Therapeutic Action of Psycho-Analysis. *International Journal of Psycho-Analysis, 41*, 16–33.

Loewald, H. W. (1985). Oedipus Complex and Development of Self. *Psychoanalytic Quarterly, 54*, 435–443.

Loewald, H. W. (2007). Internalization, Separation, Mourning, and the Superego. *Psychoanlytic Quarterly, 76*, 1113–1133.

Loewald, H. W. (2000). *The essential Loewald: Collected papers and monographs*. Hagerstown, MD: University Pub. Group.

Løgstrup, K. E. (1997). *The ethical demand*. Notre Dame, IN: University of Notre Dame Press.

MacEvoy, L. (1996). The Other Side of Intentionality. In E. Nelson, A. Kapust, & K. Still (Eds.), *Addressing Levinas: Ethics, phenomenology, and the judaic tradition* (pp. 109–118). Evanston, IL: Northwestern University Press.

Marcus, P. (2008). *Being for the other: Emmanuel Levinas, ethical living and psychoanalysis*. Milwaukee, WI: Marquette University Press.

Marcus, P. (2010). *In search of the good life: Emmanuel Levinas, psychoanalysis, and the art of living*. London: Karnac Books.

Mitchell, S. A. (1979). Twilight of the Idols: Change and Preservation in the Writings of Heinz Kohut. *Contemporary Psychoanalysis, 15*, 170–189.

Mitchell, S. A. (1983). Reflections. *Contemporary Psychoanalysis, 19*, 133–139.

Mitchell, S. A. (1984). Object Relations Theories and the Developmental Tilt. *Contemporary Psychoanalysis, 20*, 473–499.

Mitchell, S. A. (1987). Discussion. *Contemporary Psychoanalysis, 23*, 400–409.

Mitchell, S. A. (1988). *Relational concepts in psychoanalysis: An integration*. Cambridge, MA: Harvard University Press.

Mitchell, S. A. (1993). *Hope and dread in psychoanalysis*. New York: BasicBooks.

Mitchell, S. A. (1997). *Influence and autonomy in psychoanalysis*. Hillsdale, NJ: Analytic Press.

Mitchell, S. A. (1998). From Ghosts to Ancestors: The Psychoanalytic Vision of Hans Loewald. *Psychoanalytic Dialogues, 8*(6), 825–855.

Mitchell, S. A. (2000). *Relationality: From attachment to intersubjectivity*. Hillsdale, NJ: Analytic Press.

Mitchell, S. A. (2004). My Psychoanalytic Journey. *Psychoanalytic Inquiry, 24*, 531–541.

Muller, J. P. (1999). The Third as Holding the Dyad. *Psychoanalytic Dialogues, 9*(4), 471–480.

Ogden, T. H. (1986). *The matrix of the mind: Object relations and the psychoanalytic dialogue*. Northvale, NJ: J. Aronson.

Ogden, T. H. (1994). The Analytic Third: Working with Intersubjective Clinical Facts. *International Journal of Psycho-Analysis, 75*, 3–19.

Orange, D. M. (1995). *Emotional understanding: Studies in psychoanalytic epistemology*. New York: Guilford Press.

Orange, D. M. (2008). Recognition as: Intersubjective Vulnerability in the Psychoanalytic Dialogue. *International Journal of Psychoanalytic Self Psychology*, *3*, 178–194.

Orange, D. M. (2011). *The suffering stranger: Hermeneutics for everyday clinical practice*. New York: Routledge and Taylor & Francis Group.

Orange, D. M. (2013). Those Old Wineskins: Greenberg and Mitchell on Heinz Kohut's "Mixed Model". *Contemporary Psychoanalysis*, *49*, 103–112.

Orange, D. M. (2016). *Nourishing the inner life of clinicians and humanitarians: The ethical turn in psychoanalysis*. London and New York: Routledge.

Orange, D. M. (2017). *Climate crisis, psychoanalysis, and radical ethics*. London: Routledge.

Orange, D. M. (2019). Inversions: Simone Drichel on the Two Emmanuels. *Psychoanalysis, Self, and Context*, *14*(1), 23–28.

Ornstein, A. (2003). Chapter 5 Survival and Recovery: Psychoanalytic Reflections. *Progress in Self Psychology*, *19*, 85–105.

Ornstein, A. (2007). Roundtable Conversation of Child Survivors of the Holocaust. *Psychoanalytic Perspective*, *5*(1), 5–12.

Peirce, C. S., et al. (1998). *The essential Peirce: Selected philosophical writings* (Vol. 2). Bloomington: Indiana University Press.

Putnam, F. W. (1988). The Switch Process in Multiple Personality Disorder and Other State-Change Disorders. *Dissociation*, *1*, 24–32.

Racker, E. (1968). *Transference and counter-transference*. New York: International Universities Press.

Riker, J. H. (2013). The Philosophical Importance of Kohut's Notion of the Self. *International Journal of Psychalalytic Self Psychology*, *8*, 495–504.

Sander, L. W. (1995). Identity and the Experience of Specificity in a Process of Recognition: Commentary on Seligman and Shanok. *Psychoanalytic Dialogues*, *5*(4), 579–593.

Scheler, M. (1972). *On the eternal in man*. Hamden, CT: Archon Books.

Shaw, D. (2003). On the Therapeutic Action of Analytic Love. *Contemporary Psychoanalysis*, *39*, 251–278.

Shaw, D. (2014). *Traumatic narcissism: Relational systems of subjugation*. New York, NY: Routledge.

Shengold, L. (1989). *Soul murder: The effects of childhood abuse and deprivation*. New Haven: Yale University Press.

Slochower, J. A. (2013). *Holding and psychoanalysis: A relational perspective* (2nd ed.). Hove, East Sussex: Routledge.

Stern, D. N. (1985). *The interpersonal world of the infant: A view from psychoanalysis and developmental psychology*. New York: Basic Books.

Stokes, P. (2016). The Problem of Spontaneous Goodness: From Kierkegaard to Løgstrup (via Zwangzi and Eckhart). *Contintental Philosophy Review*, *49*, 139–159.

Stolorow, R. D. (2007). *Trauma and human existence: Autobiographical, psychoanalytic, and philosophical reflections*. New York: Analytic Press.

Stolorow, R. D. (2011). *World, affectivity, trauma: Heidegger and post-Cartesian psychoanalysis*. New York: Routledge.

Stolorow, R. D., Atwood, G. E., & Branchaft, B. (1994). *The intersubjective perspective*. Northvale, NJ: J. Aronson.

Sullivan, H. S. (1926). Erogenous Maturation. *Psychoanalytic Quarterly*, *13*(1), 1–15.

Sullivan, H. S., & Mullahy, P. (1948). *Conceptions of modern psychiatry*. Washington: Norton.

Taylor, C. (1989). *Sources of the self: The making of the modern identity.* Cambridge, MA: Harvard University Press.

Thelen, E., & Smith, L. (1996). *A dynamic systems approach to the development of cognition and action cognitive psychology Ser* (Reprint ed.). Retrieved from www.columbia.edu/cgi-bin/cul/resolve?clio7690076.

Troeltsch, E. (1977). *Writings on theology and religion.* Atlanta: John Knox Press.

Troeltsch, E. (1992). *The social teaching of the Christian churches.* Louisville, KY: Westminster and John Knox Press.

Winnicott, D. W. (1965). *The maturational processes and the facilitating environment: Studies in the theory of emotional development.* New York: International Universities Press.

Winnicott, D. W. (1975). *Through paediatrics to psycho-analysis* (Vol. 100). London: Hogarth Press.

Wittgenstein, L. and G. E. M. Anscombe (2003). *Philosophical investigations: the German text, with a revised English translation.* Malden, MA, Blackwell Pub.

Yerushalmi, H. (2001). Self-States and Personal Growth in Analysis. *Contemporary Psychoanalysis, 37*(3), 471–488.

Afterword

Many of the world's great religions have placed great stress on oral transmission: The early Christians before any of the Second Testament was written down, the ancient Hebrews': "hear, o Israel . . .", and the Japanese Buddhists, whose monk Join Saeki told the student who was leaving because he could not understand: just listen for a thousand days. According to Horoyuki Itsuki, we understand through hearing and though personal contact, "the school of the ear" (Itsuki, 2001, p. 134). My emphasis in this book on reparative ethical reading means to say the same thing. Like Christopher Bollas (Bollas, 2015), we psychoanalysts must now worry less about repression and more about oppression. He writes:

These days we may notice a deepening pessimism about the future. Indeed, even discussing it seems to miss the point of contemporary life, as we appear to gradually slip away from negotiating our realities, and accept a selective perception of the world that is turning hallucination into an art form. We may seek refuge and consolation in the nourishing aspects of life, falling in love, the pleasures of relationships, the meaning of raising a family, the creativity of work – but could this human resilience now be a hindrance to survival? By taking refuge in the present are we abandoning the future? (p. 538)

Contact with those who write from the standpoint of the oppressed provides us no refuge in a silent normality. But it can overcome ethical hearing deficits and connect us to others' suffering. It can change us.

Let us end by remembering once more Ludwig van Beethoven, whose encroaching deafness almost sent him to suicide:

O ye men who think or say that I am malevolent, stubborn or misanthropic, how greatly do ye wrong me . . . born with an ardent and lively temperament, even susceptible to the diversions of society, I was compelled early to isolate myself, to live in loneliness, when I at times tried to forget all this, O how harshly was I repulsed by the doubly sad experience of my bad hearing, and yet it was impossible for me to say to men speak louder, shout, for I am

deaf. Ah how could I possibly admit such an infirmity in the one sense which
should have been more perfect in me than in others, a sense which I once
possessed in highest perfection, a perfection such as few surely in my profession enjoy or have enjoyed – O I cannot do it, therefore forgive me when you
see me draw back when I would gladly mingle with you, my misfortune is
doubly painful because it must lead to my being misunderstood, for me there
can be no recreations in society of my fellows, refined intercourse, mutual
exchange of thought, only just as little as the greatest needs command may I
mix with society. I must live like an exile, if I approach near to people a hot
terror seizes upon me, a fear that I may be subjected to the danger of letting
my condition be . . . what a humiliation when one stood beside me and heard
a flute in the distance and *I heard nothing*, or someone heard *the shepherd
singing* and again I heard nothing, such incidents brought me to the verge
of despair, but little more and I would have put an end to my life – only art
it was that withheld me, ah it seemed impossible to leave the world until I
had produced all that I felt called upon me to produce, and so I endured this
wretched existence.

(Heiligenstadt Testament, 6 October 1802, emphasis in original)

Deafened himself, he taught us to hear that all are our brothers and sisters.

References

Bollas, C. (2015). Psychoanalysis in the Age of Bewilderment: On the Return of the
Oppressed. *International Journal of Psychoanalysis*, 96(3), 535–551.

Heiligenstadt Testament, 6 October 1802. http://www.lvbeethoven.com/Bio/Biography
HeiligenstadtTestament.html

Itsuki, H. (2001). *Tariki: Embracing despair, discovering peace*. Tokyo and New York:
Kodansha.

Index